The Corvette in
Literature and Culture

The Corvette in Literature and Culture

Symbolic Dimensions of America's Sports Car

JERRY W. PASSON

McFarland & Company, Inc., Publishers

Jefferson, North Carolina, and London

ISBN 978-0-7864-6284-1 (softcover : 50# alkaline paper) ∞

LIBRARY OF CONGRESS CATALOGUING-IN-PUBLICATION DATA ARE AVAILABLE

BRITISH LIBRARY CATALOGUING DATA ARE AVAILABLE

Cover art: Dana Forrester, *Concrete Heaven*, 19" × 29",
watercolor (danaforrester.com)

Manufactured in the United States of America

*McFarland & Company, Inc., Publishers
Box 611, Jefferson, North Carolina 28640
www.mcfarlandpub.com*

Table of Contents

*Between pages 116 and 117 are 8 color plates
containing 17 images*

v

Part III—Women, Sex, and Identity as Power: The Corvette, Baddest Mother of Them All

Part IV—The Corvette as Art: The Expressive Image

Acknowledgments

It is not possible to thank all of the individuals who deserve credit for their help and input. My parents would be the most obvious, for all their care and support for so many years; there were surely times when they had to wonder what I would discover that would hold my attention. Others to thank would be the friends who believed that a point would eventually come from all the wide-ranging and seemingly endless reading and discussing of everything. Among these the late Wayne L. Coleman — car enthusiast, fast driver/talker, and storyteller — who once told me, "If you don't do this, then who will?" when I told him what my topic was going to be, deserves special mention. That he will not see my *magnum opus* on the Corvette is the one major regret associated with the entire project.

Among the people involved in the research and writing of this book, a number of the Southern Illinois University faculty must be mentioned. First and foremost is Dr. Elizabeth Klaver, who served as director of this unlikely cultural study and continually offered advice and encouragement: special thanks to her for all the wise and critical words she had the grace to supply. Thanks also to the members of my committee: Drs. Veronique Maisier, Edward Brunner, Michael Molino, and Jeremy Wells. Who ever thought literature and culture could come together in the subject I chose to study? Perhaps unlikely, unpredictable subjects are the most challenging and the most in need of researching. My apologies to all the critical, literary, and cultural theories that I have coerced into appearing here; none of them were without value or failed to teach me something.

Thanks also must go out to Man Martin, author of *Days of the Endless Corvette* (2007), for our discussion of his novel, the Corvette, and life in general. Best wishes to him for his continued success as a novelist. Dana Forrester, artist and Corvette enthusiast, also deserves many thanks for his long thoughtful conversation about art, Corvettes, and how the two meet. When I needed help with aspects of art and the automobile, he gave me insights that enlightened my ideas and kept me going. His expertise and kindness are always most helpful and rewarding. Both of these individuals took the time to allow me to interview them and question their creative processes; I hope my work does each of them justice.

Of course, I am omitting other important people, but a few still need credit: Joe and Janet Winn, Jr., for years of friendship; his father, Joe Sr., and stepmother, Betty, for being the closest thing to family that I now possess; my friend Kenneth Pardue, for being a continual and reliable source of good humor in times up and down; and my fiancée, Victoria Gonzalez, who put up with, supported, encouraged, and fussed with me about getting this done, "seeing it through." I never question the honest affection and valuable counsel I receive from them.

Dr. John Hochheimer and his wife, Chris, who encouraged me to seek a publisher and gave me timely advice, along with Victoria's friend Bernadette O'Dell, who helped me pull all of this together into publishable form, deserve my heartfelt thanks as well. I remain grateful to each of these people. Each of them, and others I may not have named, played a part in the writing and publication of this work.

Introduction

Material objects in the form of personal property normally have relatively brief public lives. As commodities created for specific purposes, they persist in the marketplace and in the public consciousness until superseded by newer forms, often with new names and identities. However, a few do last and develop a distinct identity that carries with it a meaning or image that comes to possess a dynamic quality of its own. These objects may take many forms, yet one of the best examples — the automobile — enjoys a particular status as perhaps the dominant commodity of the twentieth century. In American culture, one car offers an outstanding example of a material object taking on a range of diverse cultural values over time. The Chevrolet Corvette has persisted in a competitive environment for more than fifty years and, over that time, has developed a cultural status that goes beyond what most machines or objects possess.

The Corvette has become more than a vehicle designed to transport people; it has acquired an image that exceeds the car itself. While changing over the years, the Corvette persists because it has taken on cultural and social attributes that make it an object of both power and desire. The Corvette possesses not one but many different identities, perhaps because it has taken a variety of forms that reflect a fluidity of meaning. The car signifies technology, freedom, identity (both sexual and social), and independence, among other qualities, at different times to different people.

One of the essential characteristics of this study is to investigate how the Corvette exists not in the present or past, but in all times, from its 1953 inception to the early twenty-first century and presumably beyond. This idea of a "timescape," borrowed from physics, enables a perspective that permits every moment of the Corvette's existence to be equally valued.* For example, the

---

*The quality of the individual episodes varied, but *Route 66* did deal with serious issues at times. Young Robert Duvall played a heroin addict in one show, and Buz's eventual replacement,

Corvette in the 1960–1964 television series *Route 66* becomes an emblem of American freedom, individuality, and the openness of Western culture, values that Jack Kerouac celebrated in *On the Road* (1957). However, Italian director Federico Fellini uses the Corvette in his 1960 film *La Dolce Vita* to suggest how postwar Western culture overwhelmed and frequently replaced that of the Old World with the New. In 1960, the Corvette possessed American style and virtues, yet these same values, "modern" American and Western in nature, threatened the existence of "older" European cultures. Power offers the assurance of freedom, but freedom brings with it a struggle to survive. In Robert Aldrich's 1955 film *Kiss Me Deadly*, the relatively new Corvette appears not only as a celebration of American technology, but also as an extension of the hero's violently aggressive heterosexuality — two things that remind us of the apocalyptically destructive nuclear age represented in the film.

A timescape allows all moments in time to be viewed from the same vantage point — such as masculine power, female identity, or artistic style — a perspective not limited to a set attitude or time, where we perceive a greater range of meaning and discern a more complex image. Here, alternative, even transgressive uses and views of the Corvette are to be found. The image is most frequently masculine and powerful, as in *Kiss Me Deadly*; however, it has been appropriated by women and minorities to assert an independence, even a sexuality, that does not simply rely on patriarchal white male culture. Novels such as Joan Didion's *Play It as It Lays* (1970) and Nasdijj's *Geronimo's Bones* (2004), along with the films *Cleopatra Jones* (1973) and *Rush Hour* (1998), as well as the Showtime cable series about gay friends and lovers, *Queer as Folk* (2001–2005), give us women, Native American teenagers, African Americans, and gay men driving Corvettes as a means of becoming "free" of the constraints of white, heterosexually dominant male society or of asserting an identity that belongs to themselves, not one defined by society and their surroundings. These two manifestations, the patriarchal American Corvette on one side and the Corvette in the hands of the "othered" phallic female and the socially and sexually empowered minorities on the other, form just two of the contrasting faces that the Corvette now combines in a single object.

(continued) Linc, was a U.S. Army Ranger and Vietnam veteran in 1963 while the war was still obscure and non-controversial (Ingram). Other topics included a range of social and personal ills and featured a variety of new actors who would become well known in the years to come. In 1962, the first Emmy nomination for an African American went to actress/blues singer Ethel Waters for her performance as a dying blues songstress who wishes to reunite her old group for one last show. That episode, "Goodnight, Sweet Blues," aired on 6 October 1961 (Ingram and "Awards for 'Route 66'").

The unique 1963 split-rear-window coupe was the first C2 or second generation Corvette. The 1963–1967 Sting Rays are the most iconic of Corvettes, and one of the most recognizable automotive designs ever produced. These cars convey an American sense of style and possess a presence that suggests both the power and speed of Corvette and the sophistication and affluence of the owner and the society that produced them. (GM Photo Store 53217349)

The Corvette is also an object of fashion, even art, and it manifests a style that extends beyond the realm of the automotive. Like other objects, it asserts an identity in space; its shape might be said to "stress" space and form the way a living thing does. The design of the Sting Ray and later "Mako" or "shark" Corvettes was influenced by the flowing contours of the sea creatures their names come from. The designs are biomorphic in their suggestion of vital, moving and living forms. The Corvette is also stylish in that it caters to the taste, sense of proportion, and social consciousness of its owner/drivers. In the manner that works of three-dimensional sculpture are sometimes said to "activate the space" that surrounds them, the form of an object — in this case an automobile — creates an aura of tension or energy around what might have once been perceived as only a static, material object. In modern art, there are kinetic sculptures that move and artworks that sug-gest motion while standing still, and the shapes of sports cars such as the Corvette perform in a like manner: they are meant to convey a sense of style that carries with it the feeling of a taut, powerful, even graceful form that is in motion.

While automobiles in general may be utilitarian, Zora Arkus-Duntov, the European-American engineer referred to as the "godfather of the Corvette," said that sports cars are about "emotional appeal"; a true sports car, then — like a work of art — should arouse "an exaggerated amount" of emotion (Burton, *Zora* 190). The car's purpose is not to be rational or material, but to touch human needs and desires. In a related way, the art forms termed Futurism, most notably the Italian Futurists, emphasized transportation technology (the train, the automobile, the airplane) in works that depict the power of speed and the allure of motion. For the Futurists, machine technology was not necessarily cold or inhuman, but rather captured and conveyed a sense of dynamic energy, the power to move through the world and to assert the authority of human designs over the material world. In this sense, the emotion that Corvettes offer relates to a feeling of power, power suggested in the form of the car itself and power in the speed it provides to assert its owners' existence, their identity, and their freedom from the mundane.

As a material object, the Chevrolet Corvette came into being in 1953 after General Motors' decision to create an American interpretation of the European sports car, one that became associated with the freedom of the open road. By 1963, the Sting Ray (later reintroduced as Stingray) was established as "America's sports car," with power, speed, and an aggressive, distinctly cool American image. In 1968, the sensual, curvaceous shark-bodied

Corvette premiered and came to exist in the greatest numbers, over time embodying a contrary set of images, from American power and sexuality to greed and material success. The new C4 Corvette was a 1984 update featuring high tech in an angular, aerodynamic body. It was a break with the past, and all later Corvettes would be known as C types, 1–4, each with multiple identities.* The 1997–2004 C5 and the successor C6 possess many-faceted images, as well as modern technology. All Corvettes and the different ways they are presented and portrayed are texts to be read and analyzed carefully, with an awareness of their different significance over time, according to where they are found and in whose hands they perform.

This book focuses on four distinct areas in which the Corvette and its many different uses or presentations demonstrate significations from which we may draw insights. In order to accomplish this, several areas of criticism are applied. Material culture studies, masculinity theory, feminist criticism, queer theory, and art theory are utilized as appropriate. In each case, the discussion is based on the Corvette as object and or as image. Part I will introduce the subject and discuss the first area, "The Corvette: The Empty, the American, and the Deadly Signifier" (the original that becomes America's image of itself and the danger of speed and technology out of control). Part II will be concerned with the Corvette as "The Image of Potency: The Corvette, Males, and Minorities" (aggressive sexuality, African-American males, and male domination). Part III will focus on "Women, Sex, and Identity as Power: The Corvette, Baddest Mother of Them All" (phallic females, the car as sexual power and identity). Part IV will cover the Corvette and its image as "The Corvette as Art: The Expressive Image." The conclusion, "The Corvette, Image and Object," will offer overall comments and final thoughts.

The Chevrolet Corvette was created by General Motors to take advantage of the post–World War II interest in "sports cars," an almost wholly European concept of a lightweight, maneuverable automobile that catered to a desire for not just speed, but an involvement in the process of driving.

---

*The different generations of the Corvette are usually described as C1, beginning in 1953, through C6, the model that went on sale in 2005. The nomenclature is based on body style and years produced:

C1	1953 –1962	C2	1963 –1967 (the Sting Ray Corvettes)
C3	1968 –1982	C4	1984 –1996
C5	1997 – 2004	C6	2005 – present

Each "C series" has its own distinctive style and mechanical features. Also, the "look" of each was created to carry on a certain Corvette "DNA" and continue the car's identity and image.

Sports cars were objects that demonstrated the driver's passion for motoring, and they also served to set the owner/driver apart from the usual crowd who drove large, practical, and frequently dull and uninteresting ordinary automobiles. As an American car, the Corvette followed in the tradition of the automobiles that came before it, cars such as those found in Sinclair Lewis' *Free Air* (1919) or John Steinbeck's *The Grapes of Wrath* (1939). It had to be distinctly American in some sense, while becoming a sports car as well. In 1955, a black Corvette appeared in Aldrich's film *Kiss Me Deadly*, and in this *film noir* environment the Corvette took on the characteristics that the politically liberal director saw in postwar society: an American aggression and disregard for Old World culture, a willingness to do violence to achieve our American ends, and a dehumanizing interest in technology that would come to threaten the world. As an object that was novel to American society, the Corvette was at first a new, unknown, or empty object waiting for an image to come into being.

Along with American technology, the Corvette carried with it the insistent and dominating influence of New World culture. A Corvette appears in Rome in Fellini's 1960 *La Dolce Vita* as the automobile of an American movie star there to film a new motion picture. Large, imposing, and more than a match for the Italian main character, the American male expresses aspects that are similar to the new, Western-style buildings that are replacing Rome's traditional architecture: the Old World disappears in the face of the power and progress of a "culture" that is essentially American. The Corvette reflects the dominating influence of modern, especially American, ideas with little or no regard for Europeans' taste and perception. "Americanism" may not destroy their culture, yet the richness and vitality of Europe are being drained away.

From 1960 to 1964, the television series *Route 66* came to define the image of the Corvette as the vehicle of freedom for young, adventurous Americans — particularly white males — and a representation of their ability to explore the country in an effort to discover themselves and the nation's "real" meaning. Yet, in only a few years, the Corvette also came to be associated with rebellious, wild, and threatening youth, such as those in 1967's *Hot Rods to Hell*. The Corvette was both a manifestation of America's power and prestige, and the suggestion of a dangerous undercurrent of destructive wildness that had to be restrained. The Corvette was the car of choice for many of America's newest heroes, the Gemini and Apollo astronauts. It also stood for the menace of speed and a culture that was on the edge of going out of control, like the street racing Corvette in Jan and Dean's 1964 hit song "Dead Man's Curve" in its contest with its rival, the Jaguar XKE.

Most significantly, in these works the Corvette is an object invested with "meaning." The car relates to human beings in ways that are characteristic of the field of material culture studies. The Corvette is part of person/object relationships that reveal meanings otherwise not readily apparent. In *Material Cultures* (1998), Daniel Miller writes that, by observing "the sensual and material qualities of the object, we are able to unpick [*sic*] the more subtle connections with cultural lives and values that are objectified through these forms" (9). The Corvette is a "cultural object," and "objects are not only defined by their material quality, but by their location within systems of narrative and logic laid out by social discourses" (Woodward 16). Looking at the Corvette as an "object" within social and cultural contexts allows analysis of the roles the car plays in different times and situations. Material culture studies' emphasis on objects as both "things" and bearers of meaning opens the Corvette as object to a range of interpretations.

Taken by itself, in isolation, the Corvette is only an object, not so very distinct from the multitude of machines produced as commodities over the last hundred years. Yet, if we look at the automobile as a subject of study, its impact upon and meaning within human society, especially in America, are immense. No invention is so American in its nature or interpretation. The idea that we are "a nation on wheels," a society that aspires to and cherishes its mobility, is one of our essential and defining values. Given that we as a culture tend to accept and assume this freedom of mobility (both physical and social), the automobile becomes a background, a context, for our other struggles and endeavors. In literature and popular culture, the automobile plays a significant role, as for the Joad family in *The Grapes of Wrath* or in the television series *Route 66*, yet that part is frequently subtextual, as a sign to which we grant implicit positive and negative meanings. The Corvette is an emblem, the appearance of a single example culled from the many less visible ones by time and circumstance, of the wider and deeper connection of the automobile to our own identity and personal life. While the machine changes in physical form or image, its essential and multifaceted nature — as captured by the generations of the Corvette — remains true.

The role the Corvette plays in literature, film, and television, and various other cultural manifestations, makes it an indication of how we as Americans — and sometimes those who are not Americans — see and represent ourselves. The different manifestations of the Corvette's image, in connection with people and ideas across its more than fifty years of existence, reflect a large part of American society and its sometimes contradictory views of itself. The Corvette, as found in literature and popular culture of all forms, is a signifier of complex and wide-ranging ideas. Across different places and times, it demonstrates an idealized freedom and individuality, as for Maria in the novel *Play It As It Lays*, then the deadliest or most intimate threat to our well being, as in the film *Kiss Me Deadly*. Yet again, it grants those denied a place in society (women and minorities) an opportunity to assert their existence and power. It even, in rare cases such as Man Martin's southern novel *Days of the Endless Corvette*, promises love and romance. Overall, the automobile — as represented by the Corvette — is a part of the twentieth century's literature and history.

PART I

The Corvette:
The Empty, the American,
and the Deadly Signifier

Chapter 1

Automobility

In the late nineteenth and early twentieth centuries what would be called the "automobile" came into being. In its first incarnations, which included various steam and electric versions, "horseless carriages" were the curious inventions of a few pioneers in the field of what we today would call "personal mobility." Before long these custom-fabricated, individually constructed, and novel creations became the visible signs of the wealthy, or at least the affluent, both in the United States and overseas. The internal combustion engine (ICE) soon became the powerplant of choice, giving vehicles both range and endurance. At this time, automobiles were uncommon objects, what we would today call "roads" were almost nonexistent, and a "car" was pulled by a locomotive or was the trolley car (usually horse-drawn) found on the streets of major cities. What we today think of as the freedom to travel around the country and go where we wish was, for the majority of average Americans, constrained by economic realities, a lack of available transportation, and the isolation of small towns and communities with no railroads or river traffic. America was a nation that valued mobility, yet the freedom to go, search, or wander was limited by practical concerns, and true individual mobility was a luxury.

In 1908 that began to change. Henry Ford's Model T altered the reality of American life and the way society functioned. The affordable automobile gave average people the world over a mobility and an independence that they did not possess before it came into their lives. As a mass-produced commodity priced within the means of "ordinary people," it changed American culture and the ways Americans thought and behaved. As one historian describes it, "It was more than speed. More even than sex. The automobile brought freedom," and that enhanced freedom to travel expanded the American Dream and brought new opportunities with it (Kimes 210). As "a sensual, romantic, and joyful experience," traveling by automobile promised experiences—adventures that appealed to the senses, the heart, and the intellect—that other modes of transportation did not, and it could be done with the individuality and personal choice that were characteristically American (210). In relatively short order, roads improved, and that new American attribute, "automobility," became a part of the national character. This is what we have come to expect in American society. We take our cars for granted, and we forget how the freedom they have given us has shaped the last hundred years. Automobility is what we have come to cherish and desire; however, we so depend upon our cars and assume they will be there for us that the attributes of the precious freedom they provide has come to be invested in specialized varieties: off-road vehicles (Jeeps, for example), sport utilities (SUVs), and, most noticeably, sports cars like the Corvette. Sports cars retain that cachet of individual freedom that the Model T first carried and add to it all the allure of speed and technology that seduces us into a human/machine relationship. Sports cars possess the sensuality and romance that promise us joy. Automobility is now an established affair that we consider part of all Americans' birthright.

An early example of this automotive experience is found in Sinclair Lewis' *Free Air* (1919). Lewis, himself the owner of a Model T and veteran of a cross-country excursion, writes of Milt Daggett and Claire Boltwood, unlikely lovers who discover each other on the road. Wealthy, New York-raised Claire meets small-town mechanic and repair-shop owner Milt on a transcontinental drive to the West Coast. He falls in love with her, the adventurous young female, and he follows Claire and her father to Seattle. It is on the road that the socialite and the mechanic can meet as something like equals; the physical space of the West and the demands it places on ingenuity and personal character makes the differences in social status inconsequential. The openness of America is, in this context, physically and socially complete: although Claire drives an expensive Gomez-Deperdussin roadster (referred to as "Claire's beloved") and Milt has his hot-rodded Teal "bug" roundabout, the automobility that brings them together is more powerful than the pretensions of class and property (Lewis 14).

To Claire the roadster is power, it sings "songs," and behind the wheel she feels "like a woman, not like a driver" (3). What Claire comes to possess, what will eventually change her life, is a sense of freedom and identity—not as an anonymous "driver" or the delicate, refined, upper-crust genteel lady, but as a female human being, a woman. The act of driving the open roads calls forth in her a "vicious vigor that was genius" (4). For Claire to be "vicious" and possess "genius," she has to experience the American West and face it not as a passive passenger, but as an active, engaged driver. The woman driving an automobile, the woman in command of a sports car — most obviously a Corvette — reacquires or takes for herself (at least in part) the authority over her own life that male-defined and dominated society would deny her. When she starts her car, Claire feels "that magic change which every long-distance motorist knows. Instantly she was alert, seemingly able to drive forever" (33). While Milt is independent and ingenious in his practical, intelligent western virtues — like the Virginian in Owen Wister's novel — it is Claire who grows and discovers the most about herself. The automobile, Claire's sports car, is what gives her the ability to first see and uncover her potential for life and happiness based on strength and intelligence, not passivity.

The travails and adventures of the early motorist are part of *Free Air*, but so is the nearly limitless possibility of what he or she will discover in the immense American landscape. Before the coming of the motorcar, opportunities to travel at purely individual choice were limited, and this limitation was both physical, in terms of speed and distance, and temporal, in the time it took both in waiting for transportation and in the getting to places that were out of the way. When horses, trains, and steamships dominated, individual preferences mattered less; personal freedom existed, but it had less room available, so life itself was constrained by space and time. While the fictional or cinematic image of the "cowboy" may suggest "freedom" in its purest form to us today, that freedom was frequently at a horse-drawn wagon's pace, and a day's travel might mean no more than ten to fifteen miles (Holmes 43).

That cachet or attraction that the Corvette exerts is the direct descendent of this early spirit of freedom and adventure that the new, affordable automobile brought to America. With the practical invention of the mass-produced "car," America discovered itself again, and our mental horizons opened to a wider and richer land. One analysis of *Free Air* describes how it was praised, in particular for "its emphasis on the merit of the individual rather than his or her social class or family background," and that in its pages we find both a male "western hero" and a "new American woman" (Fleming vi and vii). Both of these prefigure the variations of the two that are either connected or associated with this idea of the automobile, the Corvette in particular, in the literature and culture of our own time. In their most positive forms, these female and male characters demonstrate "the free western spirit" that we, as Americans, believe is to be found in ourselves and our society (vii). Milt and Claire are brought together by the automobile and discover a world of possibilities, romantic and social, that the new technology has uncovered. Yet technology is not without a price; as human beings are not perfect creatures, neither are the cars that become our surrogates or the reflections of our natures immune from internal flaws or the misfortunes of time and circumstance.

Not long after its coming of age as a commodity that most Americans could afford, the automobile became more than an instrument of pleasure or the source of joy, adventure, and romance. When hard times came, it was sometimes an individual or a family's only recourse, their sole access to survival. For the Joad family in John Steinbeck's *The Grapes of Wrath* (1939), the Hudson Super-Six truck that transports them and all their worldly goods is both a vehicle and a shelter: it will take them to California, and when they have no other choice, it acts as the replacement for their lost home. In point of fact, without their truck, the Joads cannot survive; the mobility it offers is their chance for another life. The life that they had, the family farm, is gone, and the road west appears to be their last and only hope. In the novel, machines are sources of power with two faces. The bright one is the truck that offers escape and a new beginning as it stands out "magically" in the morning light as the Joads leave home for the last time (Steinbeck *Grapes* 99). The other, the darker of the two, is the Caterpillar tractor (bulldozer), which "turns the land and turns us off the land" and serves to intimidate people, even to smash their dwellings and leave them homeless (Steinbeck "Grapes" essay 9). These are two aspects that recur often in the image of the automobile in general and the Corvette in particular. One is benevolent, possessing qualities that speak of the possibilities of life and encourage human endeavor; the other is ominous and frequently threatening, promising little but violence and the chance of destruction.

For the Joads, the future seems to hold some promise. While the trip is difficult, their family has a unity of purpose and a common identity that binds them together. Although dispossessed of their land and home, the family's mobility is a demonstration of their strength to endure what is sometimes described as "the destruction of a whole class of people and a way of life" (Davis 401). Also, the Hudson is apparently the family's first vehicle in some time; it is a new thing to the Joads, and Tom, recently out of prison, and his mechanically inclined younger brother Al do the driving. The young men, not their father or eldest brother, assume authority on the road. Pa is nominally in charge, yet he does not, or cannot, drive. The truck is actually a car, converted into a home on wheels, not very different in concept from the original western pioneers' Conestoga wagons. This "new thing" taken from an older form reflects the first automobiles' "horseless carriage" nickname. It also speaks of the ingenuity and self-reliance Americans value in themselves, the ability to adapt objects and machines to new uses and different purposes. Later in the twentieth century, when European sports cars come to America, they would also be modified and imitated until a distinctly American form, the Corvette, comes into being. The American automobile, in its various incarnations, suggests the inventiveness of the American people as a whole.

Once the automobile was affordable and widely available, it transformed American culture. In particular, it gave people like the Joad family a new center of their existence. They were no longer rooted to a place and totally vulnerable to the vicissitudes of bad luck or social change. Now, to their salvation or destruction, they had choices to make. As historian James N. Gregory writes in *American Exodus*:

> The automobile gave ... twentieth-century migrants a flexibility that cross-country or trans-Atlantic migrants of earlier eras did not share. By reducing the costs and inconveniences of long distance travel, it made it easy for those who were tentative or doubtful, who under other circumstances would have stayed behind, to go anyway [qtd. in Windschuttle 26].

Without the automobile, the Joads would not have a story that reaches out towards California. The "flexibility" that is forced upon them is a "freedom" with little in the way of choice, yet it is one that people marooned or abandoned in other places and other times would have grasped at.

The "ancient" Hudson truck becomes "the most important place" for the family in the moments before their departure (Steinbeck *Grapes* 99). It is not only a conveyance, a means of reaching "the promised land" of California: when the house and the fields are described as "dead," the truck is transformed into "the active thing, the living principle" of the Joads — literally, all of their lives come to center and depend upon it (99). The truck is "the new hearth, the living center of the family" (100). In a world that comes to seem defined by "limit, loss, and wandering," the Hudson carries the Joads and their spirit as a family unit; the truck unifies them, and gives a slim chance at a new life (Spangler 308). If the Joads have any stake in the American Dream, it is their automobility that lets them grasp at it. To be stationary, to possess no active motion toward a possible future, offers no more than individual and collective death. When the question "How do we live without our lives?" (meaning the people, places, and things that make up our lives) is asked silently and rhetorically, the only answer is to begin moving and to remain in motion until some resolution is found (Steinbeck 88).

The automobile, in this sense, fulfills a need that is both physical and spiritual. Al and the other Joads refer to their truck as "she," and Al personifies it when he says, "She's old an' she's ornery," before going on to describe how he has checked over the car and believes "her" to be fit enough for the journey and agreeable with the family's limited resources (Steinbeck 100–101). As French artist, poet, and film director Jean Cocteau wrote, "A car can massage organs no masseur can reach. It is the one remedy for the disorders of the great sympathetic nervous system," and the truck seems to have a life of its own that mirrors and touches the family's (Barkley). For young Al Joad, the responsibility he feels as the family's principal driver and

The Joad family in Steinbeck's 1939 novel *The Grapes of Wrath* struggle westward with hopes of a new life — even of prosperity — in the seeming paradise of California. The image of their overburdened, steaming truck in John Ford's 1940 film speaks of the promise of mobility and the power to endure hardships on the road to the future that Americans prize so highly in themselves. Other automobiles possess the same cachet of freedom and independence, even under duress (Photofest).

the bond that he forms with the old Hudson are powerful and transformative. Al is "purposeful" behind the wheel, his "whole body is listening to the
car," and his eyes are "restless" as he watches both the road and the instrument
panel (123). Al is made "one with his engine" (as if the engine powered him,
as if it were his heart, not just the Hudson's), and his "every nerve" is extended
into the truck (123). On the road, Al and the Hudson appear to be one life,
even as the text tells it, "he had become the soul of the car." As Cocteau
said, the car "touches" Al in a way that not just invokes a physical sense,
but a spiritual one. He is its "soul," and his nervous system reaches and
becomes intertwined with the Hudson's vital functions. Driving gives Al a
life and a purpose that he has not known prior to going on the road. For
the rest of the Joads, the involvement and the thrill is less, but still present.
This perception, as depicted by Arkus-Duntov, is that emotional appeal and
sense of communication that a driver feels with a car, especially a sports car,
much as Claire Boltwood was made more alive by the vitality of her Gomez-
Dep roadster and the sense of power she came to experience while driving.

The Joad family's "automobility" is composed of two parts, each of
which can be taken as an American virtue, characteristic aspects that make
the nation and its people "exceptional," according to some writers and his-
torians. In *The Road Story and the Rebel* (2006), Katie Mills breaks automobility into "autonomy" and "mobility": each of these concepts relates to
both "*physical* and *representational* spaces" (24). The autonomy of the Joads
or other characters involved with the automobile is quite real. While they
do depend on each other and on friends they make along the road to California, there is an independence of mind and spirit that unites them in a
philosophical sense with the generations of Americans who explored the
western United States and, further back in history, those who ventured across
the sea to settle in a new and unknown world. The automobile, in a personal
sense, makes "ordinary" people into potential or figurative explorers. They
have access to physical space, the surrounding world, that grants them a
freedom of mind, a psychology of openness and possibility, which, though
weighted with the chance of disaster, is itself invaluable. This is a very
American way of thinking, a way we often pride ourselves on. Along with
this is the physical freedom of mobility. Wheels rather than feet can propel
us faster and farther than the limitations of our bodies permit. Literally, a
man or woman on wheels is more powerful, if not surer of purpose, than
one on foot. Mobility, as the automobile delivers it, is *power*. The ability
to choose one's course and set an individual destination, united with the
power to go there, are part of defining one's identity, both in literature and

in real life. The Joads' situation and their story are literally and metaphorically connected with the lives most, if not all, Americans lead.

The other portion of this two-part definition is the representational aspects of *The Grapes of Wrath*. While the 1939 novel was controversial and reached thousands of readers, 1940 saw the premiere of director John Ford's film based on Steinbeck's work. In this motion picture, the author's words were given visual form, often-stark black-and-white images that resembled the photographs taken by migrant chronicler Dorothea Lange (McBride). The novel has power, but the images of the film, particularly the often-seen depiction of the overloaded truck struggling westward down Route 66, have come to represent the fictional work and the "Okie/migrant" period in America just as much as the words. Visual representations of suggested autonomy and implicit mobility have a power that has infused the automobile with status as an image that few other objects so blatantly or strongly possess. Individual automobiles, what we commonly refer to as "cars"— and who does not routinely say "my car" in a fashion that takes its significance as a sign of independence and identity for granted — may sink into our mental picture of the world and become like trees in an image of the forest, yet some (like the cinematic representation of the Joad family's truck) are given qualities perceived as outstanding or singular. This is a measure of how and why some cars have distinct identities: their images have come to embody the freedom of the Joads' truck, the promise of the road ahead, or the chance at a new and different life. Sometimes this is overridden with suggestions of affluence and/or exclusivity (such as Jay Gatsby's ostentatious and expensive roadster or a modern Mercedes-Benz or Ferrari sports car). But sports cars, for all they may cost, share an essential connection with the truck as in the novel and film. Regardless of who drives, the vehicle has that aura of freedom and the independent spirit of individual identity. The Corvette is just a car, but its "car-ness" is significant in what it says about the way it is perceived as an object and what it signifies.

The two versions of *The Grapes of Wrath* present a central idea that demands critical consideration. In the twentieth and early twenty-first centuries, words and pictures tend to combine and become striking representations of reality. As nineteenth-century photography evolved into moving images — at first silent film and later television to the eventual development of today's live, streaming video — words and pictures have moved closer together. A "picture in words" or a "picture worth a thousand words" are not substitutes for each other, but a merger of text and image into one whole perception of the world. The novel/film of *The Grapes of Wrath* are together part of the public consciousness of the story of the Joad family and what they face. To put it more plainly, these representations of the Joads are mediated by words and pictures into one complex image or set of images. This is the process that we see in modern times; as communication technology advances, the visual and print media become inextricable components of contemporary culture. The way the automobile has been and is depicted, in visual or print forms, is (along with its physical reality as a tangible object) what has determined its significance in society and what it has come to represent. The Corvette, in popular and literary culture, is a small window on this phenomenon: the object itself, along with visual or print texts, merges into a complex set of signs, signifiers, and signifieds bound together in a dynamic and changing relationship.

The resulting images or sets of images are, however, not always apparently coherent or in agreement with themselves. The story of the Joad family differs in the print and film versions of the novel. As reported by film historian Joseph McBride and Steinbeck scholar Susan Shillinglaw, the two works diverge, yet end up possessing the same overall message (McBride). The first half of the film generally matches the novel's contents, but the second half inverts the sequence of action and events. In the novel, the Joads end up driven by flood waters to a "rain-soaked barn," their truck unable to start (perhaps crippled or soon to be destroyed)—in short, with little hope left, their lives drawing to a desperate end, before Rose of Sharon's compassionate gesture of nursing a starving man (Steinbeck 443–455). In the film, the family leaves the security and comfort of a well-run government camp in search of work; riding in the cab of the truck, Ma Joad looks ahead of them and delivers the brief but powerful "we are the people" speech, a strong, determined expression of the American will to survive and ability to cope with adversity (Ford). Through these alternative endings of the same story, we see the dichotomy of the views America has of itself: the worn-out automobile that, like the family, is all but overcome by circumstance and the lack of sufficient human resources (undercut or balanced out by Rose of Sharon's sharing and human kindness), and the other the strong, hopeful vision that the freedom of autonomy and mobility will grant "the people" new beginnings and new life. The automobile and America retain these two contrary, hopeful and doomed, aspects from 1939 to 1940 and present them in the literature and popular culture to come. Steinbeck himself, after viewing Ford's film years later, thought that the differences in interpretation did not change the book's message and that the movie captured the essence of his ideas (McBride).

Chapter 2

The Deadly Signifier

Another aspect of the automobile to consider is what material culture studies critic Daniel Miller defines as "the evident humanity of the car" ("Driven" 2). The car is not made "human" in a literal sense, as in fantasies such as Disney's *The Love Bug* films or in Pixar studio's animated *Cars* (2006), but as a cultural object it is invested with qualities — virtues, vices, and desires — that reflect the humanity of its owners/creators. The automobile "has become an integral part of the cultural environment within which we see ourselves as human" (2). This "humanity" is an expression "signifying the totality of all people," yet it also "touches the specific and inalienable individuality of any particular person" (2). Claire Boltwood's roadster and the Joad family's truck signify human aspects of both individuals and society. They are not just material objects; rather than being so limited, the automobiles act in "objectifying personal and social systems of value" in the ways already described, and more, as they form "highly personal and intimate relationships" with human beings (2). While the automobile is often seen and depicted today as "the sign of our alienation" from nature or humanistic values (environmental or social questions, for example), it is in fact reasonable in many cultural contexts to see that "the car has become more a means to resist alienation than a sign of alienation" (2–3).

As to the Corvette, in literature, film, and popular culture the various incarnations of the car are tangible signs of material culture. In the form of objects, the different models of the Corvette suggest a physical reality that additionally carries the cultural weight of conflicting interpretations of the automobile, concepts that reach beyond the car into the realms of social and political concern. The "humanity" of the Corvette extends its functioning as an object and permits it to represent ideas that are "not just contradictory but convoluted in the extreme" (Miller "Driven" 2). As a single object, the Corvette is a figurative representative of the automobile/automobility culture as a whole, and given that the automobile is "a core symbol of American Culture," we should be able to see in this one select example how "overwhelmingly expressive a relationship between people and cars" has been forged in the course of the last century (23 and 22). That relationship is composed of elements of both light and darkness. The twentieth and early twenty-first centuries have witnessed a range of events that have transformed the world and how human beings relate to it and each other, so the automobile — in the image of the Corvette — is not a single sign with a set signified meaning, but a signifier with meanings that conflict and diversify over time, according to changing social and political conditions.

Film criticism often uses the term *film noir* to describe the characteristics of a body of American motion pictures produced up until approximately 1955. *Film noir*, as a concept observed by French critics during the years of World War II, suggests a "cynical treatment of the American Dream," "complicated play with gender and sexuality," and a "foregrounding of cinematic style" that draws attention to the techniques and devices of movie making (Naremore 2). Film scholar James Naremore stresses that *noir* had much to do with the "cultural and social history" of the time and that it describes "a period, a movement, and a recurrent style" (6). He writes, "The 'original' films noirs can be explained in terms of a tense, contradictory assimilation of high modernism into American culture as a whole" (7). Among other things, these films "are preoccupied with eroticism and decadence ... sexually independent women ... [and] encounters with racial 'others'" (7). Another film scholar, J. P. Telotte, believes that *film noir* struggles to discover a narrative voice featuring "new ways of expression either out of rhetorical flourish or out of need ... [in order to] convey our meanings or to account for what we perceive" (32). It seems certain that the modernism in *film noir* reveals a dystopian world that is deceptively simplistic, with hidden dangers and secrets too big to leave safely alone, and that human beings are threatened by forces beyond their control.

In one of the last and darkest *films noirs*, Robert Aldrich's 1955 *Kiss Me Deadly*, based on the Mickey Spillane novel of the same name, we have "a crucial event for the French auteurists, signaling the end of Hollywood noir" (Naremore 151). By the end of the picture, everything and everyone is destroyed; figuratively, the end of the world is at hand. The cause of this is twofold: humanity's violent, destructive nature — especially the patriarchal male need to dominate and possess — and technology that has progressed beyond what we recklessly consider twentieth-century wisdom and our power to control. In the film, machines and the technology that created them are embodied in a mysterious box containing "the whatzit," an unknown and unidentified force or thing spawned by atomic research and the development of nuclear weapons. Yet, before we encounter the box or hear the snarling, consuming sound that accompanies the light from inside, we discover the world is full of automobiles.

In *film noir* human beings frequently seem to be reduced to biological machines, creatures dependent on instinct and with limited abilities to control themselves or their fears and desires; they are dominated by situations and circumstances. *Kiss Me Deadly's* "hero," detective Mike Hammer, is heterosexually aggressive, willing and able to fight and use violence at the least provocation, and apparently scornful of all things beyond his experience and understanding. In these qualities, he is a "man of action" who feels that shrewd, cynical thinking always gets him ahead. His car is a glistening white British Jaguar XK 120 that he drives fast, a rather obvious extension of his own stylish and self-centered ego. That car is destroyed when the "bad guys" push it off the road with their large, black Cadillac limousine: the Jaguar explodes, leaving to die Hammer and the woman who would not divulge the location of the box. In fact, cars are everywhere in the film, and like the technology the box represents, they reflect a world of things — Hammer's apartment with its art objects and telephone answering machine, the modern art paintings in a private museum, the opera record by Caruso that Hammer breaks to threaten the performer who may have information — that dominates and overpowers the Old World values of civilization and culture. Hammer is ruthless and violent, and suitably enough, to replace his Jaguar the leader of the villains gives him a new, shiny black with polished chrome, Chevrolet Corvette. This is, so far as I can determine, one of the first uses of the Corvette in media other than General Motors or Chevrolet's own advertising. Since in 1953 only three hundred Corvettes were made, and only 2,780 of 3,640 produced were sold in 1954, the Corvette was something still new and uncommon in 1955 (Leffingwell 79). And the way the car is used and depicted in the film suggests one of the images that the Corvette will come to possess.

The gangsters who give Hammer the Corvette intend it to be a sweet ride, also Hammer's last. The car comes with not one, but two bombs: one easy to find, the other more subtle and hidden. Hammer is too smart to fall for this, but the connection should become clear as the movie proceeds: the Corvette with bombs wired into it and the strange box with the fiery, consuming contents both suggest a dangerous, deadly pairing of technology with human desire, the sensual, exciting automobile and the promise of money and power represented by the contents of the hot, heavy box. The desirability of the car and the technology of the nuclear age are a potentially catastrophic combination. Hammer's ready willingness to be, even pleasure in being, vicious and violent presents a masculine image that, in threatening others, neglects a concern for its own ultimate well-being and survival.

Early in the film, Christina — the woman who is tortured to death in

During the Cold War, technology offered both the promise of fulfilling human desires and of destroying the civilization that it helped build. In Robert Aldrich's 1955 film of the Mickey Spillane novel *Kiss Me Deadly*, a black Corvette with gleaming chrome and a ferocious exhaust note suggests not liberation, but destruction. Technology, in this *film noir* world, sets free the human desire to dominate others and our ability to be violent and cruel (Photofest).

order to learn where the box is hidden — tells Hammer he has "only one, real lasting love ... *you*. You're one of those self-indulgent males who thinks only about himself, his clothes, his car" (Aldrich). Yet she seems to find him attractive nonetheless. As a masculine figure, Hammer has physical power and the ability to act, but women are, to use Christina's term, "incomplete" without "Man." The character is speaking with a sense of irony, as if she sees the contradiction in a world where "Men" have patriarchal power that they cannot separate from the destructive self-centeredness, which can only conceive of using their strength for selfish ends.

Once the Corvette appears, it becomes Hammer's alter ego, "his pre-occupation with the self," a representation of his masculinity (Telotte 198). The car is a deep flawless black, with chrome mirrors and bumpers and the prominent steel teeth of the Corvette grille of that time. The front of the car, its face, looks like something predatory, ready to consume the road or other vehicles. The Corvette's aggressive appearance matches Hammer's behavior, and its engine sounds loud, assertive, drawing attention to the car's presence much as Hammer commands attention wherever he goes. The Corvette is "male" and proud of itself. Also, keeping in mind the bombs it comes with, the car is linked to the box's mysterious power. The technology of the car and of the "nuclear" box are manifestations of the same power, a masculine domination that threatens the ordinary or everyday world around us.

Furthermore, the timing of *Kiss Me Deadly* suggests this thematic context. In 1953 *The Beast from 20,000 Fathoms*, the first of the nuclear-spawned monster movies, was released. It was impressively profitable and led to *Them!*, the 1954 film of giant mutant ants created by atomic testing in the American Southwest. The age of metaphoric nuclear monsters was at hand in the world of popular motion pictures, and the box in Aldrich's movie is a more stylish and sophisticated reference to the same concern, the destructive power that humanity has unleashed and seems unlikely to be able to control. *Kiss Me Deadly*'s ending is often referred to as "apocalyptic" and is strangely in keeping with the social and cultural fears of the time regarding nuclear war, which most people thought would bring about the end of humanity (Telotte 198). However, in *Kiss Me Deadly*, the unseen "monster" is the "great whatzit" in the box, or more generally, the flawed aspects of Western culture that have generated men like Hammer, as represented in the technology they utilize to achieve their ends, like the Corvette automobile that signifies both masculine power and destructive potential.

It would seem that the automobile in general, and the Corvette in particular, possesses lingering characteristics that are both masculine and destructive based on what we find in *film noir*. While this is true, it is more complex than the mere threat of violence. In his article, "Noir's Cars: Automobility and Amoral Space in American Film Noir," Mark Osteen writes that "the auto exemplifies the desire to flout history, destiny and law, signifying freedom from rules and the dream of forging a new self" (184). In many of these films, automobiles become "amoral spaces where laws and social arrangements ... are suspended" (184). They also demonstrate the humanity of the characters as the cars "become overdetermined symbols" of human "aspirations and disappointments" (184). This identification with cars allows them to "represent the propulsive aspirations of disenfranchised people" (184). As Kris Lackey writes, the human "self" expands, and the automobile "loses its mechanical identity ... and becomes a kind of bionic prosthesis" (32). Automobiles then take on a "humanity" of their own that expresses the emotions and inner conflicts of their "more human" owners/drivers. The automobile frequently redefines human identity as it takes on, or makes possible, the expression of human wants and desires. This "American belief in mobile identity" is able to mold and shape itself according to the wishes, aspirations, and needs of the human characters (Osteen 184).

More specifically, certain cars permit greater freedom. Osteen believes that open cars — roadsters and convertibles — offer the highest degree of expression (184). In definitive terms, the convertible is "associated since its invention with youth, freedom, and rebellion." This is "convertibility," an invaluable, protean quality that brings together youth's energy, freedom's possibilities, and rebellion's promise of change (184). Yet, in the context of Hollywood's *film noir*, these virtues become, once again, negatives that threaten the individual, if not society. For example, in 1949's *Gun Crazy*, directed by Joseph H. Lewis, gun-toting outlaws Bart and Laurie stage a major robbery, escape in their convertible, and speed off momentarily free of pursuit. Their plan is to split up, then rendezvous later. However, Bart in his convertible and Laurie in hers glance at each other and, in an instant, cannot part. Desperate as the pair may be, they are still more desperate in their love for one another and cannot bear to be apart. If Bart and Laurie had not shared that look, they might have avoided their deaths at the film's conclusion, but the open cars allow that dangerous exchange of love and attraction, disclosing the couple's real weakness. For the two of them, "cars are like guns — erotic machines that enable them to evade" the dreadfulness of ordinary life (Osteen 189). The physical "openness" of the convertible provides not simply an ability to change, but a nakedness and vulnerability to the outside world. It expresses identity, but also lets the inner world of emotions and the vulnerable self be exposed. Convertibles, then, let the world see who possesses autonomy and mobility, while making the identity of those inside subject to their own flaws and the world's intrusion.

It should also be said that, outside of the Hollywood film, the automobile's "symbolic power lies in its representation as a commodity identified with its owner," and in a parallel sense, we find cinematic cars, open or enclosed, transformed into "sexual fetishes, symbols of identity, and murder weapons" as well as places of refuge or means of escape (Osteen 185). The convertible amplifies the effect all automobiles have, adding intensity and magnifying identity. As to the Corvette's place in this, in the real world the initial design of the car called for an open cockpit, like the European sports

Laurie (Peggy Cummins) and Bart (John Dall), gun-toting outlaws in Joseph H. Lewis's *Gun Crazy* (1949), seem to prefer convertibles as their vehicles of choice. The openness of the car suggests freedom, even a willingness to embrace danger and excitement; however, the same attributes are also vulnerabilities. The Corvette was conceived as an open roadster, and that freedom and exposure to the world have persisted as part of the car's nature (Photofest).

cars it imitated, and all early Corvettes — the 1953 through 1962 Cls — were open cars with fabric or removable hard tops. Significantly, the vast majority of production Corvette coupes feature removable roof sections, giving them an expressiveness and openness similar to convertibles. In effect, then, all Corvettes should be defined by that same convertibility that carries with it a dynamic image of youth, freedom, and rebellion. Thus, all Corvettes, as material objects, partake in that "aura" of the open car, and the car, as an image, asserts a symbolic power, much as do the automobiles found in print and visual media.

What we have seen so far is how one specific automobile model fits in with the American heritage of automobility in literature and popular culture and how the image of that car captures meanings intrinsic with the majority of automobiles, while becoming distinguished by an association with technology, masculinity, and the freedom of the open road. The Corvette's image may suggest a variety of meanings, yet over the car's fifty-year history its associations have become complex, confused, even contradictory: the one thing, the Corvette, is many different things, signifiers and signifieds, that all arise from diverse portrayals of the car. It is difficult to even define the classification "sports car" without running into problems. While sports cars carry an exciting, sensuous aura, they are "not dangerous *per se,*" and the term is "at best a proxy variable for [a] driver who behaves aggressively" (Ingenbleek 176–177). The image of a sports car and its "external aspects," the qualities and values we read into the material object, are bound up with the attitudes and behaviors the owners see in their own character. The Corvette projects an image, and the drivers take in and reproduce further images of the car and themselves together, sharing the qualities that the car makes exciting and desirable.

Chapter 3

The Corvette: A Scholarly Review

Scholarly research into the automobile in general and the Corvette in particular has already taken place. Yet none of the sources — theses, dissertations, essays, or critical texts — take the form or format I am attempting here. Most limit themselves to either an expansive perspective or a particularly narrow focus on aspects of the automobile, and few — if any — follow a selected example, such as the Corvette, through literature and popular culture. One of the earliest critical works is Cynthia Golomb Dettelbach's book *In the Driver's Seat: The Automobile in American Literature and Popular Culture* from 1976. Dettelbach is most concerned with the automobile's "real and symbolic capacity" and views "the relationship between literature about the car and the car itself as one of 'dialogic encounter,' a process of exchange and interaction" (xi and 4–5). As she sees it, the automobile is an "offspring of that particularly American union of space, romance, and technology," and "in a wide variety of American art forms, the car is the metaphor or microcosm of our ambivalent, dream/nightmare experiences" (5–6). These ideas are traced through a number of literary works, and Dettelbach draws similar conclusions to what we have already seen: "The anthropomorphosis or personification of the car takes the integration process [Americans becoming closer to their cars] one step further. Once the automobile is endowed with animate qualities, it can be treated as an extension of the self or even as an autonomous surrogate" (92). As she follows the automobile through novels, films, and poems, it becomes clear that cars do have a place in American literature and popular culture, one that is complex and in need of further exploration and development. While this work does not stress a single specific critical perspective, Dettelbach's analysis makes it clear that "in America, the automobile shapes — and haunts — the imagination" (120).

A book that offers a wider-ranging study of the automobile is Roger N. Casey's *Textual Vehicles: The Automobile in American Literature* (1997). Casey's focus is on the automobile and automobility in American literature in general. He views the car as "America's number-one privileged machine" and contends that the automobile has "profoundly affected the making of this nation's" literature (xi). This text is "roughly chronological" in approach, and it utilizes "structural, material cultural, and new historical" methods in what Casey terms "*a material culturalist study that privileges the literary artifact*" (original italics) (xii). "America has," according to Casey, "truly become one vast motorscape" (4). While today, in the twenty-first century, we may tend to think of the personal computer as the most intimate and important of technological machines, "most teenagers still dream of their first Corvette more than their first PC" (Casey 4). Using literary studies, "sociology, anthropology, psychology, [and] history," among other fields, Casey finds evidence that the automobile has had a powerful influence in the literature of America and that "the relationship between automobility and American culture" has been "complex" and "changing" over time (6). In its early days the automobile offered *speed*, and that rapidity of motion promised "success," which could lead in turn to wealth, much as Jay Gatsby's elegant Rolls-Royce is a sign of his achievement (29 and 50). While affluence was at first a condition of ownership, that changed, and the car became an object most Americans could purchase. To many citizens, the car was then "the ultimate representation of material culture," and this was demonstrated in the writing of the time, from Sinclair Lewis' *Dodsworth* (1929), to Erskine Caldwell's *God's Little Acre* (1933), and even William Faulkner's *Intruder in the Dust* (1948), in which he wrote, "The American really loves nothing but his automobile: not his wife his child nor his country nor even his bank-account" (71 and 83). Casey cites the "new adjective" *motorcentric*, from the early 1930s, which describes the central focus that the automobile came to have in the lives of real people and their literary counterparts (76).

"Automania" is the term Casey uses to describe the post–World War II American boom in the culture of the automobile (95). Kerouac's *On the Road* (1957) is the most outstanding representative of how the car became "an exalted machine because it could move — and move fast" (111). Nevertheless, Casey points out here that in Sal Paradise's final disillusionment with motion and the car, we witness a different phase in the relationship and culture. The automobile — in the form of the Corvette, the car American teenagers dream of or aspire to, and other cars — possesses an image that must be questioned. The postwar years present the threat of technology;

the automotive death toll on the roads and the prospect of nuclear war are aspects of the same cultural obsession with "progress." First in counterculture and Beat literature, then in more mainstream writing, the automobile suggests negative values. It threatens and corrupts the "freedom" it once signified; cars come to "insulate or isolate" people from reality (140).

In particular, the automobile may now represent the oppression of or limited opportunities for women, African Americans, and others. In their writing — such as Ralph Ellison's *Invisible Man* (1952), along with Joy Williams' *Escapes* (1990) and Louise Erdrich's *Love Medicine* (1984) — cars are instruments falsely promising what white, male America has long enjoyed. "Masculinity [white males] and automobility" appear to be "interchangeable identities in American culture," and these concepts must be critiqued and challenged by new and contemporary accounts of automotive America (Casey 168). Casey only considers "literature" in his analysis, not cinematic or other popular culture, yet he finds much the same as what, in fact, occurs: "the quest for movement and the desire for individual mobility" that "technological progress" initiates often leads to "depersonalization and dehumanization" (171). In the end, the automobile "*is* a complex symbol, a crucial icon of American culture" (original italics) and "is at the heart of American literature, as well" (173). It has led to "windshield perception," a framing of the world as if seen through a windshield, and "mechancomorphism," like biomorphism, a thinking of or seeing life in machine terms or forms; and the car has become "an emblem of desire" and "a place for sex" in America (174).

Michael L. Berger's *The Automobile in American History and Culture: A Reference Guide*, published in 2001 as part of a series called "American Popular Culture," "links together a multiple number of books in a sequence of narrative essays" that explain individual works "in a broader context within the field of American automotive studies" (ix). Berger's focus is not on literature or popular culture, so much as it is the overall place of the automobile in, as the title says, history and culture. The text concentrates on "General Industrial Histories and Biographies," "Specialized Sociological and Cultural Studies," "Political Analyses and Polemics," and "Reference and Research Sources" (Berger vii–viii). Overall, the essays communicate that "there seemed to be a good match between the nature of motor travel and what was perceived to be the national character" and that the "individualism and personal mobility that Americans always had valued" found "a new means of expression" and a "new 'escape value'" in the automobile (xix). What is also important is how the "synergy between the car and traditional

American values" came to make the automobile so incredibly significant in American society (xix). In particular, women eventually became "major beneficiaries" of the automobile; "their range of mobility began to approach that of men, and the sphere of their activities expanded accordingly" (xxi). As the car assumed a greater and more significant role in society, models differentiated, yielding a variety of types and "specialty automobiles," including "the only truly high-performance American sports car, the Chevrolet Corvette" (xxv).

Berger's work is primarily a reference text in the form of essays, each well documented and with a lengthy bibliography. Among these are "Automotive Engineering and Design," "The Automobile and American Culture," "Contemporary Socioeconomic Problems," and "Reference Works and Periodicals" (105, 205, 341, and 377). Each essay develops and supports its ideas in what seems to be an exhaustive fashion. Berger does not delve into literary works except as they may relate to the subject area of the individual essay, yet a number of ideas are suggested or points made that fit in with the ideas that may be discovered in more literature oriented or "critical" texts. In a discussion of "self-identity," he analyzes how different types of cars serve as status symbols and, as part of the material on sports cars, describes the Corvette as "America's first true contemporary 'sports car' with anything approaching decent longevity." He writes that the Corvette "began as a model and now really is a marque [a brand or series with its own distinctive character and identity] in its own right" (162). While discussing the automobile and American culture, Berger says, "Given the profound effect that the automobile has had on American culture, it is not surprising that it has influenced the development of architecture, the visual arts, and music" (205). Everything in this reference guide is not, however, one-sided in the automobile's favor: "despite the automobile's mass appeal," it "continues to pose unresolved problems for the American public" (341). As a book to consult while doing research, this is a valuable text, and — in the instances cited above and more — it suggests that certain automobiles have identities, characteristics, or significance that makes them worth studying.

Concerning the Corvette itself, two masters degree theses stand out in regards to the Corvette marque and its place in American culture. The first of these is Michele Motichka's 2003 work "Brand Loyalty in the Automotive Community: A Case Study on the Chevrolet Corvette," which looks at the Corvette and "Corvette people" from a sociological perspective. Using surveys and interviews with both owners and GM executives involved in Corvette production, she seeks to account for how the Corvette "brand" has survived for so long. Hers is "a cultural, ethnographic, qualitative case study on the Chevrolet Corvette" (3). Motichka writes that automobile manufacturers used Americans' "love of the open road and the freedom and mobility" that the car gave them to help create a culture that fixed the automobile in the American psyche (4). Through advertising in a variety of media, emotional connections to the car and the feeling "encountered while behind the wheel" became well established (8). The success of the Chevrolet Corvette is one special example of this relationship, an instance of successful image and product design that has "etched its presence on the American cultural landscape since 1953" (10). However, the Corvette does not "belong" to General Motors or Chevrolet; rather than a corporate "possession," the "brand culture owns the brand and what meaning it stands for, the company doesn't" (11). Corvette owner/drivers are "fans"— or even fanatics — who use the car "to live in and through a set of symbols ... rather than reality" (12). Corvette people develop a "sub-cultural community" that allows "group identities," even "an elitist context" to form (12).

From a sociological perspective, the Corvette answers "hidden needs" that "consumers are looking to satisfy" (Motichka 16). Among these are "emotional security, assurance of worth, ego-gratification, a sense of power, and a sense of roots" (16). While they may be intrigued by the Corvette's technology or attracted to its design and performance, it is how the car makes them feel that counts. The Corvette seems to answer part of what psychologist Abraham Maslow described as a "growth need" for "self-actualization" (qtd. in Motichka 17). Sometimes advertising and marketing lead to a "so-called legendary brand" whose values consumers "identify with"; in this case the brand has "a soul" and a "brand narrative" (22). Paraphrasing psychologist J. G. Carrier, Motichka writes, "Social and cultural meaning ... are a way to define who we are to ourselves and others. There is no inherent meaning to an object; human relationships give them meaning" (27). The Corvette community formed over time and persists today primarily because of the Corvette image and social interaction of the people involved with the car (38). The Corvette, then, is not "just another vehicle" to those attracted to the material object and sharing the values its persistent image projects.

Phillip J. Scott follows a similar line of reasoning in his 2004 thesis "The Ford Mustang and the Chevrolet Corvette: Icons in American Culture." The Corvette and the Mustang are separated in terms of price and performance, but both answer the "unyielding need for horsepower and speed" that America feels, and "the impact each vehicle has had on American culture is unmistakable, and unrivaled by any other American cars" (2 and 3). Scott points out how Corvettes have frequently been marketed as material objects of male enhancement: the "masculine driving machine" and "freedom of the road" were usually reserved for men, and women were sexual objects, decorative but rarely permitted to drive (73 and 74). He emphasizes the material objects — the cars themselves — and the media presentation — the careful cultivation of images — for both automobiles. The material objects and their images act together to generate the sales that drive further development of the object and refinement of its image; object and image conduct an interplay between themselves while soliciting the attention and emotions of the consumer, who can be male or female. "It was a combination," Scott writes, "of factors that allowed the Corvette and Mustang to become icons in American culture" (91).

Quoting researchers Marsh and Collett, Scott notes the status of the Mustang and Corvette as "icons": "The fundamental symbolism of the car is both complex and inescapable. It conjures up images of speed, excitement, and vitality ... its power and shape endow it with a sense of sexual potency. It is precisely because the car can communicate such a variety of messages that it has captured our imagination" (92–93). Part of this "iconic" positioning is due to the cars appearing in popular media, television and film. Scott points out how both the Corvette and the Mustang are perennial favorites in series television and motion pictures. Films such as *Bullitt* (1968) and television shows such as *Route 66* (1960–1964) make cars both fast and "cool," and the association with tough, masculine role models is not accidental. "*Route 66*," Scott stresses, "was the first of several television series over the decades that would make *a single automobile* the centerpiece of the series" (147–148). The American nature of the two cars, the manly actions of the leading men, and the freedom of the streets or road were, and still are, seductive to us today — at least the male "us" in the American audience. While Frank Bullitt courted danger on the streets of San Francisco, Buz and Tod explored the wide-open spaces of the American road. Others, in a variety of forms, would follow. Gender has also played a role in the way the cars are perceived. As time has passed, more women have gained access to automotive freedom and at least the suggestion of independence.

Scott includes reflections on what Corvette and Mustang owners, male and female, have to say about their cars; not surprisingly, they speak of how the cars serve as expressions of power and identity, as well as sexuality. In point of fact, Scott concludes that "it took *a series of key important events* to make the Mustang and Corvette cultural icons"; no single, unique factor seems to make for "iconic" status (205). Although he does not indulge in cultural criticism to a great degree, Scott reiterates many of the points borne out in literary and cultural works: signifiers like the Corvette survive for reasons that involve people and society, their attitudes and perceptions, and that the objects tell us something important. "Icons," historian Marshall Fishwick says, "do objectify [the] deep mythological structure of reality, revealing basic needs which go from age to age, media to media, generation to generation" (qtd. in Scott 209). The Corvette is just a car, yet its associated qualities, the characteristics the object and image suggest, do often demonstrate an "iconic" nature that speaks to human needs.

Chapter 4

The Corvette in Literature: Selected Examples

The Corvette is found in a wide range of published material. Aside from auto-enthusiast and collector works, books such as Jerry Burton's beautifully illustrated *Corvette: America's Sports Car* (2006), there are romance novels such as *The Purple Corvette* (2007), detective stories such as *L.A. Outlaws* (2008), and a variety of popular fiction in which Corvettes are the vehicles of heroes or villains — male and female. Usually the car is a signifier of an adventurous nature, sexual desirability, or the power of affluence or social position. The cars serve as material shorthand to express a character's personality or a thematic idea in the work. The quality of these varies immensely. Some are mainstream and geared to make a profit; others are simply soapboxes for the author to vent his/her social, religious, or political views. Yet some qualify as literature, with real ideas behind the use of the Corvette name and image. Following are a few representative samples of what is to be discovered when one cruises Amazon.com or does a Google search after specifying "Corvette."

Adam Johnson's novel *Parasites Like Us* (2003) presents a sad, funny, but not bitter account of a modern apocalypse: not a nuclear or global war, but a relatively "quiet" near end to humanity. Reminiscent of Don DeLillo's *White Noise* (1985), it describes the life of a college professor, Dr. Hank Hannah, an anthropologist who specializes in the culture of prehistoric Americans, the Clovis people who crossed the Bering Sea from Asia to North America. The Clovis were masters of the technology of their day, the creators of pointed and edged stone weapons — the "most dangerous weapons on earth," the "nuclear" technology of the time — that enabled them to kill to extinction what Hank estimates to be no less than thirty-five species of mammals (Johnson 8). Once his book on these people has brought him a measure of success, notoriety, and tenure, Hank acquires a custom van, a bass boat, and a Corvette. Gary Krist, in the *New York Times Book Review*, writes that *Parasites Like Us* has a "basic atmosphere" of "what you might call 'neo–White noise'—that familiar ambiance of menacing technological crisis" found in Don DeLillo's novels (Krist 7). The technological sophistication of the Clovis people, given their place and time, parallels that of humanity in the early twenty-first century, particularly their talent for "profligacy and the reckless embrace of material consumption over artistic and spiritual development." Yet, for all their accomplishments, the Clovis left behind "no art, no monuments, no shelters, few remains" (Johnson 9). Somehow, it seems, they failed to create a civilization or a society that could endure over a long span of time.

In the novel, Hank's "classic" 1972 Corvette serves as a reminder of both the technology of "modern" times and his self-absorption with his own wants and desires. Hank is a victim of "relationship troubles": his mother abandoned the family when he was a child, his stepmother has died just recently, his father frequently borrows the Corvette to chase younger women, his mentor has retired and left South Dakota for the warmer, friendlier climate of Florida, and Hank has no one he is close to or cares for. The book is described as a satire full of "inventiveness, black humor, and penetrating insight" and a "wonderful inventive, exhilarating mess," and Hank's isolated, academic, and self-centered life is one of the satire's major targets (Leber and Hand, respectively). One reviewer says that "contemporary America," as presented, is "a culture rich in everything except the warmth of human connection," and that is true; it takes catastrophe to make people forge real connections with each other (Krist 7). The crisis in *Parasites Like Us* results from the discovery of a Clovis burial site near the expansion of a Native American casino. Hank and his graduate students find, among the bones and spear points, two curious and unique clay spheres: one of them rattles when shaken, the other is ominously silent. Inside the first is what seems to be Clovis popcorn, which Hank and his companions pop and eat. When the second is opened at a "purification ceremony" at the casino, a plague is released; in ten days it kills all of humanity, every person on earth, except for the ones who ate the popcorn. The mysterious clay spheres, the end of human life, and the failure of people to form positive connections to each other all seem to resemble the strange box, the nuclear substance, and the end of the world in that last *film noir*, *Kiss Me Deadly*. In both cases, the "hero" is more self-centered than aware of the needs of others, more willing to indulge himself than do what may be best for the world at large, and quite taken with his car, in the movie a 1954 Corvette, in the novel a 1972 Stingray.

When Hank's Corvette disappears — dragged under the ice of a frozen lake while inadvertently chained to an older muscle car, a "souped-up" GTO gone "crummy with rust" — not long before the deadly, plague-containing sphere is opened, he laments, "It was more than just a car.... It was part of me" (Johnson 86 and 138). It is as if, like the Clovis people's artifacts, contemporary humanity's products don't stand the test of time either and become lost, buried in the ground or under water. Hank's identity, the one he knows prior to the coming of the plague, begins to end with the loss of "my Corvette." As he snatches the sphere full of popcorn from the Corvette, "it was as if I could see the whole history of my car at once" (137). In an instant, he recalls how the car was "the yellow 'lady slayer'" in the salesman's words and feels "the rumble of the engine" — "Oh, my willing V-8!" — as, like the dearest people in his life, the Corvette abandons him (137). When Hank misses the Russian woman he believes himself in love with, "the most beautiful paleobotanist in the state of North Dakota," he feels "the same pang I'd felt after buying the Corvette" as he realized that maybe his dreams of success and happiness would not come true (213). Later in the story, as he and the survivors try to find their way in a world now empty of the mass of humanity, he remembers and misses the car, what he referred to as "beyond extravagant" or his "baby," and one of his students labels his "macho car" (42, 120, 65).

In the end, *Parasites Like Us* presents what one reviewer calls "one of the best-realized, most realistic, and horrifying accounts of disaster" and a "terrifying, even shocking, narrative, as frighteningly understated" in its end as the novel's humor is dark and entertaining (Hand 37). The book's quality is, however, uneven; another critic refers to it as "highly original, largely entertaining, and occasionally maddening" in its "weird and ominous avalanche" of words and images ("Parasites Like Us"). Weird and funny as it may be, the novel does present a view of contemporary life and modern society so caught up in its own needs and identity — as Hank is so taken with himself, his Corvette, and his work — that it appears to have lost focus as to where it is headed and what its values, or lack of them, will say about it to future anthropologists who will study *our* remains. In the present as in the past, it seems difficult to separate a culture from its technology; one of Hank's students contends that the Clovis people, in particular the women, fashioned the potent and deadly Clovis points as both the distinctive art and weapons of their culture. What will our relics say about us? Looking back at the time before the plague, Hank believes, "The first crime against existence is hope.... [H]ope drives death's getaway car," and he finds himself comfortably resigned, in this future that seems to be an "afterlife," to a world without what we today take for granted: "You don't get to bargain [choose what you get]. If there's no Corvette, so be it. If there are no martinis or shrimp bowls, so it goes" (Johnson 37 and 332). There seems to be an echo of Kurt Vonnegut, Jr., here, the sense of humor and the resolve to accept life for what it is. Hank still remembers his Corvette, one of his personal choices, as an artifact of our time, yet as he tells one of the youngest remaining humans, once one steps "outside the cloud" of loneliness "then words and names" begin to work for you (338). The Corvette and all the objects of the old world are just signs of a civilization that held false hope for itself.

From another perspective, a moral and spiritual one, comes Brian Stewart's Christian novel *Red Corvette* (2007), almost an allegory of the Seven Deadly Sins channeled through a classic Corvette. The story begins with the car coming into focus; it is *the thing*, the material object, that suggests egotism, self-centered human nature, and the temptations of the physical — flesh and machine, wealth and power — world of mortality. The book is written with a purpose, to demonstrate the flaws and corruption of the world of "things" — false appearances that mask the truly, as in spiritually, meaningful. This is perceived from what is best described as a fundamentalist Christian perspective, a view of the world as flawed, sinful, and fallen without the acceptance of Jesus as Savior. It centers on Doug, a young lawyer who owns the Corvette, and his friend Johnny, an individual with an unclear past, who seems able to persuade, convince, and charm people, especially women, into seeing and doing things his way. Doug and Johnny bear a striking resemble to the characters of Tod and Buz from *Route 66*: one is blond, educated, and from an upper-class background, and the other is dark-haired, working class, in touch with the world of the streets, and of a less clear origin. As the Corvette first appears "reflected light shimmered like demons dancing off its smooth red metal raked curves hit by sunlight. The red Corvette shimmered as a phantom flame, torching the street" (Stewart 2). The car attracts attention, particularly that of Mindy, a sorority girl from Alpha Omega Chi, who becomes taken with the car and "slowly stroked its curves" as she flirts with Johnny (5).

If the Corvette has been portrayed or utilized as a material expression of different values, it is here the emblem of all that occurs that is evil, and this novel simplifies good and evil into two camps, the Godly who struggle but find their way, like Mindy, and the Lost, like Johnny, who do not realize how their immortal souls are at stake during their time on earth. To summarize: Johnny discovers a large bag of marijuana from a crashed smuggling plane; Mindy becomes more involved with him, using drugs and falling further from "Grace" and deeper into sin and corruption. While driving the Corvette stoned on marijuana and encouraged by Johnny's wild, reckless ways, she hits two young boys, killing one. Johnny, seeking to sell the grass and make money to buy that "New Porsche" he desires, forces her to leave the scene, and continues to entice the other characters into more and more trouble, away from God, later critically injuring a police officer who pursues the Corvette.

This is not a novel with literary pretensions; it is geared to young readers — the majority of the characters are teenagers or college students — who would be tempted by just the things depicted. And it is not subtle in its Christian proselytizing. In a place full of bad people, Johnny's compatriots in the drug trade, the narrative voice pauses to say: "By refusing to consider the possibilities of a final judgment and a reckoning for their deeds, they had in fact already sentenced themselves to an eternity of torment. They never read the book of Revelation where God pronounced the judgment of hell on those who used drugs to get high" (33). Expensive automobiles and other accouterments of ostentatious living appear frequently. Mindy has a BMW, her stepmother a Mercedes; the gangbangers and lowlifes Johnny knows have customized low-riding older Chevrolets with loud, powerful sound systems, but the narrative returns to the Corvette as manifesting a hedonism and a seductive appeal — its beauty and its speed — that evolves into a more overt and expressive evil. Once the car is "hot," Doug reports it stolen, and Johnny becomes its master. The red Corvette, a "glistening red devil," is then repainted black with airbrushed "violent red, yellow, and white flames" and a large, fanged demon in whose eyes seem to dance "shadows of tortured naked bodies (99, 129, and 130).

While all of this sounds heavy-handed in a fictional context, as an object of Christian allegory the Corvette is in keeping with the overall message of the text: the world is full of sin, our souls are at the mercy of evil's temptation, and only God's grace can save us from an afterlife of everlasting agony. A car or any other machine is not in itself an instrument of good or evil, but the author chooses to make this Corvette's image one of devilish intent. As a brand, Corvettes often signify affluence, they promise speed and freedom, and sports cars often carry connotations of physical power and sexual allure: what more readily available face for evil to wear would seem necessary for the purposes of this story? This is an incredibly narrow interpretation of an object, making it into a device that inspires fear with little or no other meaning. As might be expected, the transformed Corvette, the devil's ride, has the signature — the name — "El Destructor," the Destroyer (Stewart 130).

The Corvette, then, has many faces, and its identity shifts with the context in which it is placed and the significance that the presenter chooses to give it. As a material object with an established history and image, it offers a wide range of possible uses in any kind of textual setting. The end of *Red Corvette* comes when Johnny seeks to kill Mindy, who cannot bear what she has done and wishes to confess her guilt, thereby dragging him down with her. Like the Corvette, he too is changed: "his face transformed: filled with a cold demonic hatred, a vein pulsated in his forehead like a large horn" (Stewart 146). The car and the fallen man, the doomed soul, share the same identity. When dying, shot by the police who come to Mindy's rescue, Johnny beholds two seemingly "angelic" beings come for him, yet their fangs drip blood (146). He has died and "gone to hell"; denying salvation through Jesus, gambling "that Christianity was just a hoax," he finally asks himself, "Why didn't I just believe?" (146–147).

The Corvette here is even more extreme than the deadly box in *Kiss Me Deadly* or the plague released in *Parasites Like Us*. The two of those merely ended the world or killed off the majority of humanity; they either left the human soul alone or unspecified in its spiritual destiny. The Corvette that becomes the devil's own sports car or personifies a demon from hell is perhaps its most outrageous or even ludicrous usage. Also, if one pays attention, the Corvette in *Red Corvette* is strangely generic. It is unclear if it is a coupe or a convertible, and exactly what year or generation never becomes tangible enough to create a picture in the reader's mind. The Corvette's body is referred to as "metal" when all Corvettes are made of plastic or composite materials. The novel is so concerned with its "message" that the car is just a "vehicle" for that image of evil. Like the characters who seem merely set up to hold the place of this or that idea, no one here is as real as Tom Joad or Mike Hammer or even Hank Hannah. In this allegory, the Corvette is only a thing used to carry an overly stressed image. The many meanings of the automobile that the Corvette embodies are wasted; a richness of sign or image becomes sadly one-dimensional. As an object and an image, it is a tool of propaganda.

However, there are other Corvettes that appear in literature. One example of a "poetic Corvette" is found in William Stafford's poem "Old Blue" from the posthumous collection of new and selected poems *The Way It Is*

(1998). Stafford invokes the name "Corvette" in the first line, letting it suggest what meaning or image that word may call up for the reader. The poem first appeared in *Passwords*, Stafford's 1991 collection of poems, so this was long after *Route 66* and years of Corvette advertising had established the car's name in the mind of the public. In the opening lines the speaker declares that on some indefinite day he will start "that" Corvette, let the car speak to him and assert the authority that it possesses (236, lines 1–3).

While Stafford's poetry is often critical of modern life and the distractions of technology, his work does not suggest the interpretation that machines are inherently evil or the enemies of humanity. The title, "Old Blue," seems more like the appellation given to a dog or other faithful companion of long standing. The car here feels like the partner in a long-established and personal relationship, one that the persona in the poem looks to return to or reawaken. The Corvette, as depicted, appears to be a vehicle that has been stored away — it needs to be rocked until the wheels turn freely — in a barn or shed, as if the car, like its owner, possesses a vitality that has been put away or hidden from the world, one now in need of recovery (Stafford, lines 3–4). In this quality, "Old Blue" calls to mind Tennyson's "Ulysses" in how the individual asserts his desire for something like the life he used to have in a world where his individuality and abilities were significant. The monologue is personal, yet the sound of it is public, as if people were being addressed before one takes leave of them. While Tennyson's "Ulysses" may have ironic meaning according to the different contexts of the mythic hero's life as portrayed in literature, Stafford's "Old Blue" seems straightforward. When the speaker says he will reawaken the Corvette, it is not an idle daydream, but a statement of purpose, not a weak and fleeting thought, but a powerful intent to reclaim himself.

Critically, Stafford has been regarded as a "precursor" of the American poets who would come to emphasize "the deep image" (Rudman 109). This is not necessarily the Corvette, the car in this poem, so much as it is the image of escape, or more precisely, the material object as an image that reinforces the persona's defiance of others' conceptions and expectations. The car is the external sign of independence and self that has been locked away for too long. It could be that "Old Blue" is not the Corvette's nickname but that of the person speaking. Yet the human and the automobile identities merge together: the humanity of car, its "authority," is the outward thing that the man now claims for himself. A reviewer of this collection writes that Stafford's "specialty" is "the ultimate brutality of the small moment," and in the space of fourteen lines, a sonnet in length with no set rhymes,

we move from the questioning first words to the certainty of the final declaration, the speaker's farewell to the ties of the past (Rudman 109).

In the preface to *The Way It Is*, Naomi Shihab Nye describes Stafford's
poetry as possessing "an intense awareness of presence and absence," and in
"Old Blue" the freedom that the old Corvette promises is a *presence* that
contrasts with the *absence* found in other people who intrude on or discon-
nect with the speaker (Stafford xix). The addressees, Mona and Steve, have
failed the "I" in the poem: she found no value in him, and he refused to
support him in some way (lines 6–10). The "I" in Stafford's poetry is often
taken to be his own voice or that of someone very like or close to him. The
majority of Stafford's short poems, or lyrics, have what seems to be a male
voice and perspective, one that appears very near to his own personality.
Yet this voice is individual, not patriarchal; it may claim for itself, but it
does so on the basis of inner strength and identity, not the power to dictate
to others. In "Old Blue," like many of Stafford's poems, there is a "moment
of healing and self-fortification" that comes through "connecting with the
natural, elemental past"— a "moral strength"— that the Corvette is a touch-
stone for (Heldrich 143). The car is a positive image of the power to choose,
to still be independent and free to stay or go. The persona may be male,
but there is no masculine exclusivity in the poem. The car is not so much
a symbol of masculinity, in any sense, as it is a signifier of the human ability
to assert its own character, make decisions for itself, and follow its own
resolve.

When the speaker declares that no one can stop him once he reclaims
the Corvette and how, carrying everything of importance, he and the automobile will gain momentum (lines 4–5), it sounds like a transformation has
taken place: the "imaginative transformation of the natural world into something meaningful" (Heldrich 147). In this and Stafford's other poems, there
is frequently a posthumanist "grouping" or bringing together of agents —
animal, human, and machine — in an instant where something is realized
or a change occurs. In "Traveling Through the Dark," the driver, his car,
and the dead deer form a "group," and the consciousness of the human, the
vitality of the machine, and the moral (and mortal) example of the animal
yield an awareness that is "meaningful." In a like manner, the "I" in "Old
Blue" experiences a return to freedom that the other humans, in their devalu-
ing and refusing of him, push him toward. The use of the "Corvette" name
as an established sign lets Stafford signify the connotations of freedom, independence, and individuality that the car's image suggests. A one critic puts
it, "Stafford's language seeks signifiers or words tightly linked with their

signifieds" (Heldrich 151). In this manner, "Corvette" would appear to be part of the overall pattern of American culture, and its meanings — suggested qualities to be utilized or criticized in a subtextual way — allow creative works to present the automobile as an imaginative device to convey meaning, whether as a visual or as a written image.

In a 1992 interview with Nancy Bunge, Stafford admits that "the greatest influence on me, the voice I hear in my work, is my mother's voice" (11). So, while we may assume that a "male voice" is speaking in "Old Blue," the sentiments are wider ranging than a particular gender's insistent male dominance, and the role played by the Corvette is not necessarily that of a masculine surrogate. To use Stafford's words, the "emotional validity" that he experienced growing up comes through in his poetry, and this leads to the assumption that the desire to escape and claim authority over oneself, as expressed in the poem, is part of the human strength and vulnerability found in men *and* women (Bunge 11). To Stafford this openness to the world is a virtue — perhaps a positive corollary to the idea of "convertibility" found in *film noir*— a "readiness to learn from what's coming in from outside" that lets an individual be safely exposed to the world and other people (Bunge 14). In his family, Stafford says, there was an emphasis on "listening," and that their "attitude toward danger or toward aggression or even toward evil" was an effort to "redeem" or "save" the others, the outsiders, from themselves (Bunge 15). In "Old Blue," the speaker asserts his/her authority, as the hidden presence of the Corvette suggests it, and leaves to rediscover the relationship to the world that the others do not or will not see.

Summary

Automobiles are things, physical objects of importance in the scheme of the twentieth- and early-twenty-first century world. Sociologist Rudi Volti, in his book *Cars and Culture* (2004), writes that "more than any other artifact of modern technology, the automobile has shaped our physical environment, social relations, economy, and culture" (xix). And this is not all: automobile ownership and driving "resonate with some of our most important values and aspirations"; our cars relate to us personally, as external signs of our individuality and social position (xix). The automobile "provides an individualized and privatized" mode of transportation, yet its success is the result of "collective efforts on a massive scale" (xx). Cars are major investments of time and money, and they have acquired a hold on — if not over —

us as human beings that is just as much emotional and psychological as it may be physical.

While cars are part of our social and economic structure, their images and the qualities they have come to signify are in addition part of our consciousness. As a material object, the Corvette is not so different from many others, but over time and through various depictions in media, it has come to possess an identity and an image that gives this lineage of cars — six generations as of 2009 — a distinctly American character. This "automobile identity" in America has its vices and virtues. "Car equals freedom" seems to be an assertion that most of us accept as true, although we are sometimes troubled by the cost. As the automobile "captured the hearts, imaginations, and pocketbooks of Americans," in the minds of many people it incurred a moral price as well (Jeansonne 126). "Frustrated theologians and parents" of the early 1900s attributed a significant amount of "moral laxity" to the influence of the automobile; it was "amoral if not immoral" in its effects on a society that valued order and tradition (127–128). In particular, the automobile was an agent of corruption of youth, especially women. Reportedly, one juvenile-court judge once termed the automobile "a house of prostitution on wheels," and to this day there is no denying the sexual quality of the freedom that a car promises (128). The image of modern sports cars — Ferraris, Porsches, and Corvettes — still partakes of this "sexuality on wheels," and no owner, male or female, wishes to do without it.

Women influenced the development of the automobile in meaningful ways. Historian Glen Jeansonne says that early in automotive history "both attitudes [presumably male attitudes] and automobiles were soon forced to change to accommodate" the demands of female consumers (129–130). Women expected their cars to have appeal to "the aesthetic sense of the buyer" (130). The female influence encouraged, if not required, that automobiles develop an aura of style and that cars would have to serve not just as objects of male desire but as fashionable creations, things designed with beauty of form and color. By the time the Corvette was entering the marketplace, the desire for speed — always an essential factor in how many perceived automobiles in general — was closely followed by considerations of style. As journalist/historian Steve Thompson presents it, sports cars appealed to a segment of the automobile market in part because they were, and continue to be, "contrarian" vehicles. Corvettes and similar machines operate against the general, dull, standard car designs seen every day. The "presence and performance" of some automobiles set them apart, and that carries a cachet of individuality. Men and women desire style and freedom, especially in America, and the automobile has come to suggest those things and more.

Given the above argument for the automobile's significance as a tangible object invested with human qualities and reflecting our attitudes and desires, it should not come as a surprise that many artists have employed it to make statements about or serve as emblems of culture and society. While the masters of the patriarchy, white males, around the world were discovering the intoxication of auto ownership and driving, the attraction the car held for minorities, women, young people, and everyone with a desire for the freedom and independence of mobility could not be long contained. Before very long, and increasingly as time has passed, those deprived of mobility or who had their social or political freedom limited by tradition or law came to claim automobiles for themselves. The Corvette is not the only car in popular culture, but its presence in art and literature is a reflection of how widespread and deep our relationship with the automobile in general has become. Across more than the last fifty years, the Corvette has taken a place as one of the cars, one of the objects, that carry meaning. The automobile and automobility are an aspect of humanity now, and will continue to be so far into the distant future. As the evidence shows us, cars are measures and representations of our nature; their images are reflections of our wants and desires. Where we find the Corvette, we see what automobility means.

PART II

The Image of Potency: The Corvette, Males, and Minorities

Chapter 5

The Masculine Object

The material world is not simply composed of "things" with dormant, inactive, passive existences. When it becomes the object of human scrutiny and thought, this "world of things" is invested with meanings and associations. Human consciousness is not just reason, as in scientific research, but emotion, attitude, and attachment. The point of view that this "consciousness" creates, the one that is passed along to us, is not necessarily balanced, well thought out, or impartial. Often, the mind that sees and the voice that speaks has a perceptive base that is founded on ideas and principles that may be accepted, but uncritically regarded by society. And, sometimes, we find a work that changes perceptions or calls attention to new ways of looking at the world. Works like this emerge, frequently unexpectedly, and present new expressions of national or cultural identity. Objects, then, such as automobiles and the open road — the Corvette sports car and other vehicles — take on new or different meanings as ways of thinking about the culture develop and change over time.

One of the primary characteristics of the Corvette and its image that we discover during critical analysis is how the car has become a signifier of masculinity. This is not as simple as it may at first appear, because while the Corvette — in its original incarnation — was a corporate product, a commodity for sale, the automobile in its most general sense had already come to represent a range of meaning to the American public. While it had initially been a symbol of affluence, with the advent of Ford's Model T and other affordable cars, the automobile rapidly became the single most powerful signifier of the independence and freedom of the American people. Automobility was, and is, *power* in American culture, and there is a romance of the road that works to seduce men, making them think that masculinity does not just promise autonomy and mobility, but is to a great degree defined

49

Early in its life the Corvette went racing, where those aspects of power frequently thought of as masculine could be developed to the highest degree. Racing Corvettes have the most powerful engines and reach the highest speeds; they accelerate and corner, exerting extreme forces on both car and driver. All this *power* demands coolness under fire and control of oneself and the machine — both of which appear to be what men possess (GM Photo Store).

by them. Since our society values patriarchal power, the automobile has become a tangible sign, the proof of masculine authority, which only recently could be appropriated by "others" — those who are not white, mainstream, heteronormative males. The Corvette, as a point of focus for America's automotive dreams of freedom and masculinity, has over the last fifty years been claimed by many men with dreams of masculine power — those who claim to possess the phallus, to be "men" endowed with self-determination and social, sexual, and creative power. This masculine potency has been exercised over the land itself, over machines and technology, and — quite frequently — over American women.

In discussing this, white masculinity and the patriarchal culture of America in post–World War II literature and media need to be described. The presumption of masculine dominance and the privileged status of males, usually white, led to the dream of the open road, and the Corvette was the automobile that most blatantly took us wherever adventure was to be found. As mainstream twentieth-century American culture evolved, the Corvette and other attributes of masculinity were seized upon by "others," men outside the usual bounds of patriarchy who claimed the signifiers of power for themselves and, as society gradually permitted, took on *power* of their own, including the ownership of Corvettes. The automobile today, in the form of the Corvette, is often a signifier of desirability. The car enhances the aura of sexuality and power of the male owner, or the automobile itself becomes an object of possessive desire, an alluring signifier that promises pleasure through its very existence. The Corvette as object holds an attraction all its own and sometimes represents other desired goals or objectives: material wealth, social success, power over others, individual identity, and sexual conquest.

This analysis and discussion looks at a diverse range of masculinity through automobility, and how the Corvette signifies masculine, patriarchal, and individual qualities. These include, along with related subjects of inquiry, three primary areas where the Corvette, sometimes called by its other name — Sting Ray or Stingray — is found in literature and American culture. Representations of white masculinity and patriarchy do not begin with the Corvette, but this particular singular automobile often appears in contemporary America as a signifier of male power and masculine sexuality. By the mid-twentieth century, American technology — especially the Space Program — becomes associated with the Corvette as our "right stuff" astronauts choose Corvettes as their signature vehicles. Minority or "other" expressions of masculinity, as society opens and offers them more opportunities, take the masculine Corvette as their image to use and manipulate, intensifying its connotations of sexuality, freedom, and independence.

Each of these areas has its own focus and examples. Literary works are normally used to create a context, and particular characters or individuals and their automobiles — typically Corvettes or comparable sports cars — are looked at in detail. Since masculinity often invites sexuality, the Corvette is a vehicle for or about sex almost as much as it is a means of masculine transportation. The image of the Corvette becomes complicated over time, giving it multiple identities according to the viewer and how she/he perceives the automobile and Western society in general. As a signifier, the Corvette — like other tangible goods — is not one thing, but many. It is a commodity for sale, an object of desire, a sign of power, and a representation of sexuality.

The Corvette presents, in figurative terms, a narrative of American masculinity. This is not a fluid, linear story; it meanders, and moves in jerks and starts. While heteronormative, white masculinity in the postwar years — the time when the Corvette is first devised and built — appears to dominate at least the Western world (the Cold War and the Space Race come to mind), its performative nature makes "masculinity" both difficult to define and hard to grasp. Being masculine is powerful to the outside world, but inside, it is full of contradictions and consequences. What makes male humans "men" faces doubts and uncertainties over time; the phallus — that instrument of *power*— is not a set thing, like a penis and testicles, that can be held onto, shown to the world, or even be surely lost by a failure of control or mistake behind the wheel. As the twentieth century progresses into the twenty-first, and the six generations of the Corvette come and go, we see what it means to be masculine and how that is achieved and sustained, called into question, and redefined, only to require further clarification.

What the Corvette does as a signifier of masculinity and automobility is permit us to indirectly see part of the process that has taken place over the last fifty years and continues today. The car and the culture that it represents are suggested in the works that contain them, and the "culture of masculinity" — white, black, straight, gay, affluent and social climbing — is reflected in the evolving image of the automobile, as typified by the Corvette.

Chapter 6

Automobility, White Masculinity, and Patriarchy

On the Road

Jack Kerouac's *On the Road* is a novel that bought its author unwanted attention when it premiered in 1957. According to his friend Joyce Johnson, Kerouac "lay down obscure" the night before, and woke up "famous" (qtd. in Charters vii). Reporters, reviewers, and the American public in general took *On the Road* to be a manifesto, a living, breathing example of the new youth culture, the "Beat Generation." Yet for Kerouac, this was far from the truth. The characters might be thinly disguised versions of people — Neal Cassady, Allen Ginsberg, William Burroughs — who would become famous as figures in the so-called "Beat Movement" and after, but the book was more about young Americans saturated "with experience almost to the point of exhaustion," people who found escape from the conformity and uncertainly of post–World War II and Cold War America by going "on the road" (Johnson 120). "Beat" was a state of "exalted exhaustion" that, in Kerouac's mind, was "linked" to "a Catholic beatific vision" or "direct knowledge of God" granted to those favored or "blessed" (Charters viii). Beats were not the precursors of hippies or student protestors, but adventurers whose life of "freedom, possibility, and rebellion" had more in common with the Steinbeck characters who faced "limit, loss, and wandering" and "actively called into question the myth(s) of America" (Spangler 308).

The energy of Kerouac's writing, the flow of words to match the passing of miles and of scenery, was the chief attraction of *On the Road*. As Joyce Johnson told him, "I think you write with the same power and freedom that Dean Moriarty drives a car" (119). The heart of this speed and energy — power and freedom — is captured in the Dean Moriarty's relentless drive to get somewhere, someplace where life *is happening*, and Sal Paradise's urgent need to discover *something*, knowledge or understanding, that will give his world a center. In *The Road Story and the Rebel*, Katie Mills calls this desire a need "to escape the commonplace and immerse themselves [the Beats] in life's grand mysteries" (35). For Kerouac, the "mysteries" and any possible answers lie out where a man can find them, not the place he *is*, but where he is going. Sal begins the journey "miserably weary" and has the feeling "that everything was dead," so for him the road is a place to recover his life, his vitality as a man (Kerouac 1). Or, as journalist John Leland writes, Sal wants "to become a man, but not like the examples of manhood that surround him" (12). The energy of the writing is what he discovers, what makes the story happen. Automobiles, people, and places are the means to find himself.

For Sal, Dean is the American cowboy, the spirit of the West. Dean is "that world's purest representative, as American as the postwar automobile" (Leland 101). Sal says, "Everything was behind him, and ahead ... was the ragged and ecstatic joy of pure being" (Kerouac 195). In poet Gary Snyder's words, Dean possesses "the energy of the archetypal west, the energy of the frontier"; he drives, talks, dances, does everything almost nonstop (qtd. in Charters xxviii). If Sal is lacking in the masculine virtues of self-confidence or the aggressive will to take action, Dean is hypermasculine, doing everything at top speed: running down the road, marrying women, and fathering children — defining his masculinity as extreme, excessive, and adventurous. Between the poles of Dean and Sal, energy flows; *On the Road* is very much a tale of *men* on the road; the women they encounter are diversions, pleasant stops on a seemingly endless and restless quest. For the men, automobiles are moving spaces where their male consciousness rules, yet Dean and Sal seek to avoid conformity and to discover life as it happens moment to moment. Dean repeatedly says, "We know time," and he seems to mean that how they perceive time is under their control, or that time will bring them where and when they need to be. What they are searching for will be found or occur ahead of them; the headlong rush to get there is Dean's concern, and this drives him faster and further down the road.

There are no Corvettes in *On the Road*, but the idea of automobility dominates the action of the novel. Early in the book, Sal — too poor to own a car — hitchhikes west to reach Dean and to search for that American something that will answer his need to redeem or recover himself. Hitchhiking, as Mark Osteen points out, is "mobility without autonomy"; Sal is at the bottom, he has almost lost himself but yearns to go west, toward the unknown and the future (188). Lacking autonomy, Sal also lacks identity; he is a man, but not a complete one. He can set a direction but cannot empower himself to *move* actively or powerfully toward a goal. Later, Sal gives in to necessity and buys a bus ticket, expending his meager financial resources but gaining some measure of power and motion. When Dean and Sal finally meet, they set out, doing so usually as passengers, paying riders, in travel bureau automobiles belonging to someone else. The cars they ride in and the people they spend time with give Sal a measure of his life back. Being "on the road" with Dean, though trying, rewards him with experience. And certain cars matter more than others; some machines signify special qualities that express the nature or situation of their owners. A few of these are emblems that enhance masculinity.

In California, Sal comes to know a multigenerational family of "Okies" from Nebraska, migrant workers who travel in "a jalopy truck"—echoes of the large Joad clan and their old Hudson (Kerouac 95–96). The Okies' truck, like the Joads', suggests their homelessness, and the best hope they have is to someday acquire a trailer to go with it. Later, Dean purchases a new 1949 Hudson: he "goes broke" to buy it, drawn to the car the same way he will be attracted to new and different women (110). Dean's new car, like Camille, his second wife, is something desirable that he will not hold onto once he becomes more infatuated with something else or a new adventure. His Hudson suits Dean's manic long-distance driving habits; it is, for as long as the car lasts, a good match for his needs behind the wheel. When Dean and Sal catch a ride with "a tall, thin fag" from Kansas, they discover that his "fag Plymouth," a car with "no pickup and no real power," is what Dean calls an "effeminate car" (207). Cars with character and/or power are "manly" in Dean's conception, but cars like the slow, weak Plymouth are, at best, for women. Other cars that belong to people on the road reflect a diverse range of backgrounds, "snazzy" cars, hot rods, even a dynamite truck which briefly gives Sal a ride.

What stands out particularly are the Cadillac automobiles that Dean and Sal meet. Marylou, Dean's former wife, goes off with a nightclub owner, a girlfriend, and "a greasy old man with a roll [of money]" in a Cadillac (172). One night in San Francisco, a tenor saxophone player's "boy," a "taut little Negro with a great big Cadillac," drives a group of them "clear across Frisco without stopping once, seventy miles an hour," and this puts Dean "in ecstasies," just like the far-out jazz music that they are out on the town to hear (201). The cars, like the music, are sources of intensity, emotional and physical stimulation, and absolute concentration of his faculties for

Dean. If the cars in the novel are attributes of masculinity, then Cadillacs make men alpha males, dominant predators in the American automotive world. This is where automobility and masculinity come together most in *On the Road*. The fast, powerful car manifests the strong, virile male, regardless of his physical size, sexual prowess, or personality. Dean, flawed and totally self-absorbed, can drive like no one else, like the tenor saxman can play, and cars are his instruments. When this novel was written, Cadillacs could still, with some credibility, be considered the "Standard of the World," as the manufacturer's advertising had been claiming since 1908 ("Cadillac"). They were distinctively American, powerful, signifiers of affluence if not of wealth, and carried that aura of taste and power that men crave. Cadillacs were, in essence, in that time, what Corvettes would later come to be: instruments of masculine, if not patriarchal power; assertive signifiers of male aggression; objects that flaunted or betrayed men's egos.

In particular, there is the 1947 Cadillac limousine that Dean and Sal gain possession of. From Denver to Chicago, Dean drives this car that belongs to a "Chicago baron" (243). It is everything Dean dreams of, and he is "jumping up and down with excitement to see it," as if the Cadillac were an especially beautiful woman or an incredibly gifted be-bop musician (225). While Dean can push a normal car to 70 or 80 m.p.h., the Cadillac is able to cruise at over 110. Even Sal is pleased and impressed; "the faster we left Denver the better I felt" (227). The "big motor thrumming with immense birdlike power," Dean breaks the speedometer as the car runs at top speed (226). The Cadillac takes them into the "utter darkness," "the sea of night" of the western prairie, and Dean becomes more ecstatic. The open road unreels "with dreamlike rapidity as we roared ahead," and Dean fantasizes about what they could do with a "magnificent car" like this (231). The Cadillac is the most patriarchal of automobiles; it sits at the top of the American food chain. Sal realizes that Dean's soul is "wrapped up" in an experience like this, a masculine dream with "a fast car, a coast to reach, and a woman at the end of the road" (232).

In a sense, this *is* "freedom" as the automobile would define it for most American males. What Dean is doing, perhaps why he is the character who attracts most of the popular attention to *On the Road*, is blatantly maniacal American maleness. Extreme to be sure, but what Dean has is what so many men in the country aspire to, this freedom of the road and seemingly reckless abandonment of worries and concerns, a self-centered trust and affection for one's self, not burdened with cares about job, family, or career ... and women, the promise of sex without strings or commitment. A number of ideas hover in the atmosphere of *On the Road*, but this one may, for male readers, be the closest to the surface. While Sal's distress is real, and he is searching for that "something" he longs for, it is Dean's near embodiment in his behavior of what we know should be ours (speaking as an American male): this energy to go and do, along with the total freedom to achieve it. The "Cadillac episode" of the novel captures so much of this that it cannot be accidental. Kerouac touches something here, but it is not *his*: this is young Neal Cassady's truth, one that most American men would identify with. It is a "dream" that is both individual and patriarchal: the excess of male ego involved assumes that it is an individual desire, yet the claim to *power* is a manifestation of that need for authority we find so much of the time in dominating, unquestioning male thinking.

Eventually, Sal becomes fearful of the relentless pace of Dean's driving. "Great horrors" of crashing make him take to the floor of the back seat as the "mad Ahab at the wheel" goes on (235). Sal can no longer totally accept Dean's way of living and thinking. Although he aspires to a strength and energy like Dean's, he comes to see the danger of its excess, the focus on self that invites disaster. Near the end of the journey, Sal refers to the car as female, "her" not *it*, yet the Cadillac is clearly a "thing," an object of desire and an instrument of Dean's purpose, not a female close to his heart (239). The last night, in Chicago, Dean and Sal try to pick up girls in the Cadillac. However, by now Dean's constant pushing has made it into "our big, scarred, prophetic car" that frightens them (242). Dean, like most American males, often pushes too hard and damages the "magnificent" thing that he has possessed. When Dean and Sal deliver the Cadillac, the once fine machine is a "muddy heap," a mess that the garage attendants do not recognize (243). Masculinity, taken to the extreme, invites destruction.

Later, in New York when Sal sees Dean for the last time, Sal and his new girlfriend are in the back of a bookie's borrowed Cadillac on the way to a Duke Ellington concert. Dean is changed; he has little to say and looks worn down, battered by the road. Sal has, perhaps, learned to accept some of the pain and uncertainty of life, and Dean is without a car or even a ride. Sal is changed by being on the road, but he is not complete or redeemed. He still thinks of Dean, of that mobility and freedom, yet he knows that "nobody, nobody knows what's going to happen to anybody" (307). So our freedom is not absolute: in his preface to *Big Sur*, Kerouac writes that "the world of raging action and folly" also has "gentle sweetness"; these are the aspects of life that we must work through in order to find our own truths.

Kerouac himself was optimistic about life in America but appeared to be more cynical in his later works (Davenport 6). *On the Road* was his "road book," and while it fit in with prior novels about automobility, it does suggest that a "limitation" of the road as an ideal may have been reached. The freedom that Milt and Claire came to cherish in *Free Air* or the promise, doubtful as it might be, of mobility that the Joad family's Hudson represented in *The Grapes of Wrath* are different later in the twentieth century. The possibilities now appear to be constrained, the air not so "free." This is important in that the "magic" of automobility as represented in the Joads' truck, the Cadillac limousine in *On the Road*, and the Corvette in *Route 66* (as we shall see) all possess critical interpretations that are both favorable and unpleasant. "Automobility," while presumably open to all, was actually a white male province, and even at that, it could reveal things, flaws and secrets, that American masculinity would be uncomfortable with. In *Manhood in America: A Cultural History* (2006), sociologist Michael S. Kimmel writes that American men have had doubts, usually kept to themselves, about their position and status since early in the twentieth century. One letter to the editor of the *Nation* magazine in 1927 unhappily concluded that, as Sal Paradise or Jack Kerouac might have said, there was "no salvation in being born a man" (White 178). In the early 1930s, in *Perhaps Women*, Sherwood Anderson thought that "modern man is lost" before the power of modern machines (Kimmel 132). From what Anderson wrote, Sal — in a peculiar sense — is a "feminized man," a positive social position, because women were not at that time "enervated spiritually by the machines," while "something ... seems to be going dead in the men," just as Sal once described himself (Anderson 142). Instead of merely having "damaged" or "failed" masculinity, Sal may be an outsider in the traditional masculine world, a situation like Kerouac's own life.

Kerouac, like Sal, was reportedly an indifferent driver, not comfortable behind the wheel. In fact, Kerouac seems to have sometimes felt socially excluded, alone and isolated. Cars, Cadillacs or Corvettes, were not an essentially masculine part of his world. The child of French Canadian émigrés to the United States, Kerouac became a writer in order to find a place for himself in America. Psychoanalyst Gladys Foxe writes that Kerouac experienced the deaths of many of those close to him during the Second World War and described himself and many of his friends as "eviscerated of 1930's innocent ambition" by the world they would grow into as men (qtd. 46). Kerouac's "damaged masculinity" parallels Sal Paradise's, and his lack of a "proper manly role" — he volunteered for the U.S. Navy but was given a medical discharge and spent the war in the Merchant Marine — very likely intensified the feelings he already had of being outside or excluded (Foxe 47). Kerouac seems to have lived on the fringe of patriarchal culture, and his life after 1945 was affected by what poet Kenneth Rexroth called a "mass disaffiliation of postwar youth from a commercial, predatory and murderous society" (qtd. Foxe 50). Although Sal tries out what has been described as "the full trinity of masculine power"—"manhood" accompanied by cars and guns—he discovers little affection for or reward in them (Osteen 189). If Kerouac and Sal reject the concept that "the auto exemplifies the desire to flout history, destiny and law, signifying freedom from rules and the dream of forging a new self," then they are separated from mainstream masculinity and attempting to go their own way, no longer necessarily following Dean Moriarty's or anyone else's idea of what makes a man (Osteen 184). What of automobility and its icon, the Corvette, then?

What Kerouac and his alter ego Sal struggle with are perhaps best termed "scripts of masculinity," what Michael Kimmel says are "less about what boys and men actually *did* than what they were told they were *supposed* to do" (original italics) (7). These "scripts" help create what we should think of as "masculinity as performance" and "'public' displays of masculinity and 'private' experience and feelings" (Peel 248). There are, in point of fact, "Corvette scripts" for performance, if one observes and studies the phenomenon closely enough. Kerouac and Sal are—in their travels—looking at, through, or behind these behavioral scripts and questioning what it is they are all about. These scripts dictate or define the terms of masculinity: (1) socially and sexually active, (2) decent job and/or income, (3) acceptable home/apartment, (4) appropriate or stylish male body and appearance, (5) sexy, powerful, expensive car, and (6) suitably attractive female companion(s). These are not absolute values, but they do approximate what is expected of, and desired by, the majority of American men. The Corvette substantiates, or at least follows, one of these scripts of masculinity and enhances a suitable expression of male virtues, the other scripted behaviors. Kerouac, along with Sal, seeks to glimpse what is behind the scripts and to subtly revise them in meaningful ways. With the passage of miles and time, Sal acquires a strength of character that separates him from the relentless pace of Dean's existence. Sal may still follow the "scripts" of masculine society much of the time, as he does in Mexico, but his "outsider" or fringe character grants him an enlightened perspective.

Automobility is a promise of new places, new beginnings, or in Sal's case, the opportunity to make himself over, to escape the "Old Sal" whose life seemed like death. Many of the uses of the automobile, the Corvette most especially, in the creative works that follow *On the Road* embrace this positive, free, redemptive model for American males. As one critic says, "*On the Road* can seem without direction because its narrator is not trying to develop an identity [his own] but to escape identity ... in order to invent himself anew" (Leland 83). Men, a Corvette, and the open American road may be icons of masculinity, but they do not escape from its problems and contradictions.

Route 66

One of the key factors in the persistence of the Corvette, both as a material object — an automotive commodity that sells in the marketplace — and as an image of American culture, is how different media have used or portrayed it. An outstanding example of "product placement," as it is now termed, is the CBS television series *Route 66*. On Friday nights from 1960 through 1964, the American television audience saw two young, attractive, American males enjoy the freedom and adventure of the open road. Tod Stiles and Buz Murdoch resemble Dean Moriarty and Sal Paradise in that they are free of social obligations and willing to experience what the world (or at least North America) has to offer. More significantly, as individual episodes demonstrate, these characters are also responsible, compassionate, and open-minded about what they encounter; unlike Dean and Sal, Buz and Tod are not as "countercultural," not as much "outside" mainstream America as looking to discover what America and its people really might be. They are searching for, as Buz describes it in an early episode, a place where they will fit in. *Route 66* is quite similar to *On the Road*, but it is not the same story. While Dean and Sal seem to bounce around the country caught up in the moment and "knowing time," Buz and Tod stop in different states and various places along the way to work and become involved with the people they find there. *Route 66* is in large part about the character of America and its inhabitants. As one automotive journalist recently put it, "The freedom of mobility must define our postindustrial identity. It is this desire for independence and autonomy, a sort of unending restlessness, that finds us ever pushing 'westward'" (Neff). *On the Road* and *Route 66* share a motif— freedom and independence — but Buz and Tod are distinct characters of their own, and they share the screen and the road with a particular object, a Chevrolet Corvette, which Herbert B. Leonard, the series' executive producer, and Stirling Silliphant, its writer/cocreator, referred to as its "third character" (qtd. in Rosin 8). And the Corvette would come to have a "character" of its own.

Media historian Mark Alvey relates that Silliphant's initial proposal called for a theme of "search, unrest, uncertainty, seeking answers and looking for a way of life"—all of which sound very Kerouac-like in tone, if not in concept (qtd. in Rosin 3). The Corvette comes across as an "interested and conflicted symbol"; while it is an "expensive convertible, a status symbol," the car is Tod's "only asset," and he and Buz must work, most often manual or unskilled labor, to support it and themselves (Alvey, qtd. in Rosin 8). In the series, neither Buz nor Tod personify or anthropomorphize the Corvette; they do not call it "she" or "baby." In point of fact, they seem to take the machine as an unspoken given, more of an extension of themselves than a possession.

In using the term "extension," and in the context of the 1960s media culture, we are invoking Marshall McLuhan, whose theories of "media" include the automobile as well as print, radio, and television among the forces that shape our consciousness. If, in *Route 66*, the Corvette is a televised "extension" of Buz and Tod, then — like the automobile in the wider context of American history — it has caused "deep and lasting changes" in them and transformed their environment (McLuhan *Playboy* 237). In a 1969 interview, McLuhan said that such an extension of human thought and abilities is "an intensification, an amplification of an organ, sense or function" that alters the central nervous system, rendering the new, transmogrified "sensory balance" temporarily invisible (237). This seems true of the "deep and lasting changes" that automobility has had on American culture, and as a society we are only now developing conscious awareness of just how meaningful the automobile has become in our lives. The Corvette's image, its role as a cultural icon, begins in part with *Route 66*. The car itself is the material component of the "message" produced by the combined television/automotive media — one that as McLuhan goes on to say is also a "*massage*" (original italics) that "works over," "saturates," "molds," and "transforms" our senses (238). The "artist's creative inspiration" of the series' creators may have, as McLuhan theorizes, subliminally "sniffed out" the changes that automobility was bringing to in America in the 1960s (237–238). The Corvette took on a role in the automotive culture of the time that it has never relinquished, making it a signifier with multiple meanings and giving the car a lasting identity.

In *Route 66*, the Corvette is a patriarchal legacy, the only thing that Tod inherited after his father passed away and his business died with him, but the father figure is not a controlling or overbearing presence; the car seems to be very much just what it is. Tod seldom betrays a deep sentiment about the Corvette; in "Black November," the first episode, he quickly says, "It's not just a car," but does not develop the idea further or elaborate on its emotional ties for him or its connection to his father and their relationship (*Route 66*). In the same episode, when asked about a feeling of "unrest" or restless sensibility, Buz says, "We [presumably every American] all got it," and that what most concerns him and Tod is "just moving" with no specific goal or destination in mind. The Corvette partakes of all of this freedom and restlessness; it seems to be an object, like Buz and Tod, more at home on the road, possessed by a dream of life caught up in seeking something not named and going places, not sitting still.

The values *Route 66* promoted were "liberal" in the sense of the United States as a free, open society. The show presents a confident, not "dark," view of both America and humanity: Americans possess virtues and flaws, and there is "evil" to be found, but through perseverance and sacrifice, we progress toward a better future. It may be no coincidence that *Route 66* premiered in October of 1960, on a Friday night just after one of the Nixon/Kennedy debates (Mills 64). The combination of strength and optimism that Kennedy put forth well matched the series' own outlook. Katie Mills writes that *Route 66* "mirrors the celebratory optimism that the Beats expressed, although it was predictably more conservative in all ways" (64). However, "the road story with its hint of Beat rebellion" did act to distinguish the show from its contemporaries, and counteracted the criticism of television as a "vast wasteland" that was soon to follow with "an intuitive understanding" of how to "revitalize the troubled medium" (Mills 64–65). While "TV" is most definitely not what we should think of as "reality," the medium does respond to the wishes and desires of the viewing public, as well as influence and revise, even revitalize, the ways we see ourselves and the world around us.

Route 66's primary sponsor, the supplier of the vast majority of vehicles seen onscreen, was Chevrolet. Yet this is not to say that Buz and Tod promoted the Corvette or any other automobiles. The Corvette itself functions as a "silent partner" to its human compatriots, and the "Corvette" name is rarely used. Normally, Buz and Tod simply refer to it as "the car," which — by its distinctive singularity of title — may distinguish the Corvette as the only suitable car for young, attractive males or for a life "on the road" full of new places and people, a life of adventure. If the Corvette is an essential part of the show's atmosphere of "freedom," then it must possess the qualities that are most desirable in the context of an independent, restless lifestyle. These are summed up in the automobile's image and what its name comes to signify.

It is generally agreed upon that the "Corvette" name came from Myron Scott, the founder of Soap Box Derby racing and one of the leading photographers in the Chevrolet public relations department. In 1953, Scott chose the name from a list of three hundred possibilities proposed by Campbell-Ewald, Chevrolet's advertising agency (Burton, *Corvette* 33–34). Before then, the word "corvette" designated a class of light, fast, maneuverable warships, dating from the Age of Sail up to modern times. The name suggested speed, agility, and performance; it also carried a suitably military and masculine connotation, like life on the high seas — metaphorically another open road — and the promise of adventure. The "Corvette" name was, in a single word, *romantic*, and *Route 66*, the television series, gave the material object stories and characters with strong masculine appeal to flesh out the romance. This emotional significance, wedded to the power and technology the car acquired over time, along with the image created by *Route 66*, gave the Corvette a distinctive name and a reputation that has never left it. Automotive historian Jerry Burton writes that *Route 66* "did more to cement the Corvette into the consciousness of America than any advertisement or marketing campaign" (*Corvette* 43). "Corvette" was just a word or a term before 1953; after that time it began to be recognized as a name and a strong, independent image associated with how America presented itself to the world and thought of its own personality and character. The Corvette became a car and an image with an identity of its own.

Chapter 7

The Corvette and the Media

If there are scripts of masculinity in our society, then television in the 1960s — like today's expanded cable media and the Internet — reflected and modified or updated the scripts of its time to suit the changing face and nature of contemporary society. In 1964, *Route 66*'s last year on the air, Marshall McLuhan published *Understanding Media*. In this critical work, he proposed that the "aspiration of our time for wholeness, empathy, and depth of awareness" is "an adjunct" of contemporary — or what he called "electric" — technology (*Media* 9). The characters of Buz and Tod demonstrate or search for what could be described in just these terms; that should make them "modern," if not "modernist," individuals of the mid-twentieth century. More importantly, in a time not so long after the McCarthy Era and while the Cold War was escalating in technology — and the confrontation over Soviet missiles in Cuba was in the near future — Buz and Tod were not characters, as McLuhan writes, *"contained"* by their society or its circumstances; instead of set, predictable lives, the two of them were on the road, *"involved* in our [Americans'] lives, as we in theirs, thanks to the electric media" (*Media* 7). Buz and Tod were different versions of us, meeting ourselves somewhere out there.

McLuhan does not, in *Understanding Media*, discuss particular television programs. He does, however, point out that — as is so frequently quoted — "the medium is the message" (12). In clarifying this statement he makes clear that social and political conditions are "environments," and these "are not passive wrappings but active processes" in which "totally new" forms can come into being (12–13). To perhaps stretch this a bit, in the early days of network and broadcast television, *Route 66* was one of those new forms within the TV environment, and it changed, or at least challenged, the parameters of what was typical or expected. Buz and Tod, the

Corvette, and the American landscape were the only material constants of the series; together these acted as a "frame" for drama or action, a "new" environment for the viewers. The qualities of this "electric space" or "TV environment" became attached to or associated with what it contained: the male stars and the Corvette automobile. While the human actors went on to portray other parts, the media or electric "aura" created by *Route 66* stayed with the Corvette, giving the automobile a meaning or cachet of potent masculinity, the freedom of the American road, and the promise of adventure.

To cast this in terms more like what *Understanding Media* proposes: television re-formulated the way Americans thought of themselves and their nation as the electric medium changed their ways of perceiving. The United States was tied together or "linked" by an electronic nervous system that communicated via images and sound, powerful appeals to the conceptualizing and self-identifying processes. By giving the majority of the American public immediate, moving images — and soon, images in *color*, not just black and white — in their homes, the medium created multiple "frames" that encompassed both *what* America saw of itself and *how* it saw itself in the 1960s. As the Library and Archives of Canada website presents McLuhan's ideas, "media" of all kinds, automobiles included, "mediate our communication; their forms or structures alter how we perceive and understand the world around us"; they reshape "the ways in which individuals, societies and cultures" come to know their environments; and "technologies in a culture, like words in a poem, derive their meaning from context" ("McLuhan"). *Route 66*, and other programs, explored and developed the potential of television: by going anywhere — twenty-four states and Toronto, Canada, were used as locations over the course of the series — figuratively, the show depicted or reached into the lives and the homes of America (Rosin 6). Literally, since it was filmed "on the road," the series came to the people, not they to it, except by watching. *Route 66* promised that the action and the characters could arrive *here*, where we were, not merely take us to another place, as film and television had already proven they could do. Its form, not content, allowed TV to become a reflexive extension of ourselves, allowing us to see our own country in new or different ways. By design, *Route 66* was independent of ordinary, everyday constraints; it was "free" to roam America: the major cities, the small towns, the big sky, and all three coasts were "scripted" into the action. The Corvette became an emblem of this, what the automobility-minded public saw as a reflection of their American dream.

Yet, from today's vantage, much of this is not so simple. While we grant *Route 66*'s exploration and development of the medium of television, the series did so from a perspective that we — removed almost fifty years in time and knowledgeable of a wider America and world — readily observe to be socially and culturally limited. The Corvette only had two seats, and both of those were claimed in advance of going on the road. Its presence was predominantly white and almost exclusively male. Buz and Tod are like Dean and Sal in that their main attachment is to the road, to going places, and the people they meet form at best temporary relationships that the viewer/reader recognizes — or willingly suspends his/her disbelief — will not last. In short, *On the Road* and *Route 66* both present a homosocial world where the men possess the power of mobility and the autonomy that permits them to choose to be "free" of conventional lives and limited choices. For others, minorities regardless of gender and most especially women, "the road" is not readily available, and "freedom" is not obtainable except at great personal cost.

Writing about "the phallus (or its absence)" in his work *Masculine Domination,* Pierre Bourdieu traces the phallogocentric view of the world back to a "division into relational genders, male and female," that centralizes power and identity, "the specifically male point of honour," in a distinctly masculine authority (qtd. in Fowler 470). From what we discover in *On the Road* and *Route 66*, this is very much what the "worldview" of the mid-twentieth century does. The male characters appropriate automobility and its symbols for themselves, granting "others" restricted access according to a state of "authority" that is almost exclusively Western, white, and male. As sociologist Bridget Fowler writes, "The 'social arbitrary' of gender domination is tied into natural differences or even converted into 'nature'": masculinity is central to the structure of power in society, and this is cloaked in a false appearance that Bourdieu terms "biological nature," yielding a "naturalized social construction" that assures continued male domination (470). While Dean and Sal seem to exist "outside" society as part of their Beat status, they do enjoy a freedom and independence that is granted to them because of their masculinity. The women they encounter on the road are uniformly either "rooted" to a place and situation or limited to traveling under the authority and protection of men. Sal's affair with his Mexican girlfriend Terry ends with his promise to "see her in New York," which both of them know is extremely unlikely. In a like manner, Dean's marriage to Camille in California seems to be his most enduring female relationship, yet she rarely — if ever — accompanies him on the road and has little mobility or autonomy of her own, except by default when Dean is absent.

In *Route 66*, the Corvette serves as "masculine territory," and the car takes on that aura of male power and authority. Fowler says that "masculine domination is a characteristic ... of specific symbolic structures associated historically with phallogocentric presuppositions," and the automobile is a site of several of these (471). The Corvette becomes "symbolic" of masculinity. To carry this further, following Bourdieu's reasoning, Fowler states that "the social constructions of masculinity and femininity are actually *written on the body*" (original italics), and in this case the Corvette is itself a stand-in for the male body and the car's "masculinity" has been "written on it" by its presentation on television and in other media (471). The popularity of the car is in part its acquired "masculine" nature and an associated "machine" or "object" personality that carries male connotations of power and identity, what Mills refers to when she calls the Corvette "a status symbol of masculine power and (upward) mobility" (69). As an object, an expensive sports car, the Corvette is also a possession that demands some financial resources. To put it plainly, the Corvette requires, in a capitalist, free-market system, that someone purchase the car to gain the benefit of its masculine image and aura of power. As Bourdieu states, economic power — that Western, white males have access to — can be converted into the "symbolic capital" of the fast, sexy, desirable automobile and other objects (Fowler 481). Stylish mobility has an economic aspect that goes along with its masculine virtues of freedom and independence. We do not expect Dean or Sal, or any of the Joad family, to drive a Corvette, but they do possess identity that is related to their vehicle and the mobility it provides. The Corvette serves to extend and enhance masculinity, as so many products on the market in the twentieth century have promised to do. Behind the wheel of a "Vette," a man feels *like a man* and knows who he is. The car's identity reinforces the performance of masculinity.

Historical studies researchers Mark Peel, Barbara Caine, and Christina Twomey make the observation that masculinity as a form or manifestation of power and identity is "often best studied in those places where it is most under question and where men's emotional investments in some of its specific historical and contemporary forms are most clearly revealed" (249). When automobility lets men take to the road, it places them in contexts where they can be tested; however, the testing process itself is a sign of prospective manhood, a qualification that has already been met. "Manhood [is] the object of a quest," and when masculinity is "questioned, or problematic," men "strive to assure themselves or others that there is something solid or lasting about one or another version of masculinity" (Peel 249). The

Corvette projects a predatory heterosexuality and a masculine aggression — just as Buz and Tod innocently and predictably chase "girls" or are willing to fight to assert their strength of body and character — that is usually more implicit than overt and offensive. The symbol, like the men who ride in it, asserts its confidence quietly, unspeaking, but sure of the unstated nature of its masculinity.

Anthropologist Matthew C. Gutmann writes that masculinity is, in part, "anything that men think and do to be men"; in "different cultural contexts," men "perform their own" and look to other men to observe how "other's manhood" is expressed (386). It is not so much that one is born male, as it is that a male human can demonstrate an acceptable level of "'performative excellence' of manliness" in his society and cultural environment (Gutmann 386). Following established ideas of performativity in masculinity studies, Israeli sociologist Gabriela Spector-Mersel says that demonstrating masculinity is often more a matter of "*doing* rather than *being*" (original italics) (69). Accordingly, men are "expected to show different masculine 'faces' within different contexts," and over the course of the *Route 66* series, this is just what Buz and Tod do (Spector-Mersel 69). Along with the "third character" Corvette, they "perform" the masculine scripts and embrace marginally rebellious yet acceptably constructive roles that may stretch the limits of 1960s television, but only in an entertaining and adventurously masculine manner. The characters may question the status quo of the place they visit but rarely threaten mainstream concepts of law and order. Their masculinity is assumed to be a sign of the strength of their character and principles; what they ride in is a manifestation of the virtues they embody in their actions and articulate when they speak. The Corvette is a man's car.

The scripts of "Western hegemonic masculinity" are supported, although with liberal sensibility and appropriately heroic male compassion, by *Route 66* (Spector-Mersel 68). Jack Kerouac himself disliked the show and wrote to a friend that *On the Road*, "unlike the Television [*sic*] cheap imitation ... called 'Route 66,'" had "no fist fights, gun fights or horror of that kind at all" (qtd. in Mills 64). What Kerouac did not point out was that *Route 66* shared much of its atmosphere of male camaraderie with *On the Road* and that the two works both emphasize the masculine nature of the road as well as the "essential maleness" of the freedom and independence that automobility offered. It might be beneficial here to recall what Joyce Johnson said, that Kerouac wrote "with the same *power and freedom* that Dean Moriarty drives a car." The added italics stress those distinctly — or so men may suppose — masculine qualities of the road, that it takes a *power* intrinsic to masculinity to go out on the road and face the world, and that the *freedom* found there is one that is most suited to masculine virtues and character. Neither of these is, of course, true. Women of all kinds and non-white males also may enjoy the power and freedom of the road; gender, race, political beliefs, and even sexual orientation are not essential qualities. To state it another way, it was not just that driving the Corvette seemed forbidden to women and minorities, but even as riders — those to be helped or confronted as the adventures continued — they could only share in a severely limited fashion in its style, power, and identity.

If, looking back at the 1950s or 1960s, we wish to characterize the masculinity of that era as evil and/or oppressive, biased racially as well as sexually, we are not given much direct supporting evidence in either *On the Road* or *Route 66*. The assumption of white, masculine superiority is quiet and often understated. Masculinity is taken as normative, the socially accepted standard for independence or heroism; as one critic describes it, the "homosocial [male centered] culture of male heterosexuality" is presumed to be the measure of autonomy and mobility (Wiegman 31). For women and minorities, the standard values — or so they often appear — are dignified sacrifice or stoic endurance, not taking a heroic stance against social injustice or fighting for a just cause. The dominant view of "others" in American society at that time seems to be much like Sal Paradise's: while he longs to be "a Negro" on occasion, his privileged, outside view of the lives African Americans lead is highly romanticized, making them more soulful, feeling, and emotionally connected — like a song he has heard — than engaged in a struggle for existence in the face of oppression. And few, if any, of the major male characters in these works treat women as equals or as capable of free, independent lives that are empowered in any substantive way. Yet a few episodes of *Route 66* do show signs of this unthinking, self-assured patriarchal bias, and the nature of phallogocentric white male society does become clear in subtle, indirect ways. The Corvette sits in the background, confident and unperturbed, while Buz and Tod discover new or questionable aspects of masculinity and patriarchy.

In "Good Night, Sweet Blues," Buz and Tod come to the aid of dying former blues singer Jennie Henderson (singer/performer Ethel Waters). All Jennie wishes is to be reunited with the members of the band she performed with years ago. Buz and Tod make this possible for her, finding the men, bringing them to Jennie, and witnessing a last performance before she dies. The point here should be that "the boys" with the Corvette have the agency, the power to accomplish this; Jennie herself and the African American community around her do not. Buz and Tod's involvement with her is the key to the reunion and the "happy ending" as the black male performers — one a prominent trial lawyer, another in prison, others successful musicians — gather one last time. The cast here, in 1961, is almost all African American, and Ethel Waters was nominated for an Emmy for her performance, the first such for an African American, but the actual power to make Jennie's dream reality comes from Buz and Tod. Neither the minority males nor the woman are able to cause the desired action: it is only after masculine white males become concerned that it happens. Except for the convict former musician, none of these men betrays a rebellious or dissatisfied attitude with American society, and even he sees his imprisonment as a consequence of his own actions, not a result of any social injustice. Generally speaking, in *Route 66* African Americans are much as they appear in *On the Road*, relatively invisible or consigned to the background in minor roles; militancy or outspokenness rarely surface. American society, although not perfect, is shown as being on the right course.

If African Americans are presumably subordinate, or only play significant roles on few occasions, then it is women who are most obviously characterized as weak, in need of rescue, or as lacking the ability to redeem themselves or bring about positive change. Masculine strength and virtue may often be defined in terms of the relative position occupied by women, and that place means not being *too* strong or independent and having only limited mobility or resources. While Dean and Sal seldom, if ever, come to the "rescue" of a damsel in distress, Buz and Tod make a career of it. However, not every episode of *Route 66* presents an ineffectual, feminine woman — recall the "fag car," weak Plymouth in *On the Road*. Some female characters stand out and attract critical attention because of their strength and ability to define themselves while determining their own course of action.

In "A Month of Sundays," Buz and Tod meet Arline Simms, a successful actress who has returned to her hometown. Arline is uncompromising in her thought and action; she demands and takes what she wants and needs by force of will and assertiveness. This is, naturally, both off-putting and incredibly attractive: Buz and Tod are taken with her, yet she shows little interest. When Buz pursues her, asking if she would like to ride into town in the Corvette, Arline — good-looking and well-dressed — holds out her hand for the car keys. The rarity of this gesture is noteworthy: she expects to drive the Corvette, to be in command. Buz responds by saying that that is not the way "the game" is played. Arline is not behaving in a "bitchy" manner; instead, she challenges the assumption of male authority, the man's ability to dictate to women. This follows what Eve Kosofsky Sedgwick writes in *Between Men* (1985), that "patriarchal heterosexuality can best be discussed in terms of one or another form of the traffic in women; it is the use of women as exchangeable, perhaps symbolic, property for the primary purpose of cementing the bonds of men with men" (26). While most women in *Route 66* conform to this idea, and often act as "exchangeable" in the game between men, Arline refuses to play. She answers, "My game, my rules," and does not back down. The contest of wills here, in 1961, seems to usually occur in an argument, but this is a negotiation of the gender relationship, one that Buz anticipates winning. He replies, "In the battle of the sexes, men make the rules"; then Arline says, "Win the battle, lose the war," and turns and continues on her way.

Here there is a pause, Buz thinking, wondering; then he steps out of the car and gives Arline the keys. This seems like a small detail, yet the male has surrendered control of the masculine vehicle, metaphorically surrendered himself, to a woman's control. Arline asserts herself as "nonexchangeable," and a large part of her power and powerful desirability comes from knowing her own mind and her own desires. Again, this is not dominating, domineering, or hostile femininity; it is more a sense of power, of phallic identity, what might be called being a "phallic female," or what Judith Halberstam refers to as "female masculinity" ("The Good, the Bad, and the Ugly" 344).

Although Arline's case sounds promisingly feminist, it is not. Buz falls in love with Arline, yet this is all doomed — as might be expected. Her source of strength, of "female masculinity," is conditional, not total; she is not someone any woman can be or would wish to be. Unknown to Buz, Arline is soon to die from lupus and does not know how long she will survive: hence, the "Month of Sundays" she wants her life to be. Without her impending death, Arline would be a powerful female character, yet the narrative predicates her strength on an awareness of certain death soon to come. When a woman goes against, to use Judith Kegan Gardiner's phrase, "masculinity's normative association with sexual and cultural power," she risks punishment for defying "the natural order of things" (23). It seems to be a trick of masculine narrative that females are only empowered due to extremes of circumstance; they cannot be granted autonomy and/or mobility unless the situation is at least dire, if not deadly. The fact of the matter is that the powerful female is a doomed role to play; she cannot last long. In the context of the masculine world, the woman with a strong sense of identity or the ability to control herself and the world around her has no place. The structure of the television reality, the male-dominated narratives and the control of the medium by men, and the "real" world impose limits on female self-determination. Arline drives the Corvette, is entrusted with it on her own, but cannot claim it for herself. Her beauty and brains are not enough to allow her to live.

If the phallic or powerful female does not die, then masculinity as the structuring force in society compels her to another extreme. In the *Route 66* episode "How Much a Pound Is Albatross?" Buz and Tod encounter Vicki, a blonde motorcyclist who makes trouble for them immediately. After causing, or contributing to, a traffic accident, Vicki is arrested. She has no identification, no registration for her motorcycle, and speaks in a strangely uncooperative — that is unfemale — and enigmatic manner. Rather than acceptable, socially sanctioned "female passivity," Vicki demonstrates a quiet, insistent independence of body and mind. If "white male masculinity [is] equivalent to political personhood and public power," as Halberstam describes it, then Vicki rejects, even defies, the "masculinity" of patriarchal society ("The Good, the Bad, and the Ugly" 345). If a woman can publicly present a "powerful and active alternative to female passivity," she may offer females and males outside the normative, heterosexual culture an "alternative mode of masculinity" (345). Clearly, Vicki brings trouble with her to town.

Buz talks Tod into putting the Corvette up to guarantee her bail. Vicki, we learn in the end, is the heir to a fortune, her entire family having been killed in a plane crash. Since that time, she has lived this way, rejecting society's conception of responsible behavior, traveling the country, going where and doing what she wishes. And she speaks only in terms of getting close to life, never directly revealing personal details, even to the psychiatrist sent to interview her. While Buz is taken with her, buying her a fashionably female dress for her court appearance, she prefers Tod, who has doubts about Vicki and the wisdom of getting involved with her. Like Arline, Vicki does not fit the "female role"; she works to actively defy rules and preconceptions. Vicki has, in a way, rejected masculine automobility by riding a motorcycle, a "bike," the ride of outsiders or those who wish to marginalize or separate themselves from "polite society." Cars, the Corvette included, seem too patriarchal, too mainstream for her. Tellingly, when lost out in the desert with her on the motorcycle, Tod — the Corvette owner — comments that she has taken on the man's dominate role and that someone — himself — is struggling to adjust. Instead of the "social power" and "social dominance" he and the male audience are accustomed to, Tod faces a "healthy, invigorated, and active" female who assumes what should be his role of, as Halberstam calls it, "essential masculinity" (351 and 354)

Taller than Buz and Tod, intelligent and educated, and quietly defiant, Vicki is like the Arline character in that she is a powerful female. Yet, again in the narrative of 1960s American culture, she cannot function or have a role in a society predicated on masculinity as the defining social role. The message delivered in most *Route 66* episodes is the conventional "men come to the rescue, men make the rules" common in Western culture. In the few cases when women demonstrate female autonomy and claim mobility, they are almost uniformly either doomed or cast out, ostracized from masculine-defined social structures by death or physical exclusion. In this, *Route 66* seems typical of the popular entertainment of its time, and these qualities are most visible once one is years removed from the American culture that it reflects and was a part of. At the conclusion of "How Much a Pound Is Albatross?" Vicki — emotionally distant from what was formerly her own life — is, as she predicted near the beginning, sentenced to leave town and never return. She is not punished, as the "normal" male might be, but sent "outside," where she already exists, into a social limbo where females who cannot conform to patriarchal standards must live. When Buz and Tod drive off in the Corvette, Vicki takes another, less-traveled road. Vicki possesses automobility, but without being male, having a place in the Corvette/phallogo-centric world, the road cannot be her home, yet she is not welcome anywhere else unless she learns to conform. Female masculinity threatens the social and political order and must be suppressed or exiled.

By the late twentieth and early twenty-first centuries, ideas of masculinity and femininity are dynamic and continually evolving. As Halberstam writes, "Embodiment, identification, social privilege, racial and class formation, and desire" are issues that apply to both males and females ("The Good, the Bad, and the Ugly" 355). *Route 66* and other works offer a glance back at how issues we can examine in detail and depth today are contained, or at least suggested, in the popular entertainment of the past. The "cult of masculinity"— if we can call it that — in the late 1950s and early 1960s descended upon the Corvette, making it an excellent example of how "power works through bodies and desires," usually human ones, but sometimes machines (355).

Chapter 8

The Sting Ray, the Space Race, and Masculine Technology

The early 1960s did not last forever. Major changes came about. The Cold War, Vietnam, the Civil Rights Movement, the Space Race, and other events altered society, not merely in America, but around the world. The original C1 Corvette was transformed into the most famous, the "coolest" of cars, as later chosen by the auto enthusiast readers of *Automobile* magazine, the 1963–1967 Sting Ray ("100 Coolest Cars"). The Corvette Sting Rays are, even today, perhaps the ultimate Corvettes, the ones all others are compared to and aspire to equal. In the sixties, style mattered, and during its short five-year life span, the Sting Ray became significant in ways that persist to today. What the C2 Sting Ray added to the Corvette's image, and what would be perpetuated forevermore, was a sense of the design as art, not just masculine, but a union of technology and style. The original Stings Rays — the name was revived for the C3 in the late 1960s and 1970s as "Stingray" — were, in the field of modern automotive design, "works of art," ostentatious objects that broadened and deepened the Corvette mystique. They were also the most powerful Corvettes yet: 427-cubic-inch V8 engines routinely made four hundred horsepower that was available to anyone who could afford the price. Power and masculinity, styling "cues" still found in Corvettes almost fifty years later, and names — 427, Z06, ZR1— came into being during the years 1965–1967. These cars were European influenced in style, but distinctly American in power and masculine appeal.

This impression of the Sting Ray as an instrument of masculine empowerment has endured, and — at least cinematically — been projected into the future. In the film *Star Trek* (2009), twenty-third-century adolescent James T. Kirk takes his stepfather's "antique" 1965 Corvette Sting Ray for a testosterone-stimulating joyride, destroying the car and almost himself in the process. An almost three-hundred-year-old sports car is still a potent signifier of masculinity, style, and power, even in an age of travel to the stars. As the motion picture presents it, the Sting Ray must be an irresistible temptation to the youthful human. The Corvette brings together many of the desirable qualities that adult males must possess: it has unmistakable style, projects an image of power, and demands disciplined control if one is to master it completely. These "manly virtues" are in keeping with Captain Kirk, who is the central character. Although seemingly reckless on occasion, he is heterosexually active, demonstrates determination and aggressive qualities, and seeks to dominate situations — never accepting that he cannot somehow devise a way to win: as Kirk says, "I don't believe in 'No Win' situations" (Abrams). The choice of the Sting Ray allows the motion picture narrative to signify several things at once: a spirit of adventure that is central to the entire *Star Trek* storyline, the boldness and daring of the individual who will grow into its leading figure and hero, and the unquestionable masculinity of the story's main character. The Corvette appears only briefly in this film, as in others, yet its image serves to introduce or represent the qualities of the "hero" — stereotypically male — who leads the action of the film and performs the essentially "male" role. The masculine figure saves the day, comes to the rescue, struggles against adversity, and triumphs over the forces of evil in the end. If he drives a Corvette, the hero is so much easier to identify.

Physical or situational dominance is not the only form that masculinity can take. In the modern world, a man's ability to surpass others financially is also a manifestation of strength, not just the power of the body, but the metaphorical force available to the man who has superior resources. Wealth can be a sign of manhood; the man with *more* is the better man. As the "Chicago baron" in *On the Road* owned a Cadillac limousine, men today purchase a variety of automobiles to stand for their masculine power. The Corvette does not claim to be at the pinnacle of the world's automotive hierarchy; however, it does claim a curious or special place: it is fast and stylish, yet occupies a middle ground of affordability and exclusivity that grants it both mass-market status along with a rare and almost exotic cachet.

In F. Scott Fitzgerald's *The Great Gatsby* (1925), Jay Gatsby's pride and joy is not his house, the mansion in West Egg, but his car. As an American, as a man living in a culture that places a premium on automobility, Gatsby's car is a personal, even intimate object, a better signifier of masculinity than an elaborate dwelling. The mobility of the automobile permits a man to demonstrate his exclusive taste and relative wealth anywhere the car takes him. Gatsby's automobile is "gorgeous," and it seems to reflect "that resourcefulness of movement that is so peculiarly American" (Fitzgerald 64). In the man, Gatsby himself, this "quality" breaks through his controlled manner in "the shape of restlessness" (64). This same restlessness takes a variety of forms in American culture, perhaps it is our most distinguishing national characteristic, and the automobile — for us — signifies that need to move, to be in motion. While the image of the car can be static and stationary, it is more suitably and properly thought of as moving, and stylish sports cars — Gatsby's car is a "sports car" despite its size and weight — capture a feeling of restless motion even while sitting still.

Gatsby's automobile is "a rich cream color, bright with nickel, swollen here and there in its monstrous length with triumphant hat-boxes and supper-boxes and tool-boxes" (Fitzgerald 64). The description of the automobile as "rich" and "bright" conveys a sense of Gatsby's social position and suggests how affluence can represent dominance through material objects. Even more tellingly, the car is "swollen" along its "monstrous length," surely connoting phallic masculinity in the extreme. His car is a signifier of what Gatsby aspires to, a machine that reflects his desire to acquire objects, his lost love Daisy being the principal objective. In the novel, men dominate the wealthy upper class, and women become "things" to be possessed. Females have, or gain, social position by birth or marriage, but the power and the money is in the hands of men. Women seem to be merely the most desirable of objects; a wife or mistress is not the key to power, but possession or "ownership" of her is a signifier of masculinity that can be presented to other males as proof of manhood, potency, virility, and power. Women and cars are indications of a man's social and cultural autonomy, his ability to determine and control his own course of action. "Mobility" here is not just physical; the motion the car offers is an outward sign of the affluent male's ability to move from place to place and woman to woman without regard for negative consequences for himself. Masculinity may not be the source of actual power or position in society, but in itself it is an *assurance of power*.

From a critical perspective, automobiles and women — as objects of male desire and acquisition — are signifiers of what Thorstein Veblen termed "conspicuous consumption" in *The Great Gatsby* and in contemporary society (47). The more powerful and ostentatious the car, the more beautiful and desirable the woman, the greater the aura of power — presumably both affluent and sexual — that the man can bask in. Veblen wrote that the apparent incentives for "ownership" of property, especially women, have been an inclination, on the part of men, to "dominance and coercion"; the usefulness of owned people as signifiers of the "prowess of the owner"; and the "utility" of people to provide services (36). The automobile is a tangible signifier of a man's ability to impose his will on other, "lesser" individuals; an expensive, powerful car feeds the ego of its owner or driver. Tom Buchanan, Daisy's husband, exerts his power of ownership over her, but Gatsby counteracts this by acquiring possessions, such as his car, that demonstrate his own relative strength and masculinity.

While Daisy may seem to be the object of Gatsby's desire, it could be that what he truly wants is the power to create and define himself, which appears to have been Sal Paradise's heart's desire in *On the Road*. Daisy is only the best outward signifier of what Gatsby wishes to see in himself, the power to have anything or anyone he chooses. Looked at closely, the masculinity of Gatsby's automobile — its rich, bright, swollen, monstrous, and triumphant nature — stand for the better man he wants to be. For many men, this is the role the Corvette plays. The car's relative affordability makes it available to those who have upper-class taste or pretensions, yet it also offers the speed and power that can be read or felt as sexual potency, figuratively if not literally. The difference in Gatsby's phallic machine and the Corvette as object is one of degree, not of kind. Men want to be what they think women desire, the potent machine.

Veblen also believed that people "emulate" the tastes of those socially and economically above them (70). Owning a potent but reasonably priced sports car allows one to imitate the very well-to-do who can purchase the most expensive, exclusive automobiles, like Gatsby's car — the Ferraris, Lamborghinis, and Bugattis of the rich and powerful whose rarified and elite tastes are cultivated in the extreme. This affection for the elite and expensive is often expressed as a longing for things that "gratify our taste, our sense of the beautiful," as Veblen describes it (84). This, in part, explains why we feel an attraction to certain objects, the force of their beauty draws us toward them. Gatsby might use this as a rationale for his fascination for Daisy and for his gorgeous automobile: both are compellingly beautiful. And the language used to depict women and cars is often quite similar; even when the sexuality and physical beauty of the object are not emphasized in words, the quality of subjective desire is still there behind any objective description. Yet Veblen also points out the error of using beauty as the motivation in object relationships: "The superior gratification derived from the use and contemplation of costly and supposedly beautiful products is, commonly, in great measure a gratification of our sense of costliness masquerading under the name of beauty" (85). Perhaps Gatsby's love for Daisy, or his automobile, is just as much founded on their exclusivity and difficulty in obtaining. If he could have had Daisy without going to so much trouble, would she have been worth the effort? The object of desire may not be so innocent then; its "costliness" in terms of necessary expense or sacrifice of time and resources may be a large part of its attraction. In terms of a car like the Corvette, if it were too affordable and too many of them available in the consumer market, then the subjective value would be less. The desire for the car or the woman is predicated on the fact that not just anyone can purchase it or win her. The ability to acquire a rare or difficult to obtain object is a reflection of the masculinity and male attributes of the possessor, much as in the expression — popular among men — "he who dies with the most toys wins." Gatsby, and the majority of Western males, appear to be motivated by a desire to outdo one another: cars, women, and "toys" are often merely markers in the game. The faster, more powerful automobile — the Corvette — enhances perceived masculinity.

The Space Race began in the 1950s, not long after the Corvette came into being. The launch of Sputnik in 1957 and the earth orbit by a Soviet cosmonaut in 1961 created a technological race for space that was a "high frontier" counterpart to the Cold War. Not weapons, but machines that could expand human mobility upward and outward were the newest components of the Arms Race. Yet it was the men who would fly in these machines that may have been the biggest part of the challenge. Who would they be? As Tom Wolfe describes in *The Right Stuff* (1979), both civilian and military authorities looked at what they already had, fighter pilots and test pilots who had demonstrated coolness under extreme circumstances and showed "manly courage in the face of physical danger" (130). This "righteous stuff" was the most masculine of virtues, an absolute faith in oneself and one's ability to confront adverse circumstances and bring a recalcitrant machine — such as that newest of technological devices, the rocket ship — under human control (Wolfe 130).

The Cold War in outer space was a struggle for dominance, a patriarchal contest of who had the best science and the most advanced technology. It was, in a way, a struggle between men, not nations, for the sharpest edge of masculinity. The nation whose men — scientists and astronauts, military and political leaders — were the best and most daring would win, and the other would be second place, no better than the Miss Congeniality of nations. Wolfe writes that, in the minds of America's leaders, this contest for "the high ground" meant "nothing less than *control of the heavens* was at stake" (original italics) (54). Thus, in the thoughts of many leaders on both sides, the Space Race was an epic contest, one that required the service of heroes. In fact, according to John McCormack, U.S. Speaker of the House at that time, America faced "national extinction" if the U.S. could not catch up to the Soviets. The "survival of the free world — indeed, all the world" hung in the balance (qtd. in Wolfe 55). The free world needed warriors, men who could face uncertainty and death with that most manly virtue, American coolness under fire.

Those chosen to be the first United States astronauts, the Mercury Seven, all possessed competitive instincts, a drive to excel, and a confidence in themselves that were superlatively masculine. What American male could not aspire to be like them, if not one of them? The car of choice was the Chevrolet Corvette. There were several reasons for this. The immediate and practical one was that Jim Rathmann, a Florida Chevrolet dealer and 1960 Indianapolis 500-winning race car driver, brokered a deal with General Motors that gave the original Seven each a new Corvette. As journalist and NBC newsman Jay Barbree describes it, Rathmann's logic was that the public relations and advertising benefits would far exceed the cost of the Corvettes (Barbree 35). This was in 1960, the same year *Route 66* premiered, so the American public and the world were given a double incentive to pay attention to and admire Chevrolet's sports car: the Corvette starred as the adventurous hero of a successful television series, and it was the preferred ride of America's bravest and fastest men. Given the American public's desire for heroes and an already-established love affair with the automobile, coupled with the affluence of the post–World War II years, the Corvette was positioned not just properly, but perfectly to capture the multiple auras of the freedom of the open road, the adventurous spirit of America, and the new technology that would carry the newest heroes into space. And the car itself was fast.

The astronauts drove their Corvettes the way the designers intended. Most of the astronauts were young, and although married, many were more wild than tame, used to the fastest jets and "pushing the envelope," looking for the outer limits of a machine's performance. What car, other than a few European sports cars, would suit such men other than a Corvette? Test pilots and fighter pilots are encouraged, even taught, to be aggressive and competitive, and the astronauts wanted to be the first or best in space and the fastest on the ground. This was the other, and personal, reason that Corvettes were popular with the astronauts. The men valued their image as fast and in control of situations, and the Corvette let them demonstrate that while looking "cool." They also competed with each other for flight status and in performance tests, and the Corvette allowed them to express those competitive instincts. The Corvette and the astronauts were much alike, and they suited each other.

Wolfe writes that, among the astronauts, if one had "any natural instincts at all, with any true devotion to the holy coordinates [those standards of manhood only the best or the bravest could reach]," he "either possessed or was eating his heart out for the sort of car that Alan Shepard had, which was a Corvette" or drove "some kind of hot car ... something that would enable you to hang your hide out over the edge with a little class" (105). The "mother's milk" of competition pushed the astronauts "to see who could get the most speed out of anything," and "each astronaut's personal Corvette was at the top of the list" (Barbree 35). Rat-racing their often Rathmann hot-rodded Corvettes two or three at a time down the road near the launch complex at Cape Canaveral was a favorite pastime for many of them (Barbree 35–37). When Corvette owner Shepard, the first American into space, called on John Glenn, the first American to orbit the earth, "to loosen up a little bit" from his straight-arrow, clean-living, old-school Presbyterian ways, he reportedly said, "What you need is a sports car.... It'll do you good, John" (Wolfe 140). According to Wolfe, one morning when the Mercury Seven came into the astronaut office at Cape Canaveral, someone had written a "big inscription" on the blackboard: "Definition of a sports car: a hedge against male menopause" (140). That seems to sum up the attitude of the majority, if not all, of America's astronauts.

Jim Lovell, the mission commander for Apollo 13 and one of the "Next Nine," the second group of American astronauts, remembers that "those were the days we [the astronauts] had Corvettes," on the commentary track he and his wife, Marilyn, provided for Ron Howard's film *Apollo 13* (1995). In the media, film and television, Corvettes are often presented as the vehicles of the astronauts. In director James L. Brooks' *Terms of Endearment* (1983), retired astronaut, raconteur, and notorious womanizer Garrett Breedlove (Jack Nicholson) is rarely without his silver Stingray coupe. He is aggressively charming, hard drinking, and reckless, as when he drives his Corvette on the beach, steering with his feet while sitting on the open roof. This sequence might be, in part, a demonstration of the "holy coordinates," that enticing edge-of-the-envelope performance expected of an American astronaut, the bold figure who lives the adventures the rest of us dream of.

In *Apollo 13*, based on his memoir *Lost Moon* (1994), we first see Jim Lovell (Tom Hanks) driving through traffic in his red Corvette on July 20, 1969, the night of the first moon landing. Immediately, we know this "guy" is someone special, and as soon as he reaches home, he is surrounded by his fellow astronauts and their wives and children. Later, not long before the ill-fated moon mission, the red Corvette stutters, stumbles, and stops while the Lovells are on their way to an evening out. It is a bad omen. The car stands for not just the men who fly to the moon, but the technology — primarily the product of a phallogocentric, masculine culture — that they rely on to take them there and return safely. As Apollo 13 lifts off, one of the other astronauts watches, standing next to his gold 427 Corvette; the technology of both rocket and automobile linked together — through the man who masters *both*— and connected to the overwhelming power of the machines men have devised. Technology may be the most obvious representation of Western masculine culture. Its ability to "conquer" space is its latest and best manifestation. The "right stuff" applies to machines as well as men; the Corvette represents successfully controlled power.

Yet *Apollo 13* reflects something else, the fallibility of that male culture, how at critical points in time it is forced to re-evaluate itself and struggle against adversity. In a way, *Apollo 13* is about how men and the culture that sustains them must confront and adapt to circumstances they cannot control. And an "unmanly" loss of control is one of, perhaps the most, trying of all the situations any male can face. From this perspective, the film depicts how the astronauts on the disabled spacecraft and the predominately male NASA culture of technology, face a "crisis of masculinity" in which their resolve and ability to think in new paradigms and create innovative solutions is tested. As we might expect, they triumph, and the three astronauts return home having proven themselves. Control of themselves, their machines, and other human beings is — to recall Veblen's description of "ownership"— characteristic of Western masculinity.

If masculine virtues in the twentieth century are being discussed, the work of Ernest Hemingway surely comes to mind. While he is popularly known as the virile proponent of "grace under pressure"— surely another name for "the righteous stuff" the American astronauts all possessed — recent scholarship proposes more complex ideas about Hemingway's writing. In *Ernest Hemingway: Machismo and Masochism* (2005), Richard Fantina describes the critical attention now being paid to how "machismo ... coexists with an alternative, masochistic sexuality" in Hemingway (*EH* 1). There is, sad to say, no "Hemingway Corvette," yet related ideas of masculinity are readily discovered. Fantina notes that "far from upholding the image of the macho warrior, he [Hemingway] often suggests a profoundly submissive and passive side to his sexuality" (*EH* 1). This complex view of masculine sexuality reveals how, according to one critic, "traditional concepts of masculinity ... are too emotionally restrictive and in need of change" (Fore 82). From what we find in the Corvette's association with masculinity, this is undeniably true, but not frequently or easily addressed.

In *The Sun Also Rises* (1926), Jake Barnes with his damaged masculinity, his unspecified but tragic "phallic divestiture" — to use Kaja Silverman's terminology — faces life without functional masculinity at the same time is he both in love with the desirable Lady Brett Ashley and surrounded by a world in desperate need of a strong and confident male presence (qtd. in Fantina, *EH* 27). Like Wolfe's astronauts, Jake himself was once a man with what was presumably "the right stuff": he was a fighter pilot in the First World War, one ingloriously downed by circumstance — not enemy action — and who gave "more than your life" in the words of an Italian colonel (Hemingway 24). If Jake had flown in World War II or the Korean Conflict, if he had not been wounded in that "rotten way," he might have spent days driving his Corvette around the Cape and chased tail, all those astronaut groupies, in his free time.

Jake Barnes is a fictional character not unlike in masculine virtue the real life astronauts who flew into space. The essential point here is that the qualities of "manliness" defined as "righteous" are still found in Jake; it is only his male equipment that is missing in action. Although Jake is emotionally damaged, what thinking and feeling man in the twentieth century is not, and what actually defines a man? Jake's physical sexuality may be damaged beyond repair, but does that make him like a gay male who does not desire women, or does it render him more a woman than a man since he cannot perform the primary male sexual function? Writing about the post–World War I era, critic Greg Forter says that Hemingway and other modernist authors formulated a "reaction to the loss of masculine authority and potency" in the face of "the onslaught of a destructive and emasculating modernity," one that — in Fantina's words — was "characterized by a nostalgia for a 'disappearing ideal of male autonomy'" (qtd. in Fantina, *EH* 26 and "Hemingway's Masochism" 86).

It seems that what the Corvette signifies in the middle and late twentieth and early twenty-first centuries is caught up in the questions of masculinity that metaphorically invoke Jake Barnes' impossible dilemma and what some individuals call the "crisis of masculinity" confronting all males who bother to be self-aware in our time. While the Corvette as a material object and as an image is on the surface a positive expression of masculine potency, power, and control — the "right stuff" all men aspire to — it also (quietly, barely more than a whisper), speaks of doubts about potency, the uncertainty of masculine power, and the failure of male control. As in the near disaster of Apollo 13, Jake's antiheroic and emasculating wound, and the general sense of unease all men feel about having to "perform" masculinity over and over again, the Corvette also suggests an uncertainty, even a lack of male confidence, that all of us face but do not admit to openly or honestly. Corvettes allow us to cover up that anxiety with a self-assured exterior, a winning Hemingway-hero smile, and an ironic sense of humor.

Masculine behavior may frequently be extreme, and sometimes foolish or funny, but it always has one serious component, a willingness to flirt — and "flirt" may be precisely the right word because danger usually has a sexual allure about it — with danger or to do things to excess. This boldness could be a consequence of male, testosterone-induced excess enthusiasm for life, as Dean Moriarty displayed, but it also must be considered as socially constructed. What the public looked up to and what the press celebrated was the daring and courage of the astronauts, as on the Apollo 13 mission, and for many of them this was not something they could turn off at will or leave behind when the time for heroics was past. As social scientists have observed, masculinity often manifests itself in places and times "where it is most under question" and where "emotional investments" in its forms are "most clearly revealed" (Peel 249). The environment the astronauts worked in and the public attention they received fostered behavior that gave proof of their possessing "the stuff" that makes men masculine. American males admired the manhood and masculinity of the astronauts. The Corvette, by its nature a "performance car," gained appeal and an even greater masculine personality by becoming the sports car of choice of first the Mercury, then the Gemini and Apollo astronauts. Advanced technology and the ability to control it were qualities that were associated with the American space program, along with a patriotic sense of pride and achievement; these rubbed off on the Corvette and stayed with the car through future generations.

The HBO mini-series *From the Earth to the Moon* (2005), executive producer Tom Hanks, gives a larger, more nuanced view of the American astronauts than any popular motion picture. While there are masculine heroics, there are also failures and flaws, affection and humor, and a humanity to the men and women that films about the space program frequently sacrifice in favor of romance or action. The astronauts and their wives become human beings. Corvettes are part of this atmosphere. Alan Shepard (Ted Levine) has a white C1 roadster, while Jim Lovell (Mark Harmon) drives a blue C3 Stingray; historically, according to photos and personal accounts, both cars are accurate and factual. If that is not enough, the crew of Apollo 12 bears even more support for the astronaut/Corvette connection. In the episode "That's All There Is," each of the astronauts on that flight has a Corvette Stingray coupe (*From the Earth to the Moon*). Moreover, they are such close friends that they have matching cars, gold with black trim, and their appropriate crew assignments — CMDR for the mission commander and so on — painted on the driver's side doors. From photographs from that time, one can see that these are truthful depictions of the men and their Corvettes. So, in this case, the car represents not just masculinity or technology, but the relationship of the cars' owner/drivers. It comes to stand for a fraternity of three, masculine bonding that speaks for a homosocial society among the astronauts as a community. Or, by extension perhaps, among all male Corvette owners, astronauts or not.

If the connection between the Corvette and contemporary, masculine technology seems tenuous, then we can look to another example. In his book *Future Energy* (2007), journalist Bill Paul writes of the coming changes in the way we use and consume energy, especially the role of the oil companies as providers of alternative sources of energy and how the automobile industry, American and foreign, is going to change and adapt in the future. The only U.S. manufacturer described as potentially doing "best" in the new "technology-driven environment" is General Motors, and the car Paul selects to stand for its future is "perhaps the most iconic symbol of the freedom of open road in America — the Chevrolet Corvette" (123–124).

The Corvette is not a hybrid or an "economy car" by any stretch of the imagination, yet it does bring together a blend of American style, fuel efficiency — "25-plus miles to the gallon on the open road" — and power that appeals to many U.S. car buyers (Paul 124). The Corvette is the "one American car *model*" (original italics) that Paul includes on his "watch list" of automobile companies and car models (125). The reason is a mixture of image and substance: the Corvette makes Paul's list "as a symbol of the spirit that I feel must guide the new oil industry" (125). In terms of Americans' love affair with the automobile, Paul quotes an Internet blogger who writes that automobiles "present us with the possible. Freedom of movement. Personal mobility." And, the blogger adds, "Owning a car has become a rite of passage to personal independence." Our "national culture" is constructed "around this concept of personal mobility. It sets the parameters of our space and time" (qtd. 126). The automobile helps define American identity, and the Corvette is the most prominent example, the most intense instance of the man/car relationship.

A case in point is Terry Berkson's book *Corvette Odyssey* (2004). As in the film *Corvette Summer* (1978), the story centers on a missing Corvette, a red 1963 convertible. In 1979, on the day the author's son is born, the Sting Ray is stolen. For Berkson, the quest to find and recover his Corvette becomes an obsession. The subtitle of the memoir, *The True Story of One Man's Path to Roadster Redemption*, reveals how much Berkson identified with the Corvette: its rescue would be his "redemption." Finding it almost costs him his family, yet he cannot let go of the need to be reunited with the car. French artist, poet, and film director Jean Cocteau once wrote, "A car can massage organs no masseur can reach. It is the one remedy for the disorders of the great sympathetic nervous system" (Barkley). As Cocteau said, the Corvette touches something in Berkson that his wife and children do not, and they are unable to understand his need. The car is part of his masculine identity, as Corvettes often become for their owners. *Corvette Odyssey*'s epigraph is from Norman Mailer: "All you can ever ask from the worst of experiences is that they deepen our knowledge of the tragic" (personal letter from Mailer to Berkson). For the Corvette addicted or afflicted, the car can only be replaced by another, better, or more desirable Corvette, if its place can be taken at all. The loss of a Corvette is a wound to the heart of one's male identity; as Mailer wrote, the "knowledge of the tragic" comes from the bitter experience of a damaged psyche. Berkson's Corvette is a part of him, not a replaceable, material object. He is wounded, damaged, without it. Like Hemingway's sexually disabled Jake Barnes, he is incomplete — psychologically, if not physically — until the Sting Ray is restored to him.

Writing in *Plastic Ozone Daydream* (2000), a compilation of essays from the Longhorn Corvette Club BULLetin of Austin, Texas, Floyd Orr says, "Time passes slowly when you're a Corvette. You age like a vampire: you do it, but at a pace that is wonderfully slow," and "the Corvette is such an integral part of American culture that every model has its defenders" (63 and 64). Berkson's connection to his Corvette is how an owner, usually male, often thinks: the model or age of the Corvette does not matter, but having one and being able to define oneself as such becomes essential. The number of Corvettes still living is a measure of how close the cars and their owners become. According to James Schefter's *All Corvettes Are Red* (1996), the chronicle of the 1997 C5 Corvette's development, the one millionth Corvette was produced in 1992, and "by 1996 almost 1,100,000 Corvettes had been built and close to a million of them were still on the road.... Many of those people [owners] are fanatics" (36). Orr's writing on the Corvette experience and Berkson's devotion to his car are testaments to the truth of

Cocteau's words. Neither Cocteau nor Mailer uses the word "identity," how a person's "disorders" or "experiences" can be organized and answered by a possession such as an automobile, yet identity is tied up with our sexuality and definition of ourselves. Corvettes fill a need for many male owners, much as female sexual partners help confirm masculine identity. And that identity may sometimes find its values and integrity questioned; it sometimes becomes self-destructive as it conflicts with others and pursues its own need for confirmation of its superiority.

The relationship between men and their automobiles comes through in music as well as film and literature. The best single depiction of the Corvette's "destructive" aspect as a representation of masculinity and technology is Jan and Dean's "Dead Man's Curve" (1964) in which the drivers of a Sting Ray and a "shiny, new Jag" XKE meet late one Friday night and agree to race (Jan and Dean). In the song, the "gender role expectations and stereotypical notions" of masculine competition using automobiles are also reflections of European/American rivalry, the drive for dominance characteristic of nations as well as men, and the race ends in a deadly accident (Compton). As Anglo-African Cultural Studies scholar Paul Gilroy contends, the "active, dynamic social forces" that the automobile creates in society appear represented in the "hot rod" Corvette and the "sophisticated" XKE. "Dead Man's Curve" also reflects a class struggle, a contest of automotive masculinity between working- and middle-class American males, the Corvette's market, and those of a perceived elitist upper class. Later, Dean's accident driving his own 1966 Sting Ray added to the car's masculine image of vitality and speed, reinforcing its exciting, manly image. While there was greater interest in highway safety and a developing environmental movement in the late 1960s and onward until today, the masculine image of the Corvette often far outweighed all other concerns. The American "romance" with the Corvette continues today, especially for men. The car's speed and power, the danger that excites and the sometimes unspoken potential for destruction, are persistent parts of its allure.

In director T. C. Frank's film *Billy Jack* (1971), the town boss's violent, prejudiced, and cowardly son drives a gold Corvette convertible. His association with the Corvette criticizes supposed American values, our obsession with "things" and power over others; these are, in the most negative sense, two of the masculine character traits most often found in Western culture. According to the counterculture of the time, the products of mass consumerist society were signifiers of the exploitive materialism of Western, white, male thinking, and in the film, the Corvette manifests the negative aspects of patriarchy. The Corvette becomes two-faced — one evil, the other good — depending on the viewer and his/her political and social sympathies. The traditional masculine virtues are open to criticism. If the Corvette were confident and self-assuredly masculine in *Route 66*, it now becomes an object to be reinterpreted and used by "others" in society to signify their own purposes and represent slightly different aspects of male consciousness. Corvette ownership is no longer limited to white, heteronormative males, although its aura of masculine power remains, and it continues to serve as a signifier of empowered sexual identity. The Corvette image is reimagined, but its masculinity remains powerful and unchanged.

Chapter 9

The Corvette and
Black Masculinity

Bill Paul writes that, for Americans and a growing portion of the world's population, the automobile is "the ultimate *freedom* machine" (original italics), and the Corvette stands for that image, perhaps American in origin but not in meaning and significance, of "having fun behind the wheel" that many around the world see and aspire to (177 and 198). The "image value" of the Corvette is this combination of style, efficient technology, and aura of freedom and fun that the global, not just American, energy and car industries must maintain. Automobiles, no matter how fuel efficient, must remain "freedom machines" like the Corvette. Otherwise, the ideals of autonomy and mobility, which the world — as Veblen might say — has come to "emulate" in its climb to upward mobility, would be compromised and freedom lost.

Arguably, three of the least free groups of American, male human beings have been African Americans, gays (regardless of race and ethnicity), and Native Americans — some of whom prefer the name "American Indians." The history of oppression presents us with people who have had almost no control over their lives or ability to move, either socially or spatially. As we have seen, mobility and autonomy are, if not essential, then at least vital to the American way of living. To have no mobility, even if one is otherwise "free," means fewer choices, less quality of life, and little hope for the future. To possess masculinity, even alternative or nonstandard forms, men are expected to have a measure of control over themselves and their lives, yet these three groups have traditionally been denied just those qualities of masculine virtue. Dean and Sal, Buz and Tod, Jay Gatsby, and America's astronauts were all men with access to these manifestations of power; they were also uniformly mainstream white males. However, in recent years we find accounts where men from oppressed backgrounds or socially invisible origins claim automobility and appropriate the outward signs of freedom and independence for themselves. In point of fact, there are specific instances of males seemingly outside the established white, heterosexual, and European-American patriarchal society taking Corvettes as their personal vehicles and using the car's image to promote a powerful masculinity of their own.

In films such as *Passenger 57* (1992), an airline security expert; *Rush Hour* (1998) and *Showtime* (2002), police detectives; and *Seven Pounds* (2008), an aerospace engineer and team leader — all African American males — drive a variety of Corvettes that serve as signifiers of masculine power or empowerment, affluence or accomplishment, and a confident, and self-assured sexuality (Hooks, Ratner, Dey, and Muccino). Each of these African American men exhibits a confident outward manner and a clear place in his social and professional world — even if others sometimes act to deny him or circumstances confront him with extreme challenges. According to Richard Delgado and Jean Stefancic, authors of *Critical Race Theory* (2001), there are a number of ways through which the truth behind false or misleading — yet socially accepted — ideas about racial minorities can be revealed and negative stereotypes counteracted. Oppressed people are endowed with power when they are given a "voice-of-color" that speaks with authority (9). Originating in law and legal studies, Critical Race Theory calls on "legal storytelling," or what is termed "counterstorytelling," and other methods to act against the narratives that white, patriarchal society uses to enforce its power and to characterize nonwhite or "other" human beings as creatures with less reason, strength, or ability than their "betters" (39 and 42–43). These counternarratives often "challenge, displace, or mock these pernicious narratives and beliefs" that society, or the legal system, allows to be told about people of color or those marginalized by the dominant culture (Delgado 43).

The black male characters in these films act in ways that are strong and decisive; even the comic or action nature of the films allows for the positive nature of the heroes' masculinity to be made clear. Security expert Wesley Snipes, in *Passenger 57*, and police detectives Chris Tucker and Eddie Murphy, in *Rush Hour* and *Showtime*, perform masculinity in ways that are in keeping with what the mass media audience has come to expect of its leading male figures. While they may express themselves in black vernacular or indulge, as Tucker does, in "loudtalking" or in Snipes' trademark line, "Always bet on Black," the Corvettes they drive — a red C4 convertible for Snipes, a black C3 for Tucker, and a silver C5 coupe for Murphy — speak of acceptable masculinities that obey familiar, normative ideas of white male behavior. The narrative counterstories these motion pictures convey depict African American males as loyal to their friends or partners, brave, professionally and financially successful, and sexually attractive in a manner that is not particularly threatening or outside the range of masculinity found in white male leading men. The films present another side to the negative images frequently employed to make African American men appear less "human" than white counterparts.

Their Corvettes are meaningful signifiers of the masculine qualities of their drivers. The cars are powerful, yet confirm the men's presumed acceptance of masculine responsibility and discipline to go along with their intelligence, strength, and independence. The Corvettes suggest the controlled power that helps define masculinity; they grant automobility and bring the African American males into the masculine fold, not as sheep but as appropriately wolfish members of society. The African American Corvette owners/drivers possess that assurance of power and identity that enables the characters to act as men, and nothing less, in their narrative structures. The cars are, metaphorically, extensions of the male personality, images of how the men look at themselves from a confident, secure perspective. If white masculinity is being appropriated by these characters along with their Corvettes, if black and white males become "brothers" in a shared masculinity, its "whiteness" appears to be superseded or augmented by heightened and insistent assertions of black or "other" identity. In fact, this association continues the "bad boy" social/cultural boundaries-stretcher identity that the Corvette cultivated in the past, its "living-on-the-edge" but belonging astronaut quality. Masculine Corvette sexuality is, if anything, further stressed and given emphasis by the manner in which black males drive Corvettes and use its masculinity, power, and identity to enhance their own.

What is less clear from a critical point of view is the complexity of this masculinity. Critical Race Theory also uses the concept of "intersectionality," of the multiple roles or complicating factors that should give depth and humanity to a person. Intersectionality is "the examination of race, sex, class, national origin, and sexual orientation, and how this combination plays out in various settings" (Delgado 51). What we do not see in many depictions of African American and other minority males in these films and others is a complexity beyond "maleness." The characters perform masculinity well, but they are not intersectional; they rarely develop a depth of "race, sex, class," and so on that creates masculinity in a fuller, richer sense.

In other words, they are just as limited as many white American males in similar roles. Masculinity is, in the majority of cases, played narrowly in popular entertainment. Men of various ethnicities and origins take on a uniformity of masculine behavior that subsumes all but the most obvious and predictable appearances and behaviors. While both black and white males may take the Corvette and its image as their own, they may be less able to manipulate the image of the car and more likely to be "taken in" by its long-standing identity, along with its ability to grow and mutate over time and with conditions. The image of the Corvette may be bigger and stronger than the power of individual males to mold it to their wills; instead, it could be the image of the car that accepts them and absorbs whatever subtleties they seek to bring to it. The Corvette image, by its protean and dynamic nature, defeats attempts to redefine it by appropriating those who would alter its purpose and identity. The car wins, as powerful males always do.

The case could also be made that these characters are heteronormative and follow the well-established pattern of male sexuality to ensure a broad, general appeal to as wide an audience as possible. The films may portray them as action heroes, comic figures, or sympathetic males, but in almost all occurrences, African American men in media present behaviors that would permit the substitution of other ethnicities without significant change to the characters' personality or behavior. The addition of the Corvette usually helps reinforce the masculine nature of African American males in ways that enhance their performance within a context of accepted, normative masculinity. Few of them would be caught dead riding Pee Wee Herman's bicycle. These men may be rebellious, but they are — by and large — no more agents of significant social change or menaces to the established order than Buz or Tod. The confirmation of masculinity, via the Corvette, is one of "belonging" to the culture of American masculinity and individuality, but not of making new statements about alternative kinds of male identity or different ways of expressing maleness in the American context.

The question of masculinity and identification with the Corvette as both object and image is, at its most fundamental level, an issue of power. For masculinity, controlled power is the essence of everything else; the phallus — whether actual or figurative — is *the sign* of power, and material objects, actions, and behaviors are external manifestations of internal, personal power. Sociologist Johnnie David Spraggins, Jr., in his essay "African-American Masculinity: Power and Expression," writes, "The dimension of power is another way [in addition to being 'breadwinners,' marriage, and fatherhood] for masculinity expression in the U.S. Meanings of gendered expressions of power [for African American males] may be more explicit and direct, and public displays of power may be more accepted" (46). Spraggins is particularly concerned with the possession of firearms by African American males and what this means; however, since the automobile, along with the gun, is one of the archetypal signifiers of masculinity, many of the same implications may apply.

As other researchers have noted, cultural expressions have three "principal constituents": "texts, producers, and an audience" (Spraggins 46). Whether the text is Colt .45 or Corvette, the object suggests "power" to those in the public or private audience, men and women, and this — socially and psychologically — often serves to enhance the masculinity of the producer, the driver/gunman. The larger, the more powerful the gun; the faster, the more expensive and exclusive the car — think of Dirty Harry's .44 Magnum or Gatsby's "monstrous" roadster — the more potent the masculinity of the man. In the majority of the films mentioned earlier, both cars and guns reflect the masculinity of the central character. He is comfortable and capable with both, and not afraid to confront opponents, usually other men, who are willing to attempt to outdrive or outshoot him. The contest of power is explicit, yet the competition for masculinity is implicit. In the "continuum of power, prestige, and status," there is a hierarchy of "several masculinities," and according to the terms of the place, time, and situation, masculinity is "negotiated" by what a man says, does, and possesses: guns, cars, and women included (Spraggins 47). As one researcher has pointed out, "the assumption and possession of an array of privileges ... are denied most black men," so the cinematic versions of these men are frequently granted the power and prestige that all but a relative few of them may find wanting in real life (qtd. in Spraggins 48). Firearms and Corvettes — and other "instruments of power" — are used in popular entertainment and real life to suggest that "autonomy and control over people and things which masculinity supposedly engenders" (Spraggins 48). Yet, as in other cases, masculinity is at best a conditional state; it must continually be performed and, on occasion, faces something that points to its flaws and vulnerabilities.

One example is *Seven Pounds* (2008), a film starring and in part produced by Will Smith, the leading man and hero of popular and successful vehicles such as *Independence Day* (1996), and more dramatic efforts such as *The Pursuit of Happyness* (2006). Smith has worked to strike a balance between tough characters proficient with aircraft, automobiles, weapons, and women, and more nuanced, down-to-earth men with the realistic challenges of making a living and becoming successful husbands and fathers. Read as follows, we can look at *Seven Pounds* as a film that explores and develops ideas about what masculinity is, how it affects and deceives us, and possible consequences for men who cannot adapt to more open and sensitive ways of facing life and the changes it often brings. Smith's costar, Rosario Dawson — who portrays Emily Posa, a young woman in need of a heart transplant — described *Seven Pounds* as an "emotional film for men," one that many men told her made them cry (Rodriguez 102). Smith himself said the film showed "options in life for redemption and finding yourself again" (Samuels 66). This may be the case because it presents no less than two specifically different interpretations of masculinity, neither of which is as simplistic as the macho African American heroes so often depicted, men with a "colorless nature" and in keeping with well-established standards of heteronormative patriarchal masculinity.

Director Gabriele Muccino chose to structure the film by means of a narrative present, in which we witness Ben Thomas (Will Smith) acting to donate parts of himself — a lobe of his liver, a kidney, bone marrow, and finally his heart — to people in need whom he determines to be worthy, of good moral character with both kind and selfless natures. The "why" of this is not explained, and Thomas' own character betrays few signs of what it is that drives him. What is slowly revealed, by dreams or momentary reflection, is that Ben holds himself responsible for the deaths of seven people, one of them his fiancée. The flashbacks or recollections show that he was an aerospace corporate executive, a brilliant engineer — an MIT graduate — with an expensive, stylish beach house and all the other markers of success. Among these was a classic 1967 427 Corvette Sting Ray coupe — that "coolest of cars" mentioned earlier. The car goes with his lifestyle: 1967 427s are desirable automobiles, exotic artifacts of American automotive art. After forty years, Corvettes like Ben's are indications of both a taste for the rare and expensive, and an interest in fine machinery, vehicles with both physical power and an alluring aura of sexuality. The car appears to be an extension of Ben's own character, and it is very similar to the convertible young Jim Kirk takes for a joyride more than two centuries later and destroys. The Corvette mystique crosses time and ethnicity; it gets at a core value, or essence, of masculinity. The automobile is sometimes not just a car.

For Ben, the Corvette is, like his girlfriend and his other treasures, a manifestation of his autonomy, that "mature psychological independence and the freedom of choice that comes with it" (Adams 160). It is also the instrument of death for the seven people he kills by an instant's loss of control, attention paid to his fiancée's new engagement ring and a text message on his Blackberry at a moment he should have had his eyes on the road. When a man loses control, his masculinity is called into question; in this case, Ben's self-image, how he thinks of himself as a man, is shattered by what he has done. This sense of *control* is "one dimension of having power," one of the central qualities for male identity, and "a valued aspect of masculinity" (Spraggins 53). For a man, African American or other ethnicity, with Ben's accomplishments and drive to succeed, control is an essential part of his life. The destruction of the car, the taking of human life, and the loss of his wife-to-be are actions that destroy Ben's masculinity. Without the "control" that in part defines masculinity, he cannot go on.

The only atonement is the sacrifice, the seven "pounds of flesh," an effort to balance out the harm that he has done, to make things right, a final assertion of his power to take action. His masculine strength and spirit, as demonstrated by the Corvette and other possessions, once lost cannot be regained; he is, then, dead already and only looking for a way out, a conclusion that will benefit others. In a bit of irony, Ben has a longstanding fascination with the Box Jellyfish, a beautiful and deadly sea creature that he will use to kill himself. His car, the Sting Ray, is named for a stinging member of the ray family, and it has brought death to Ben's seven victims.

Yet this is not all. Looked at differently, Ben's masculinity, although tested by the accident and his remorse for what he has done, is not destroyed. Rather than having his life emptied by what has happened, it is his masculinity that sustains him and demands that he give up parts of himself, lastly his own heart. Masculinity is not destroyed but pushed to the extreme. It is a "warrior" masculine trait to sacrifice oneself for one's fellows, like the samurai's ritual suicide, a last statement of a man's resolve and ability to decide his own actions. This is one of those "carefully crafted performances [of masculinity] that deliver a single critical message: pride, strength, and control" (qtd. in Jamison 46). Ben is not out of control but caught up in an obligation to reassert his authority and, silently, proclaim his masculine ability to live or die as he so chooses. His masculinity is powerful, but it leads him to kill himself. While this is a problem, it is not without explication. Looked at from an outside, or objective, perspective, Ben commits suicide to restore a "balance" to the world, to put back into seven lives a portion of what he took from seven others. It appears to be a moral act, atonement for masculinity lost due to a failure to control himself and the immediate world around him, his "masculine horizon" of things and actions.

If the Corvette was an extension of his own identity, he now makes the organs and tissues he can donate "spare parts" for other people.

Paul Gilroy, author of *The Black Atlantic* (1993), among other works, states that modern automobiles are "pre-eminent symbols of power and prestige" and "manifestations of wealth as well as elements of wholly unprecedented personal autonomy," yet also "probably the most destructive and seductive commodities around us" ("Driving While Black" 82). He goes on to propose that in "much twentieth century social science," the automobile and "the social and cultural relations it created and reinforced are ... rapidly passed over, naturalized or simply ignored" (82). This is particularly true "in black culture," because of "the uniquely intense association of cars and freedom" (82). In the case of Will Smith's characterization of Ben Thomas, the Corvette automobile is an emblem of all these concerns. His Sting Ray is both the signifier of his "power and prestige" and the "destructive and seductive" commodity that gives him joy and creates tragedy. Rather than either the "destruction of masculinity" or "masculinity driven to extreme" interpretations, Gilroy's ideas suggest that Ben's situation is a consequence of broader cultural significance; the "traditions of flight, restlessness and mobility" characteristic of American society are components of "the cultures of compensation with which some American blacks have salved the chronic injuries of racialized hierarchy" (84). While race is not visibly a factor in Ben's life and choice of death, in the context of masculine behavior and African American manhood, it would be meaningful.

Ben is not simply a victim of his own assumptions of masculinity, but of a wider and deeper troubling of America men. This is especially true for male African Americans because of their special "restlessness" and desire for freedom based on the forces within a racialized society. The destruction of the Sting Ray could potentially be an awakening for Ben, a traumatic opportunity to realize that life must consist of more than the outward, tangible signifiers of affluence and success. An obsession with material things, at the expense of his humanity, along with the Western concept of masculinity — a patriarchal and predominantly white male culture that values property and ownership — do not necessarily demand his own death. The accident is not just a "personal" incident, but one re-enacted and repeated, in various forms, by contemporary culture and technology as a whole. Ben's "surrender" or acceptance is part of going along with the illusion of masculinity. He is not, as he assumes, compelled to sacrifice himself. According to Gilroy, it should be possible for him, like other African Americans, to achieve something similar to what W.E.B. DuBois termed "double consciousness" and then go beyond that to reach "a higher and better selfhood" (Interview, *Darkmatter*). But Ben resists change and external support.

Writing in the *Journal of Feminist Family Therapy*, clinical psychologists Desiree Compton and Markie L. C. Blumer state that Ben Thomas' character is "struggling between two desires — intimacy and isolation." He is unable to live with the way his life has gone and unable to change, apparently suffering from Post-Traumatic Stress Syndrome (PTSD). One particular aspect of his crisis is the "stereotypic notion that men solve problems on their own," which suggests that masculinity requires self-reliance and often rejects outside help, in this case treatment and/or therapy (Compton). The "totemic, sublime power" of material success and its objects, like the Corvette and his own commodified body, along with the "gender role expectations and stereotypical notions associated with men," limit his thinking and his choices (Gilroy "Driving" 85, Compton). In fact, by seeking "redemption" through donating body parts — and, in the end, his life — Ben makes himself no more than "an object," denying his own humanity in an attempt to escape his feelings, whether guilt for the past or affection for the character of Emily. This is a denial of his subjective ability to exceed the bounds of Western, masculine thinking. Transatlantic black culture, Gilroy contends, offers the world a means of "de-provincializing" American/European thought; applied correctly, this should allow Ben to synthesize a masculinity beyond simplistic, even deterministic, white patriarchal culture (Interview, *Transition*). But he does not, and so he dies.

Traditional Western concepts of masculinity, combined with technology, as in *Kiss Me Deadly* (1955) with its glowing nuclear material and aggressive violence suggested by the then-new Corvette, often become deadly. Not just in a global sense, as in nuclear war, but in a personal one: enhanced and further strengthened by the instruments of technological culture, masculinity frequently yields a loss of humanity in men, a sacrifice "of the heart" similar to the circumstances under which Ben aims to conclude his life. And this is not necessary, even with that intimate, personal machine, the automobile. The relationship between human beings and automobiles, what Daniel Miller refers to as "the humanity of the car," does not have to be out of control (2).

In a 2006 interview with *Transition: An International Review*, Gilroy describes his latest cultural studies project: "I want to denature people's relationship with automotive transport and represent their romance with the automobile as part of our complicity with an unsustainable social and political order in the world" (Gilroy). Automobiles in general, and presumably the Corvette in particular, are signifiers in contemporary modern life of the "relationship between *identity* and *property*" (Gilroy, Interview, *Transition*). The Corvette is a tangible object, but it is also — in its image and how many of us think of it and respond to that image emotionally — for many owner/drivers, a merging of personal identity with real physical property. This may seem to be an extreme, outrageous statement, but as with Ben Thomas in *Seven Pounds*, the Corvette takes on the significance of a "personal object": something intimate that reflects the human half of the relationship's image of self and sense of identity. The destruction of the Sting Ray in this film is, figuratively, the destruction of Ben himself. His "romance with the automobile" is part of his sense of identity.

The persistence of the Corvette over the past fifty years is tied to its masculine image and appeal as an instrument of power and sexuality. Gilroy says that there is a "fluidity of culture," that it has "liquid characteristics" (Interview, *Transition*). In its nearly-exclusive domain in automotive and popular culture, the Corvette possesses something like this. Its "liquidity" of image and character permits the car to suggest different attributes and take on new meanings over time. Journalist Bill Paul looks at the Corvette and sees a model image for the future of the oil and/or automotive industries. Gilroy looks at automobiles as "devastating" in their physical and social presence, and in the Corvette, would most likely see an excellent example of the "romance" that renders human beings accomplices in the continuation of that "unsustainable social and political order" that threatens the world. Both associations may be valid. If the Corvette stands for so much of what automobiles in general have become, it has come to own a complex image. Cars have "shiny authority" and "antisocial prestige"; the hold they have over us "reveals how particular objects and technologies can in effect become active, dynamic social forces" (Gilroy, "Driving" 89). The automobile is "among the most destructive technological innovations to have been produced on this planet," yet it is indisputable that many of us love them so (90).

If the Corvette is one of masculinity's uncontestable love objects, it is also part of a complex relationship mixing sex and gender in dynamic and puzzling ways. The masculine male loves and desires his Corvette; he also, if heteronormative, desires and loves women — the sexier and more alluring, the better. Yet the desires and the roles sometimes become intertwined. If African American males have taken on the characteristics of masculinity that the Corvette suggests, then they must suffer — even to extremes — the gender and sexual mixing of desire that women and Corvettes come to present. For black males, the "gendered expressions of power" that reflect masculine sexuality may be particularly "explicit and direct," and if these are made in or to the public, then "displays of [masculine] power may be more accepted" (Spraggins 46).

This is what occurs in probably the best known of all "Corvette songs," the one most blatantly sexual and striking, Prince's "Little Red Corvette" from his 1982 album *1999*. A black male sings of a beautiful, desirable woman he met one Saturday night — perhaps the night *after* "Dead Man's Curve." She is the type who believes in becoming sexually involved, a brief affair, then leaving, cutting the male off from her attention and affection, and he should have know better. But when he discovers how sexually demanding she truly is, the woman appears far too "fast," lustfully active and independent. The name "red Corvette" is how the song refers to her; she is the tantalizing female "love machine" he wishes to achieve masculine control over. The image of the Corvette signifies his fascination with her. She attracts him; female sexuality unites with the car's suggestive nature, becoming inseparable. The fast, powerful automobile and the overtly, intensely sexual woman become a single image: one that is "pleasurable in form," yet "threatening in content" (Mulvey part I B). If an African American male's sexuality is "more explicit and direct" than would normally be found in white, heteronormative males, then his desire for the woman is even more intense, passionate, and physical — at least in how he might articulate and express it in a public performance. To the man singing, the Corvette and the woman are kindred spirits. They possess their victims' hearts and minds: promising fulfillment, they inflame a man's passion, then frustrate his masculine desire for control. The Corvette/woman tempts, then defies him. She is a wild, enchanting thing who casts a spell over her male victim; like the lady in Keats' poem, she becomes "La Belle Corvette Sans Merci." The male, black or white, finds his masculine control threatened by the strength of his own sexual desire for her. She seems to take control and drive the relationship.

The first line of "Little Red Corvette" gives us a clue to the woman's nature. Prince tells us that the man should have recognized the transitory nature of their passion by the way she parked her car, perhaps a Corvette: "sideways" across a space, claiming territory and/or asserting a powerful sense of self-identity. She performs a "diagonal move" reminiscent of how Maria Wyeth in *Play It as It Lays* (1970) maneuvers her Corvette quickly and skillfully across traffic on the California freeway. Prince's promiscuous, sexually aggressive lady asserts herself; the car's looks and power match her own. In her identity and sexuality she is as confident as the "red Corvette" name suggests. The song makes her an object of sexual fascination, one the singer cannot forget. Her passion and his desire for her haunt him.

Prince himself is noted for his many relationships with young, attractive women: Vanity, Sheila E., Apollonia, and Sheena Easton among them. While his style of dress and self-presentation — in performance and on album covers — may seem effeminate, or at least metrosexual, Prince is actively heterosexual. In fact, many of his songs stress *sex* as the most significant component of life. Passion drives the majority of characters in his music or the personae he assumes while performing. One song, "Pussy Control," from the 1998 boxed set *Crystal Ball*, is similar to "Little Red Corvette" in how it depicts a female who gains wealth and social status by controlling her sexuality and selectively granting access to those who will further her ambitions. In "Pussy Control," the speaker is again male, and he tells the story of the woman's successful rise to power over herself and others. No automobile, as metaphor or material object, appears in the song; the sexual content is carried through the man's description of the woman herself and the "object" that she uses to assert her identity.

From a critical perspective, "Little Red Corvette" is an example of what Laura Mulvey in "Visual Pleasure and Narrative Cinema" (1975) describes as "the male gaze." This is the song's real focus. The male recollection of *her* frames the action and the telling; the "man's role" is "the active one forwarding the story" (Mulvey part III A). Although the woman is powerful in her sexuality, her identity is constrained. She never speaks and is not given a name, only an identity as "little red Corvette," an attractive but inanimate being, not a person. The storytelling male remains in control of the narrative and its emotional content; his masculinity — whether black or white — is to some degree protected by the assumption of narrative control. As Mulvey cites Budd Boetticher's description of the female role, "What counts is what the heroine provokes, or rather what she represents. She is the one, or rather the love or fear she inspires in the hero, or else the concern he feels for her, who makes him act the way he does. In herself the woman has not the slightest importance" (qtd. part III A). The "red Corvette" image conveys her powerful attraction; it is also popularly taken to be a euphemism for her "hot" and desirable private parts, a direct allusion to the seat or core of her sexuality, her vulva. The woman is reduced to an intimate body part, which stands for her whole being and personality. The personification of the automobile is sexual, yet she/it remains a "thing" to be driven or made love to by the narrative male voice. By assuming control of the narrative, the male remains in his position of power over her: she is still the object of his desire. The song, the "telling" of the story, is his means of maintaining his masculine authority; the empowering "male gaze" functions as a manifestation of power. Whether the "gazer" is black or white, the power of masculinity is preserved.

Unusual as it may sound, Prince's song thematically resembles the painting *L'Origine du Monde* (1866) by Gustave Courbet, a work of realistic art that shows the spread legs and genitalia of a young woman whose face cannot be seen, presumably just after intercourse. "Little Red Corvette" and *L'Origine* both present the "origin of life," the female's ability to be passionate and sexual, but reduce the woman to an object, not a human being. The "Corvette" is a metaphor for something, in this case a woman, "hot" or desirable. Prince uses the name and image of the Corvette to sum up how sexually provocative and attractive the woman is; the car itself is figuratively one object of male desire standing in for another. The Corvette attracts "the male gaze" as the woman does, and both help confirm the masculine identity of the onlooker, his privileged "bearer of the look" status (Mulvey part III B). From this male perspective, desire and humanity are male, and females/Corvettes are suitable subjects for domination/possession.

"Little Red Corvette" objectifies the female by means of the male gaze. Another song that embodies the African American masculine perspective is LL Cool J's "Going Back to Cali," from his album *Walk Like a Panther* (1989). Except in this work, the gaze is directed not at a specific female, but back upon the male himself, creating a public face or image of strength and power for the black singer/performer. Where Prince's song focuses on the female through the male storyteller, "Going Back to Cali" centers on the man himself. The song promotes ideas of *identity* and *property* much like what Gilroy discusses. As observed before, the automobile and the African American male often manifest a relationship at least as intense, in the public domain, as that between white males and their cars. More extreme social and cultural circumstances make for more emphatic relationships.

As seen on www.mtv.com, the music video for the song prominently features the Corvette that LL Cool J — James T. Smith — sings of in the opening lines: a cool black Corvette convertible. The song's black Stingray is distinctive, individualized by its glistening chrome, a custom steering wheel, and Daytons (expensive aftermarket wire wheels); its engine sings while passing all the less potent cars on the road. The sleek onscreen convertible is not quite as individualized as the one in the song, but it is still a masculine, eye-grabbing presence. And as LL Cool J — "Ladies Love Cool James" — comments, several women are somewhere waiting for his return.

The car, as *property*, is an extension of the young African American's *identity*; the "coolness" and sexuality it projects are reflections of his own. As Gilroy says, "Being racially oppressed might be to bind you ever more closely to a particular sense" of this relationship between how people define themselves and the objects that they use to signify that identity (Interview, *Transition*).

The Corvette in this song and video is not a signifier of white patriarchal masculinity, as in *Route 66*, but has rather been appropriated by LL Cool J as a signifier of his own black male power. From the early 1960s to the late 1980s, the United States changed significantly; emblems of patriarchal culture became more and more available to "others," those outside that "closed world" of white, male property and identity. The "romance with the automobile" could be embraced, and the Corvette possessed — like a "phallic trophy," perhaps — by those in need of powerful symbols of independence and freedom. As it was in *Route 66*, the Corvette retains its sexual appeal and aura of male personality, but LL Cool J makes it "black," taking command of the machine and himself.

The "Going Back to Cali" video is about power, how the young man in it performs as a strong, confident male. Implicitly, he is telling a story to his public and to his rivals — in the rap music scene of the time the repeated lines, "Going back to Cali [California]," are an implicit statement by the Queens, New York-born LL Cool J that he has left nothing behind on the West Coast to go back for. More than this, the video makes clear that the Corvette also suggests *sexual* power and a masculine presence that draws women. What the song may make a subtext, the visual medium makes clear: LL Cool J lives up to his name. Young, slender, sexy women are seen again and again; cleavage is displayed, and shapely figures and pleasing faces are juxtaposed with LL Cool J that make him seem to be the object of a "female gaze." And these are, uniformly and without exception, young white women — presumably "California girls." They touch him, he responds: black male sexuality is quickly presented. Even the visual style, black and white with an almost constantly moving camera, makes for a *film noir* look that conveys a tension in the air. Yet there are no white agents of control, no Caucasian patriarchy, only the young African American male and his black Corvette and those women.

African American public intellectual Cornel West, in *Race Matters* (1993), writes that "black sexuality is virtually taboo" in the majority of American culture, yet "it is virtually impossible to talk candidly about race without talking about sex" (120). In the "Going Back to Cali" video there is explicitly an eroticism surrounding LL Cool J; however, as in the song, he holds back, denies the women their influence over him, and leaves. Race and sex mix together in the song and video, as West suggests, but in contrast to Prince's "Little Red Corvette," the male figure maintains total control and never doubts his ability to exert power and authority over himself as well as others. LL Cool J sits confidently behind the wheel of the Corvette and drives, just as he drives the narrative, and his masculinity does not yield to a "little red Corvette" or any other external forces. There may be a "crucial link between black sexuality and black power in America," and, if so, the Corvette — as used as an automobile and a signifier by African American males — along with other "objects of masculinity," may come to suggest "different self-images and strategies of acquiring power in the patriarchal structures of white America and black communities" (West 126 and 127). Masculinity and identity can be maintained and reinforced by the correct choice of property; Corvettes are one outstanding example.

Chapter 10

Gay Masculinity, Automobility, and "Other" Identities

The Showtime cable television network series *Queer as Folk* (2000–2005), based on a British series of the same title, was a successful, critically well-regarded show for five seasons. At the center of its cast of predominantly gay and lesbian characters was the handsome, brilliant Brian Kinney, advertising executive, "love machine," and aggressively homosexual male. Brian is a sexual predator, master of the gay club scene, and at thirty years of age near the peak of his personal, sexual, and professional powers. In season three, episode three, in order to reward himself and salve his wounded pride over a "failed romance," he goes hunting. His object is not a suitable lover — he has that — but a machine to match his ego, status, and lifestyle. What Brian pursues and purchases is a classic 1970 Corvette Stingray convertible (*Queer as Folk* QAF). The car, in age and image, is an external alter ego. In a cast commentary on the Episode One DVD Special Edition, actor Gale Harold, who portrays Brian, points out the Jeep from the first two seasons and says, "Don't you think he'd [Brian] drive something a little more [...] sexy than a Jeep?" Clearly, the Corvette seems to be the answer. And it is not merely the sexuality of the car that is desired; it is also an expression of masculine power, an essential quality of Brian's nature.

While he is aggressively gay, Brian does not seek lasting relationships, preferring intense sexual affairs that he is free to break off whenever he pleases. Aside from his sexual orientation, the character is everything most Western, heterosexual males would aspire to be. He is not effeminately gay, except perhaps in a metrosexual way: he pays close attention to himself, his image, his haircut, taste in clothes, the objects he chooses to bring into his life — like his Mies van der Rohe coffee table. Central to his character is a sense of not just superiority, but of masculine supremacy. Feminist critic

Marilyn Frye comments, in "Lesbian Feminism and the Gay Rights Movement," that for many gay men their homosexuality is "congruent with a logical extension of straight male-supremacist culture" (144). And in "Foucault and the Fortunes of Queer Theory," G. S. Rousseau writes that, in the present, homosexuality faces "the extremes of empowerment, on the one hand, and symbolic dismemberment on the other" (401). All three points are captured in Brian's personality. He has become personally and professionally empowered, yet he continues to acquire suitable symbols to represent a supreme view of his masculine self. Although by definition "queer," Brian has power and authority.

His attitude toward heterosexuals is quite simple; in the very first episode, he declares that there are two kinds of straight people, "those who will hate you to your face, and those who will hate you behind your back" (QAF). In this manner, Brian sets up not just an opposition between "straight people" of all kinds and gay men and lesbian women, but what appears to be a personal challenge to meet and oppose this way of thinking and these people. He seems driven by an antagonism, even at times, a quiet, unrelenting, self-centered hostility toward the world. Brian embodies what Frye calls "this cosmic male arrogance" that grants a "presumption of the almost universal right to fuck — to assert his individual male dominance over all that is not himself by using it for his phallic gratification or self-assertion at either a physical or a symbolic level" ("Feminism" 142). One of the symbolic artifacts Brian selects is the Stingray, a signifier of masculinity appropriated from heterosexual mainstream culture that he now claims as his own. The car is a manifestation of what has been termed homosexual desire's "unique power to disrupt and subvert" that Brian channels into a public representation of his own identity (Rousseau 410). The Corvette is not "gay," but it is forcefully and openly masculine.

Yet it seems that it is not actually the straight world that is the object of Brian's rage. More accurately it is what Cultural Studies/Queer Theory scholar Nikki Sullivan, paraphrasing Judith Butler and Monique Wittig, calls "a complex matrix of discourses, institutions, and so on, that has become normalized in our culture, thus making particular relationships, lifestyles, and identities, seem natural, ahistorical, and universal" (39). In other words, Brian is at war with heteronormativity, the expectations and demands of a presumably heterosexual world. He finds deep, fatal flaws in gays and lesbians who seek to mirror heterosexuality or create a safe, stable homosexual lifestyle, complete with family life. His response to the world that seems not to want him is this masculine interest in "power," a "network of relations," that he can use productively (Sullivan 42). Brian defines himself as "queer," in the way that author David Halperin calls "*whatever* is at odds with the normal, the legitimate, the dominant" (qtd. in Sullivan 43).

If explicated satisfactorily, it is clear that Brian Kinney is not unlike other American males noted for their masculine qualities. Like Mike Hammer in *Kiss Me Deadly* (1955), he is aggressive, willing to dominate others to get his way and to gain sexual favors. Brian is also like Tom Joad in *The Grapes of Wrath* (1939), in that—when his family or community is threatened—he accepts responsibility for others at the risk of his own well-being, although he refuses to do so openly. He additionally resembles Sal Paradise of *On the Road* (1957) in that he is, without articulating the sentiment to anyone, in search of something outside himself that he needs to complete or redeem his life. He even calls to mind Gatsby, of *The Great Gatsby* (1925), in how objects, his automobile in particular, come to be an extension of himself and his masculinity.

In the first appearance of the Corvette, Brian drives into view and the car aggressively fills the screen with its physical presence—similar to the way its new master dominates places and situations—while the soundtrack features the driving beat of a song which stresses the need to take control and dominate (QAF season three, episode three). The Corvette is an expression of Brian's alpha male aggression, personal and sexual, and his continual quest to control, if not dominate, people and activities, at which he is incredibly successful. As one gay African American male, speaking of manhood and masculinity, told researcher Sheila J. Wise, "To be a man is to be strong. To be in control, to be in power. To be in control of your emotions.... To the extent you can be in control, you're going to be in control. To be a real man[,] which means being powerful and in control of your emotions, [is] to be in control as much of your own life as you can be" (9).

This articulates what Brian Kinney puts into action as a lifestyle. For a gay American male in a patriarchal society that often demands he hide his sexual orientation, casts him out for expressing his sexuality, or actively opposes his ambitions, "control" is a *potent* force—and *potency* is meant both sexually and in the sense of agency. Brian will not be denied his ability to achieve power. Much as what has been called "female masculinity," this means that masculinity—in its positive sense of a strong personal identity and the ability to make choices independent of normative social pressures—is open to gay and lesbian individuals: masculinity "does not belong to men [presumably heterosexual], has not been produced by men, and does not properly express male heterosexuality" (Halberstam 241). Brian demonstrates this over the course of the series by creating his own advertising firm, acquiring wealth in the process, and eventually purchasing his favorite night club, aptly named "Babylon," to become ruler, or "master," of his environment.

Queer Theory questions the assumptions many people make about gender, sex, and sexuality. *Queer as Folk* parallels this inquiry in a popular format. While Brian is the central and most outspoken and controversial, the other characters present a range of identities and problems faced by gay males and lesbian females. There is, for a heterosexual audience, a bit of initial discomfort and unease in viewing, but this soon fades. The gay and lesbian becomes "normal" once the characters are accepted as "people" first, and alternatively sexually orientated second. That is, in part, what *QAF* is about: the "normalcy" of non-heterosexual life. This may sometimes be deceptive, yet most of the things — love, family, friends, a measure of success and security in everyday life — that straight men and women value are those to which these characters aspire. The "edge," the point of difference between gay/lesbian and straight, mostly comes through in Brian Kinney, the one who refuses to "go along" or fit into anyone else's criteria. His male response to the outside world is distinctly antagonistic and masculine, just like his Corvette.

In *Bodies That Matter*, Judith Butler writes that performativity is "the power of discourse to produce effects through reiteration," and in *QAF* this can be seen in Brian's words and actions (20). He speaks and acts in ways that articulate what it means to be both gay and successful in American society, balancing male aggression with sexuality and control. His rise is configured through the use of "vectors of power," and — since his profession and expertise is advertising — Brian uses both the spoken word and images to manifest a discourse that could be called "gay masculinity" (Butler 18). Brian's life and work, as his Corvette represents, moves in the direction of what Butler calls "a radical resignification of the symbolic domain" (241).

The Corvette is a tool, a phallic symbolic object that Brian can utilize to present his identity to the world. It has emotional appeal for him, making a statement, perhaps exaggerated, that he rules or at least demands respect. It is also a source of autonomy and mobility. In the first scene in which the Stingray appears, Brian suggests that he and his best friend Michael leave *now*, from Pittsburgh, and drive straight through to New York City: a "road trip," two gay men — a queer Buz and Tod, Dean and Sal — "on the road" to adventure. Two seasons later, when Michael needs transportation out of town in an emergency, Brian immediately pitches him the keys to the Corvette; the car carries an aura of control of one's destiny, the ability to not just physically "escape" present circumstances, but to bring about change, to grant agency and masculine power to whomever comes to possess it.

By the conclusion of the episode that introduces the Corvette, Brian has re-established himself—there was never any doubt—as the craftiest, most able to surprise, shock, and manipulate others, and fittest to rule of all those he meets. In the end, he drives off in his dark green with gold pin-stripes Corvette, in the company of a new and handsome one-night stand. The Stingray's aggressive exhaust note merges with the insistent beat of the soundtrack. Now, as the car moves out of sight down the alley into the dark, the song that was heard when the Corvette was first seen plays over the closing credits. Again, we hear about the necessity of possessing power, of being the one who has control (QAF season three, episode three). The lyrics describe Brian's reassertion of masculine supremacy, even if it is gay, and seemingly confined to him alone, at the apex of the food chain.

In the series' final episode at the end of season five, Brian's friend, Michael—now happily committed to a male partner of his own—looks him in the eye and says, "You'll always be young, you'll always be beautiful, you're Brian Kinney"; all of which sounds very like what Corvette lovers would say of their cars (QAF season five, episode twenty). Like the "time passes slowly ... at a pace that is wonderfully slow" that Orr uses to describe Corvettes, Brian is—in his own eyes and those of his closest friend—a "classic," someone/something whose image will always be held in admiration: "young" and "beautiful" forever. The identity of the character and the image of the car are "fixed in time" by the qualities that they possess and the associations that people have for them: the iconic Corvette and the icon of gay masculinity. The two of them "live" at a different pace than mortal beings. Michael does not mean that Brian will literally be "young" and "beautiful"—although Brian, doubtless, would insist so. Instead, he is articulating his love and admiration for Brian: the "manliness," strength of will, and individuality that make up his identity. In another sense, what Michael so loves in Brian is the quality that the majority of males — straight or gay — value: a passionate rage to live and be active and creative. The homosexual and heterosexual appear to cross paths, to some degree, in what gives a "real" man his masculine virtues. His Corvette is the most visible of the objects that Brian uses to publicly reinforce that image; it is masculinity and power rolled into one.

A different perspective on the Corvette arises in Nasdijj's *Geronimo's Bones* (2004). The book's subtitle, *A Memoir of My Brother and Me*, describes the content of the work; the narrator, looking back over forty years, recollects his difficult but rewarding life. As teenagers, sons of a white cowboy and a Navaho woman, in 1963 he and his younger brother stole a new red Corvette — a "Corvette Grand Sport II Roadster" complete with "the image of a naked woman" imposed on the foam dice hanging from the rearview mirror — from a "New Jersey chop shop" and headed west for California (Nasdijj 87 and 101). They grew up as migrant laborers, much like the dispossessed Joad family, and continually traveled the country, on the road and homeless. But unlike the Joads, they did not have the family structure and support. Their mother is a kind, loving alcoholic, and she dies drunk in the ditch alongside the road one night. After that, they are raised by "the Cowboy," as he is sometimes called, "one tough, mad, cold son-of-a-bitch," a man called "the devil" by his other, Mexican family (2 and 93).

Geronimo's Bones is a dark variation of *Route 66*. Tod and Buz, light and dark, are mirrored in the two mixed-race boys, the narrator almost blond and Anglo, and his brother — Tso, their mother's nickname for him, "the Smarter One" — with his "long black Navaho hair," a "darker, thinner [male] version of Brigitte Bardot" (Nasdijj 97). The "memoir" is like *On the Road* turned inside out: the boys are not exactly out in search of something; instead, they are on the run, trying to escape their desperate, meager lives. Most especially they are fleeing their father: a violent, physically, psychologically, and sexually abusive man. Years later, Nasdijj calls him "the demon in all my nightmares and the reason my brother sometimes took refuge in the darkness under beds" (287). It seems clear, given the boys' mixture of Anglo and Indian ancestry, that their father stands for everything that is cruel and evil in white, male patriarchal culture. He is a, or even *the*, personification of the forces that led the war to destroy the Native Americans and their culture. Additionally, he is the image of any or all abusive male figures, a man who — after his wife dies — brings "whores" home, then forces his young sons into bed with the women. As an account of the experiences of people growing up outside any mainstream American society, black or white, the book itself is cruel, making the reader "see" what life might be like for the people at the bottom and at the doubtful mercy of a hostile, racist culture.

Booklist called *Geronimo's Bones* a "pain-filled" memoir that many will find "hard to read" and described the writing as "raw" and "emotional" (Huntley 1259). *Publisher's Weekly* said the book "juggles sardonic anger and full-out hilarity" in a "lyric memoir" (66–67). And *Library Journal* wrote that "Nasdijj's lyrical, almost poetic writing entrances" even while depicting "unbelievable pain" (Brodie 134–135). *Kirkus Reviews* said the purpose of the writing was to find "a way back into the grotesque swarm of horrors and a way forward to give a whole new breadth to the meaning of survival" (73). The work seems to capture the love between two brothers who grow up without a choice in a harsh, nearly unbearable situation.

It is no wonder that a Corvette comes to embody the boys' dream of escape: "We saw that car as the ultimate symbol of freedom," the narrator remembers (Nasdijj 100). Like the Corvette in *Route 66* or the Joad family truck, this machine carries all the promise of the open road and a chance at a new and different life. As Nasdijj describes it when he looks at the Corvette, "*Freedom for my soul. A band of angels coming after me,*" and the car is "not unlike a new and gleaming chariot made by the gods" (100 and 99). The Corvette is hope, a dream come true. The boys steal it, along with all the money their father had hidden away after winning at gambling, and hit the road west. The Corvette, as the image of American freedom and independence, has penetrated even into the farthest levels of society. It both suggests the power of patriarchal culture, yet also offers an avenue of escape to freedom.

But ... Nasdijj does not exist. The "memoir" is a work of fiction; the real author is Tim Barrus, a white male known prior to Nasdijj's series of successful works as an author of gay and/or sadomasochistic fiction. Nasdijj and his works are a now well-known "Navahoax"; "all of his work was a literary fraud perpetrated by a middle-aged white writer" (Chaikivsky). Barrus, writing as Nasdijj, was nominated for a National Magazine Award for a June 1999 essay in *Esquire*, and *The Boy and the Dog Are Sleeping* (2003) won a 2004 PEN/Beyond Margins Award (Fleisher). Native-American writer Sherman Alexie, author of *The Lone Ranger and Tonto Fist Fight in Heaven* (1993), writes that Barrus "cynically co-opted as a literary style the very real suffering endured by generations of real Indians ... caused by very real American aggression." Where does this leave the book's use of the Corvette as an icon of freedom? The answer is that the image Nasdijj/Barrus used is more real than the characters he created or "borrowed" for his "memoir." The Corvette, in *Geronimo's Bones* or elsewhere, has by now established itself over time as an image suitable for appropriation, by anyone who wishes to use it, to represent freedom, power, and control.

While we have seen how the Corvette has come to express that American passion for freedom and independence, as well as affluence and social status, the spirit of automobility is not limited to the Corvette. As mentioned earlier, the Joads' lowly truck, Gatsby's ostentatious roadster, and the Jaguar

XKE can embody similar qualities. But none of these quite suggests masculinity as well as the Corvette. Masculinity is about both power and control, and most Corvettes demonstrate these virtues exceptionally well. Taken together, for a large number of men, these are near spiritual qualities, not just temporary, but eternal in their necessity. No Corvette appears in David Seals' *Powwow Highway* (1990), but the car in this novel does definitely show its "spiritual" power in a Native-American context.

The essential story of *Powwow Highway* is, once more, a journey down America's roads. Geographically, it occurs from the Lame Deer Cheyenne Reservation in Montana to Santa Fe, New Mexico — a roughly north-south axis complicated by side trips to other places. Spiritually, the "road trip" is a visionary quest for regaining touch with the true nature of being an American Indian, a Cheyenne, and a warrior. Philbert Bono is like Sal Paradise: he seeks spiritual renewal. But the difference between *Powwow Highway* and other works is that the major characters are people truly outside Western white culture. Philbert and Buddy Red Bird, a Marine Vietnam veteran and militant member of the American Indian Movement (AIM), start out outside the United States, on the reservation, and then journey to the sacred places of the Cheyenne. The America we know is the alien-invader world to them, the conqueror of their people. On "the Res," they live inside what Seals calls "the Indian Problem": the poverty, unemployment, alcoholism, and purposelessness many Indians know so well (Seals "Another Sioux Uprising in the Black Hills"). It's *Route 66* and *On the Road* yet again, but the vague, poignant longing or spiritual void Sal feels is this time rooted in an American Indian sense of everything lost or corrupted, a culture destroyed. "Indian masculinity" would seem to be a joke.

The novel begins with the car, a 1964 Buick LeSabre with the engine from a '55 Chevy, mag hubcaps, racing slicks, the nest from a family of skunks, and a shit-brown — once bright red — exterior resulting from an engine fire (Seals *Powwow* viii–xi). Seals writes, "This is the story of a machine and of the people who made a story of its movements and of what happened to the machine and its people" (vii). The old Buick is far from a Corvette, but Indians could only dream of Corvettes, not possess them, and Philbert's dream is to become a Cheyenne warrior and to gather the tokens of spiritual power, "medicine," that will make him whole.

Automobility here is something different from how it is found in other works. Masculinity is certainly part of it, but for the character of Philbert, the Buick is not so much a machine as a spiritual partner: it is "Protector," his "war pony" (1). The old car, when it first starts, is "like so many American dreams resurrected back to reality" (x). The Buick comes to have a tribal identity and a role to play. It is "the talisman of [against] the whiteman, the medicine to explain modern spirits that ailed and healed the redman of his technological woes, the sacred bundle to protect the superstitious Morning Star People from the whiteman's evils" (1). While the Corvette may be a western symbol of power and control, prestige and status, these are the qualities lacking in the people of the reservation. Only by escaping this world, spiritually rather than physically, can the "mysteries of the world" be grasped and "absolute moments of purity" be achieved (5). In her review of the film based on the novel, *New York Times* critic Janet Maslin says that Philbert demonstrates a "determination to find some kind of spiritual core in contemporary American Indian life." This is "automobility" done a bit differently.

What the Corvette hasn't shown in works studied thus far is a spiritual quality. It may make a political or sociological statement, but in speaking for the modern automobile, the Corvette seems strangely silent on matters of the spirit. Is this a reflection of the limitations of technology or of interpretation or of owner/drivers? The automobile is rooted in this material world, but can it move into a realm of spirit, can it be transformed into an "immaterial" idea? The narrative voice in *Powwow Highway* says,

> There are two parts to every story: the part that is believable and the part that is not. It is impossible to determine which of the two is the truth and which of the two is a lie, for a lie is an extension of the truth and nobody knows what the hell the truth is. Perhaps it is a lie that is so exciting and preposterous that it has to be true. But nobody really knows [159].

Given this bit of wisdom, if an object speaks to the human spirit, it can be a spiritual artifact; the test is in the performance. What an artifact has to give is the test of its spiritual value.

In *Powwow Highway*, the car takes Philbert, and even Buddy, who seems at first unwilling to be changed, on a spiritual journey. Philbert's warrior name, who he seeks to become, is "Whirlwind" (2). At one point in the novel, Philbert/Whirlwind stops a Caterpillar snowplow about to bury the Buick, a tractor very much like the one that smashed the Joads' home and ripped up their land (188–189). When he realizes that he gains "religious strength from history," yet "the whiteman" does not, Philbert becomes powerful and is then spiritually fortified by the ghosts at Fort Robinson, Nebraska (180). Automobility at times manifests itself as both a physical and a psychic means of travel; it is transformative. While we tend to focus on the material and the tangible, on occasion other things matter more.

The result of this "spiritual automobility" is that a Cheyenne warrior experiences "an untranslatable aura of unreal freedom, an Indian reality at implausible odds with the rational world of whitemen" (273). Philbert and the old Buick become "one" at a crucial moment, and Protector is then "more than a machine" (275). In the end the Buick expires after giving its all. It crashes and burns, but delivers everyone safely in the direction of home. Without its Cheyenne spirit, the car is again only an object, "the dead American thing his people no longer wanted" (293).

Seals writes in his online essay "Another Sioux Uprising in the Black Hills" that "we [the Native American population] don't trust America at all, anymore," and he sees problems of corruption in tribal government, indifference of Americans in general, and a widespread disregard — even a contempt for American Indian concerns and suffering — as something still not addressed by either the American people or their predominantly white and uncaring leadership. Although his novel presents hope, in Seals' opinion Indians in America only receive the respect and attention they demand or take for themselves. While automobility unites the rest of us, for his people life continues to be a struggle to survive.

In Ridley Scott's *Thelma & Louise* (1991), masculine culture includes law-enforcement agencies, tractor-trailer trucks, abusive and sexist males, and one Corvette — the one driven by Thelma's husband, Darryl. His red Corvette is closely linked with Darryl's self-centered, conceited "masculine" nature. He primps his hair, twirls his keys, gives Thelma orders, and wears a gold — undoubtedly as fake as he is — necklace reading "The 1 [One]": all signs of what he takes for being "in charge," sexually aggressive, and compellingly masculine. He drives the Corvette, called "a macho symbol in itself" by one critic, with the t-tops out to ensure admiring females see him, and it bears a vanity plate that reads, again reflecting his self-concept, "The 1" (Cooper 286). Darryl, obviously little better than a buffoon, is Thelma's spouse, making it painfully clear how little choice, decision-making power, or good judgment she possessed in marrying him.

In point of fact, Darryl's persona is not so very different from that of Harlan, the man who attempts to rape Thelma. It is more a matter of degree, than of kind. Female frustration *with* and anger in response *to* this assumed male supremacy and natural superiority is what many, so it seems, of the women in the audience recognize in themselves: unequal relationships and partner bonds with males who see themselves as entitled, dominant, and with total authority in their hands. Actress Susan Sarandon, who portrayed Louise, believes that real women identified with the title characters, since

In Ridley Scott's *Thelma & Louise* (1991), two women rebel after years of male domination. Once beyond their accepted roles, they become powerful and independent, both female and fully human. The patriarchal power structure, American society in general, that they confront is typified in Thelma's self-centered husband Darrell, owner of a red Corvette (and matching neck chain) with "The 1 [One]" as his personalized plate, a car similar to the one pictured here (Roger Viollet/Getty Images).

they expressed "a little bit of every woman's rage and rebellion" (qtd. in Cooper 279). In this context, the Corvette is a questionable, false signifier of "manliness," unless it is a masculinity that is hollow to its core, one that must — out of necessity — be challenged at some point. In this particular film, the red Corvette suggests falsely puffed-up male pride and ego — like the rooster's inflated comb — all part of masculine attitudes toward and desire to control women. One Corvette sums up how patriarchal males feel.

As a device, a shortcut to meaning, the Corvette suggests male values, even a masculine personality; as a signifier of masculinity and power, it is intrinsically connected with all the other mechanisms or instruments of its kind. Patriarchy is a network of power, with those who have access claiming greater or lesser amounts of authority and control. As a masculine signifier, the Corvette often stands for the power of male culture, its ability to use machines and technology according to its ideological principles: while this may be open to "others," the male nature of "power" remains unchanged. It seeks to dominate, or at least control, its environment and circumstances.

Summary

Masculinity and automobility are normally compatible, even complementary. However, the supposition of masculinity often overlays automobility with a cultural attitude that the road and the freedom it offers are primarily the province of males; the territory is not suited to those outside the heteronormative or culturally approved values of performance and behavior: "others" need not venture out. The American Corvette is not the exclusive symbol of autonomy and mobility; there are others. But the Corvette is, so very often, a signifier of masculine power, the ability to dominate and control, that the car becomes desirable to those who are not "traditionally male" or do not have the recognized ability to define themselves or their place in the world. The car's image is sexually powerful and attractive; it invites attention and desire. Men of different ethnicity and social class use it to reflect their own potent masculinity or make the Corvette an object of desire. Over time, the Corvette has developed an identity of its own distinct from any human individual.

Although culture dictates much of what characters in films, novels, and songs do, we have an inclination to forget that we are part of the cultural — phallogocentric, heteronormative, masculine, and so on — environment. What the characters in creative works do negotiates reality. In large part, the Corvette as a material object has come to represent a range of diverse interpretations that reflect "real" concerns about independence and freedom, the nature of masculinity, and who has power and control in our society and of our behavior. This is not limited to any one group or time in the last fifty years; the Corvette moves through time, existing in the timescape of isolated yet connected spots of signification. It is not one thing, but many, with complex significance given whoever rests his "male gaze" upon it.

And, as the next chapter will show, sexuality, masculinity — in its wider meaning of power, authority — and automobility are not limited to those socially, politically, or physically identified as males. Women, as well as (sometimes better than) men, can acquire Corvettes and utilize them — or other cars that borrow from and share signifier status — to demonstrate *their* power to go "on the road" or to assert their authority over themselves and their identities as independent and self-determined human beings. What men do, women can do; the Corvette does not care who drives, so long as she does it with style and remains in control.

The 1990–1995 ZR-1 Corvettes were among the fastest, most powerful cars available in a time when the American automobile industry was adapting to the demands of fuel economy, product quality, and a global market (GM Photo Store).

If the Corvette lacked sophistication in its earlier incarnations, the 1997–2004 C5 became directly comparable with the world's best. It integrated Corvette styling cues from previous generations with the latest performance features (GM Photo Store).

The 2005 C6 Corvette had a 400 b.h.p. V8 engine and a top speed of more than 180 m.p.h. It was a "freedom machine"—a powerful object that Americans intuitively understand (GM Photo Store).

In Man Martin's novel *Days of the Endless Corvette* (2007), the 1953 Corvette, like the one pictured, is not just a valuable old car that mechanic Earl Mulvaney maintains, but also a suggestion of the love between two people who may always be apart. Yet again, the Corvette is a bundle of stories (Giulio Marcocchi/ Getty Images Entertainment/Getty Images).

After over fifty years of racing, Corvettes are recognized as fast, powerful, and always distinctly American. Their engine sound and aggressive, muscular styling are among their signature characteristics (Darrell Ingham/Getty Images Sport/Getty Images).

In the *Rush Hour* films, Jackie Chan (passenger) and Chris Tucker's (driver) Corvette convertible seems perfect for the crime fighting partners. Once emboding the masculine strength of white, male patriarchy, the Corvette was readily appropriated by others (Eric Ford/Getty Images Entertainment/ Getty Images).

Many of America's astronaut heroes in the 1960s and 1970s drove Corvettes. The Apollo 12 crew — Al Bean (left), Dick Gordon (center), and Pete Conrad (right) — had matching, personalized Stingrays, vehicles that reflected their courage, fascination with performance and technology, and competitive nature (Ralph Morse/Time & Life Pictures/Getty Images).

From 1960 to 1964 *Route 66* brought two young men and the Corvette they shared into America's homes. Although Buz (George Maharis, standing) and Tod (Martin Milner, in car) engaged in a restless search for adventure, the series emphasized a spirit of American virtue in spite of problems or flaws. The Corvette, as the third cast member, never lost that liberating, exciting aura (CBS Photo Archive/CBS/Getty Images).

Concept car Corvettes come in a multitude of forms. Many are produced by Chevrolet; more still are created by aftermarket custom shops or major automobile designers, such as Italdesign, which debuted its Corvette Moray in 2003. The Moray stresses the Corvette's distinctive American identity (Italdesign Giugiaro Photo Archive).

In Ridley Scott's *Thelma & Louise* (1991), the title characters react against a society in which men intimidate and suppress women. Louise (Susan Sarandon, left) and Thelma (Geena Davis, right) take on new personas, female and free, but do not escape masculine retribution. Their elegant 1966 Thunderbird convertible suggests openness to new experience and the freedom to explore — like the Corvette in *Route 66* (Photofest).

The 2009 Corvette ZR1 is the fastest, most powerful road-going Corvette ever, a car that joins — or challenges — European supercars at the pinnacle of automotive performance (Joel Saget/AFP/Getty Images).

In the Showtime series *Queer as Folk* (2000–05), a 1970 Corvette Stingray convertible much like this one is an image of power used by the assertively gay, professionally successful, and sexually predatory Brian Kinney. As male, gay, and empowered, Brian chooses objects that reflect his affluence and self-image (GM Photo Store).

Corvette "concept cars" reflect the car's evolution and the dreams of its designers. While some are pure styling exercises, the 1963 Mako Shark I (rear) reflects the form and style of the 1963–1967 Stingrays, albeit taken to extremes, and the 1965 Mako Shark II (front) looks very much like a customized 1968–1982 Corvette (GM Photo Store).

The 1956 C1 Corvette was an important styling revision in the first generation's overall design. Along with the introduction of the V8 engine in 1955, the new looks reinvigorated the car. The "side coves," often in contrasting colors, became a trademark characteristic (GM Photo Store).

Top: In the 1967 427 Corvette Sting Ray, the *power* of the machine is obvious. In Gabriele Muccino's *Seven Pounds* (2008), Ben Thomas (Will Smith), a successful aerospace engineer, drives a Sting Ray similar to the one shown — and his masculinity seems secure (GM Photo Store). *Bottom:* The original 1953–1962 C1 Corvettes underwent significant evolution, as did their image. While the Corvette suggested youthful freedom and independence, it also could represent rebellion against the established social order (GM Photo Store).

America on the Move: 50s Sporty Cars

"A WORK OF ART," proclaimed the Museum of Modern Art in New York, describing the low-slung Studebaker Starliner, the only American car in the 1953 exhibition, "Ten Automobiles." Considered by many as "the first American sports car," the sophisticated, European-styled hardtop was designed to appeal to younger drivers.

The '52 Nash Healey was the ultimate hybrid sports car. Its American-made Nash engine was shipped to England for a Donald Healey-engineered chassis and then to Italy for a Pinin Farina-sports car body—then back to the U.S. Although the car enjoyed amazing success at the Le Mans sports car race in France, its list price of nearly $6,000—principally due to shipping costs—priced it out of the market.

In January 1953 the Chevrolet Corvette, a fiberglass-bodied, two-seater, was unveiled at the GM Motorama at New York's Waldorf Astoria Hotel. Under the design direction of GM stylist Harley Earl, the Corvette captured the public's imagination with its sleek styling and sense of fun. All 300 models produced in the first year were hand-built and white, with a red interior and black convertible top.

Henry J. Kaiser, who had turned to automobile production after World War II, eventually teamed up with master designer Howard

Twenty 37c Self-adhesive Stamps · Five Separate Designs

"Dutch" Darrin, of Packard fame, to develop a fiberglass sports car that would be known as the Kaiser Darrin. Introduced in 1954, the two-seater featured retractable doors that slid forward into the front fenders and a three-position convertible top. A victim of the soft car market, only 435 Kaiser Darrins were made.

In 1955 Ford introduced its flashy Thunderbird, dubbing it "a sports car with luxury." In road competition with the Corvette, there was little difference in performance. But the Thunderbird—boasting a steel body, interchangeable hard and soft tops, roll-up windows, and other luxury options—outsold the Corvette.

These five sporty cars of the '50s have been captured at stamp size by renowned automobile artist Art M. "Fitz" Fitzpatrick of Carlsbad, California. Designer of the Darrin Packard 4-door convertible and hard-top sedans, Fitzpatrick went on to set the advertising standard with his award-winning art at General Motors for more than 20 years.

FORD THUNDERBIRD

CHEVROLET CORVETTE

STUDEBAKER STARLINER

NASH HEALEY

KAISER DARRIN

Artwork and photography courtesy Art M. Fitzpatrick. Sports car engraving courtesy Carl T. Hermann. Ford and Thunderbird, ™ Ford Motor Company. Kaiser Darrin and Nash Healey are trademarks of DaimlerChrysler Corporation. General Motors Corvette Trademarks used under license to the USPS.

Stamps printed by Ashton Potter (USA) Ltd. (APU) / No. 743 in a series / August 20, 2005 / Printed in U.S.A. / © 2005 United States Postal Service

UNITED STATES POSTAL SERVICE®

In the 1950s various American sports cars appeared, only to vanish shortly with a few exceptions. The "America on the Move: 50s Sporty Cars" stamps from the U.S. Postal Service pay tribute to five of these: the 1953 Studebaker Starliner, 1954 Kaiser Darrin, 1953 Corvette, 1952 Nash Healey, and 1955 Thunderbird. The stamps, as art, suggest how cars have become cultural artifacts (U.S. Postal Service).

PART III

Women, Sex, and Identity as Power: The Corvette, Baddest Mother of Them All

Chapter 11

The Gendered Object

The automobile as a significant material object and automobility as a dominant, frequently masculine, idea in global — no longer just Western — culture are found, as we have seen, in a wide range of media. Yet, much of the time, the car and the freedom to move — as the Corvette has come to signify — are predicated on being male or possessing the attributes of masculinity. This has been a limiting factor, both in thought and action, for female human beings. Autonomy is often denied to women, and mobility is not considered a "natural" attribute of femininity. In fact, female autonomy and a strong, feminine sense of self have been perceived as threats to the established social order, an unnatural manifestation of displaced identity, or a not so covert sign of deviant female sexuality. The "social order" is, more often than not, taken to mean patriarchal culture, "unnatural" is defined as anything not sanctioned by the accepted mores and behaviors of that culture, and "female deviancy" carries the stigma of nonstandard — that is to say, powerful and self-determining — assertions of women's sexuality.

Empowered women, those with authority over themselves or who desire physical, social, or sexual emancipation, frequently struggle with and against the "orderly," usually heteronormative and phallogocentric, masculine culture, along with its "male gaze." In many instances, the Corvette — or a substitute that borrows its ability to signify power and independence — serves as their literal vehicle. Figuratively, if not in fact, these women achieve a measure of what Judith Halberstam calls "female masculinity," phallic femininity, and self-determination (1). In the essay "Are Mothers Persons?" from her book *Unbearable Weight* (1993), Susan Bordo does not use the term "automobility," but does stress women's need for "subjectivity, authority, embodied consciousness, and personal integrity" — all conceptions that relate to, or share values with, this combination of autonomy and mobility (96).

The Corvette, as a machine and a material object, actually has an androgynous or even asexual nature (shocking as it may be to admit): its masculine or feminine qualities are more a matter of perception than actuality. As Pierre Bourdieu would remind us, the taste or conditioned perceptiveness of the viewer, the *habitus* (male or female), constructs the final or total perception of the automobile (101). The Corvette, or other object, may have masculine or feminine characteristics — the shape of a particular contour, the angular or curved form that a certain view presents.

If female, these qualities are most often couched by male viewers in terms of women's body parts or attributes with sexual overtones. For example, the large, pointed, chrome bumper "breasts" on cars from the late 1940s and early 1960s were sometimes referred to as Dagmars or "Dagmar bumpers," after an especially shapely and well-endowed female television performer (Fitzgerald, "Dagmar Bumpers"; Martin, "Dagmar"). The outline of a particularly "female" automotive form most often has pleasing, to the masculine eye, contours to its rear fenders or "hips," giving the car a "behind" that elicits the male desire to touch, even caress, it. The current C6 Corvette has this alluring shape to its muscular but female body. Male qualities are usually connotations of power or an aggressive, assertive form, not a rounded or shapely expanse of automotive bodywork. The "muscle cars" of the 1960s were noted for their horsepower and torque ratings, their ability to accelerate — usually 0 to 60 m.p.h. and through the quarter mile — and their "masculine" proportions: most often big, angular shapes not known for how they turned or stopped. Pickup trucks and today's SUVs may be perceived as "male" even when the overall form is more rounded than squared off; their physical presence and size grant them masculine connotations.

Male vehicles seem to possess "shoulders" or broad, relatively bulky shapes, while female automobiles have a curvaceous or sensuous form. Both may be sensual and sexually attractive, but they are not the same, and any gender perception is strikingly different. Sports cars, like the Corvette or Porsche 911, balance masculine power with the more feminine grace — think of a football player or professional fighter combined with a ballerina or female figure skater — in a form that carries physical power melded with a preciseness of motion and flowing style. The term frequently applied to extremely powerful automobiles — such as the 205 m.p.h., 638-horsepower 2009 ZR1 Corvette — is "potent," a word that reeks of masculinity, testosterone, and sexual performance ("First Look"). Yet the same Corvette, when it debuted in automobile enthusiast publications in February 2008, was variously referred to as "The King," "The Devil's Own Vette" (a play on "the

Corvette from Hell" nickname for the ZR-1 of the past), and "The Mother of All Vettes" (Swan, Markus, and Sherman). The Corvette's sexuality might be constant, but its gender identity is variable, so long as it bears an aura of speed and power (although taken to be a masculine signifier, the *power* of the car means more than the masculine or feminine appellation). Presumably, the "Mother of All Corvettes" is, in the parlance of "bad mothers," either male or female — *badness* trumping all other qualities.

Female objects have suggestive, sensual physical contours; male objects express or possess a tangible feeling of power. Masculine and feminine connotations are carefully separated from one another in the majority of cases. However "female" a beautiful automobile might be, its power and speed are taken to be "male" characteristics. Bodywork might be "female" and voluptuous (perhaps "brawny," like a female bodybuilder), but the engine and the car's performance would be "impressive" or — to use an overworked masculine phrase — "awesome." The maleness or femaleness of the Corvette's qualities depends more on the viewer and the context, along with the intent of the artist/designer, than intrinsic values in the car itself. This may not have been true in the 1950s and the early to mid–1960s, the time of *Route 66* and the first generation Corvettes — when masculinity dominated American culture — but during the Sting Ray years, 1965–1967, interpretations began to change, and the styling of the car became more important. If the feminine Corvette was behind the scenes in the car's initial years, it becomes more assertive and powerful as time goes on. In a variety of creative works from that time to the present, the Corvette's identity grows and develops, becoming less male and more of a diverse, fluid signifier — carrying male and female, positive and negative associations. The car's "potency" is not simply masculine, but protean, allowing women to embrace, share, counter, or expand its meaning. Female potency, feminine power in all its aspects, is really an important, pressing question in the majority of works that involve women and Corvettes.

Until we invest an object with signifying status and a cultural identity, even a machine that interacts with us in ways we construe as intimate and personal — such as a sports car like the Corvette — exists merely as what it is, a three-dimensional form and an image in the consciousness of those who come to know and recognize it. Its power to signify outside itself may be narrowly circumscribed. Yet, pondering it more deeply, if human minds create an object and human hands give it shape and form, how can it not present or depict some aspect of human thought and feeling? Will the tangible object and its image, as it becomes part of our lives, not take on new and unexpected, even uncontrolled significance? And human thinking seems inevitably tied to, in some cases unavoidably obsessed with, *gender*. In its literary and cultural depictions over time, the Corvette becomes increasingly associated not just with males and masculine faults and virtues, as we are aware, but with diverse, dynamic, and changing female characters — along with ideas about women and femininity that demand our attention and call into question what was once assumed to be true.

This part of the book looks at how women and Corvettes are found or come together in a range of creative works. The male presumption of power they confront is not factual, but contrived and situational. Women, as well as men, strive for control of their lives, and while patriarchal culture does favor the masculine, its nature as a structure of "power" cannot absolutely deny the authority and control that these women and their vehicles are able to develop or seize for themselves. This is what we discover in creative works during the cultural lifespan of the Corvette, and the car becomes one of the signifiers women choose as signs of their automobility.

Modern women struggle to take command of their bodies, their "personal space," and the external world. In novels or cinema, the outside — the natural landscape or urban environment — is frequently an expression of women's interior existence. Women do battle with physical and psychological oppression through both internal and external means; the acquisition of a Corvette or other potent signifier does not assure freedom, but it is a step toward independence. The automobile is *both* a signifier of the power over them *and* the appropriation of power to escape or defy the forces that oppress: it both conflicts with and supports female empowerment. The works described here, *Play It as It Lays* (1970) and *Thelma & Louise* (1991) among them, present women asserting a desire for control of their own lives and struggling to have a Corvette or signifier of their own. If women can become "men," that is, equally human, then the Corvette can become feminine when women want or need it to be. The car belongs to them, and any power it possesses or confers is theirs.

Chapter 12

The "Female" Corvette and the Struggle for Freedom and Identity

Play It As It Lays

In Joan Didion's *Play It as It Lays* (1970), Maria Wyeth, a thirty-one-year-old actress and former New York fashion model, faces a life that seems absolutely empty, without meaning or purpose. Divorced from Carter Lang, a young up-and-coming film director, and mother of Kate, an institutionalized four year old with "soft down on her spine and an aberrant chemical in her brain," Maria is confronted with the uncertain prospects of what will happen to her now, in the Hollywood of the late 1960s, after having an unborn child, most likely not her ex-husband's, aborted at his insistence (5). *Play It as It Lays* is what one critic calls "a picture of personal dread and anxiety, of alienation and absurdity lurking within and without"; it is also an existential novel that is "uniquely feminine" without being "blatantly feminist" (Geherin 64–65 and 68–69). Another refers to the novel as "an unbroken circuit of exhaustion, spiritual paralysis, dread, and vacuous persistence" existing in "a seemingly merciless present" (Coale 164 and 162). Maria wants change, escape, discovery of something that will give her back her life.

As a woman, she is doubly trapped (all the male characters are also enclosed) in a "social world"—not just Hollywood or even America, but the whole of postmodern time — seemingly ruled by Kierkegaard's "aesthetic mode," which takes "immediate pleasure" as "its sole imperative," and women appear to be merely objects at the doubtful mercy of male desire (Chabot 55). Maria, institutionalized "for her own good" as the narrative of the novel proceeds, exists in what feels like a world parallel to T.S. Eliot's *The Waste Land* (1922), where "so raw are her nerves that she will not let herself feel any further" (Chabot 60). Didion's work is a "Hollywood novel," in the vein of precursors such as Nathanael West's *The Day of the Locust* (1939), but it is about the whole of the late-twentieth-century world; Hollywood is only the setting, the metaphor that is reminiscent of both Eliot's land in need of water and spiritual rebirth and Maria's own home, the ghost town once called Silver Wells in the Nevada desert — now the site of, in an echo of the deadly technology of *Kiss Me Deadly*, a missile test range. Critic Richard B. Gehman, writing about West's fiction, describes Hollywood as "a microcosm" of America; "everything that is wrong with life in the United States is to be found there in rare purity," and the "unreality" of the motion picture business makes for a "half-world" that is not our own but very close to us: remarks that apply to Didion's novel as well (xviii–xx).

What Maria craves most is not love and affection — commodities to be bought or bartered away in her present environment — but control. If the social structure of Hollywood, and American society in general, does not allow for female independence, it does grant mobility. What autonomy and freedom Maria creates for herself comes from driving her Corvette, endlessly speeding down the California freeways. This is not to say that Maria goes anywhere with a purpose; she simply drives, moving down the road at 70 m.p.h., sometimes eating a hard-boiled egg or stopping to drink a Coke. Plagued by bad dreams, she sleeps fitfully at night, and the daytime driving — "seven thousand miles on the Corvette" in a single month — sometimes gives her a satisfaction that nothing else provides (18).

Driving the Corvette, usually barefoot to better feel the car's power through the pedals — perhaps to interact more intimately with her car than with any human beings — Maria attempts things that challenge her. With the Corvette, Maria feels empowered — dare we say sufficiently "potent" — to take on a difficult task, a demanding maneuver through freeway traffic that appears to be a private, emotionally, and even sexually pleasing assertion of Maria's own inner strength and ability to assume control: "Again and again she returned to an intricate stretch ... where successful passage required a diagonal move across four lanes of traffic. On the afternoon she finally did it without once braking or once losing the beat on the radio she was exhilarated, and that night slept dreamlessly" (16). The Corvette lets Maria feel something undiluted or real and immediate that little, if anything else — whether sex or drugs or even her unemotional, unresponsive daughter — can supply. Maria does not drive the Corvette naked, does not have sex either in or with the car, but it is one of her few truly rewarding and personal relationships. Piloting it successfully, making that "diagonal move" across the stresses and unrelenting flow of traffic, answers a need she has, although the exhilaration — like the high of alcohol or marijuana — does not last. But for a brief while Maria does have *control* of her situation and herself.

The experience she shares with her Corvette touches Maria in a way that maybe nothing else does. The automobile can, if used with skill and in perfect coordination with the present moment, give her a positive thrill that sex with any and all partners does not ("making love" does not really appear in the novel; sex is just as barren of meaning for Maria as for the women in Eliot's long poem), and afterward she sleeps deeply and peacefully. Perhaps the only other intimacy that makes her feel a similar way is when she remembers thoroughly brushing Kate's hair, working out all "the tangles into fine golden strands," but Kate does not respond to Maria's caresses the way the Corvette does (43). In her best moments with the Corvette, Maria falls into a "rhythm," a oneness with the machine that matches what Didion, in a 1999 interview, said most excites her about writing: "When the rhythm comes ... you go into over-drive. When a book starts to move and you know you can go with it. Between then and the time you finish it is a good period" (Frumkes 2).

Additionally, Didion herself during the time she composed *Play It as It Lays* was a Corvette owner and driver. The cover of her collection of nonfiction *We Tell Ourselves Stories in Order to Live* (2006) is a photograph taken some years ago, showing a youthful Didion behind the wheel of her white 1970 Corvette Stingray, smoking a cigarette, looking into the camera with a pensive — maybe haughtily confident — expression. It is a photograph of Didion that can be found over and over again; presumably it captures a quality in her that the Corvette brings out. In her Stingray, Didion does not look like the petite, slender, unassuming woman she is to this day (or so she describes herself in her writing); instead, she looks "in charge," as if she disdains the picture-taking but sits still for it anyway, a Maria-like pose: saying, "Yes, think of me *this way*." In this and other photos of Didion and her Corvette to be discovered online through Google.com, we see her in or next to the car, as if— as in Maria's case — there is a relationship between them, and Didion looks pleased or amused to be photographed with her Corvette. Much of the rest of the time, over the course of years, she appears in pictures alone, without even her husband as company. As if the Corvette for Didion, like Maria, is a source of security, as if the car gives her a sense of self as Maria's does for her in the novel.

In her 1976 essay "Bureaucrats," from *The White Album* (1979), Didion writes that the LA "freeway experience [is] ... the only secular communion Los Angeles has" (238). To participate in this demands "a total surrender, a concentration so intense as to seem as kind of narcosis, a rapture-of-the-freeway. The mind goes clean. The rhythm takes over.... The moment is dangerous. The exhilaration is in doing it" (239). Although this is nonfiction and years after *Play It as It Lays*, the description fits perfectly with what Maria and her Corvette experience: there is a pleasure, a joy, in the accomplishment. As British architect and critic Reyner Banham observed in 1971, "As you acquire the special skills involved [...] the freeways become a special way of being alive ... the extreme concentration required in Los Angeles seems to bring on a state of heightened awareness that some locals find mystical" (qtd. in Didion 239). What Didion shares with her Corvette and what she and Banham discover in and on the LA freeways is the real manifestation of how the image, the signifying value, and physical being of the car come together with the driving experience of the road to affirm, strangely all at once, a human ability to feel empowered and to be able to lose one's self in moments of intense physical and mental involvement. Automobility becomes not just a practical, but a "mystical" state that offers fulfillment of human wants and needs. Maybe this, to go back to "the Righteous Stuff" of the American astronauts, is part of the rush of danger and speed to be experienced when pushing the edge of the envelope, of going all out with one's abilities, in the air or on the ground.

Yet Maria does not escape for long. While the Corvette becomes more of her "home" than either the house in Beverly Hills, for which Carter pays the rent, or the apartment she later moves to, sooner or later she must interact, to some degree, with the people around her. Maria does not do this well; she suffers from ... it is difficult to say just what, at least a neurosis, more likely a psychosis. Patriarchal culture dominates her life; like other women, she is a warm body, a commodity to be desired and discarded. The "Hollywood establishment" is entirely male and very caught up in expressions — sexual, verbal, and social — of its phallic masculinity: the "gangster" lawyer, said to be a "great admirer" of Maria, reportedly praises her as "not a cunt," not just a female body part (27). At a party, he observes "contemplatively" a "very young girl" and comments, "I'd like to get into that" — as in sleep with, get laid by, and so on (36). The response of BZ, Maria's gay/bisexual producer friend, is "I wouldn't call it the impossible dream" (36). The single powerful female — the one who can be "free" and independent at will — is Carlotta, BZ's mother, who is as cynical and patriarchal as any of the males (her $35 million entitles her to be): she pays BZ and his wife Helene to stay married, regardless of who sleeps with whom or what happens (26 and 48). Didion's Hollywood, like everywhere else, respects money and power; ethics and morality come a distant second to making "deals" and pursuing that "aesthetic mode" that values personal pleasure above all else. No one in the novel is immune from suffering lapses of decency and compassion; none of the other characters questions the motives and meaning of it all as much as Maria does. And she tries to drive her Corvette away from it all.

Exactly what Maria suffers from is uncertain — suicidal impulses, perhaps, like the emotional and psychic exhaustion that causes BZ to overdose on Seconal and die in her arms (Didion 213). But suicide is a manifestation of some deeper ill. The abortion is also part of it; Maria's thoughts of how "the tissue" was disposed of lead to nightmares of cold rooms and obstructed plumbing. In his essay "Didion's Disorders," Samuel Coale writes that "the idea of sex scarring 'the female with the male's totem' adds to this distinctly female vision [sexual surrender and infant death] of the world in Didion's eyes" (166). A portion of Maria's emotional "scarring" is how outside forces, usually masculine and patriarchal, have used and dominated her life. Carter Lang's career as a director began with an underground film called *Maria*, featuring Maria in the role of herself, living her life in New York as a model, doing all the things great and small that signified her thoughts and feelings (Didion 20). Carter, in a word, *stole* something of Maria's life, then made her his exclusive property, his wife; his "success" begins with what he takes from her.

More theoretically, Maria suffers from "ontological insecurity," a psychological state proposed by Scottish psychiatrist and "existential psychologist" R. D. Laing (Geherin 70). In this condition, "the individual lacks a firm sense of his [her] own identity in a world which seems threatening to him [her] at all times" (qtd. in Geherin 70). While Laing's ideas about the existential nature of psychiatric illnesses remain controversial, this breakdown in the "sense of continuity in regard to the events in one's own life" does very well describe Maria's thinking and feeling as rendered in *Play It as It Lays*; she very much struggles to find or recover "a positive view of self, the world, and the future" ("Ontological security"). She fights to bridge that "great divide between fact and feelings" that Laing called a "product of our own schizoid construction"; Maria is isolated in her Hollywood world and torn apart by the apparent conflict — at least within her psyche — of "facts and feelings" (qtd. in Itten 11).

Her Corvette is a means, a device, to help her temporarily hold this "nightmarish burning" and "random world of chance" together in some cogent form (Geherin 74). Aimless, endless automobility is her way of buying time. Through the Corvette, Maria can inhabit a small space that grants her some agency and momentary purpose — both limited, but necessary to her survival. R. D. Laing wrote that the "*presence*" of another person, "so immediate to our sensibility ... eludes being pinned down entirely objectively.... The moment we snap into this sense of the immediate presence of the other, movements express intentions, and we are back into the realm of human *conduct*, however vestigial (original italics)" (qtd. in Groth). While the Corvette may carry overtones of masculinity and patriarchal culture, Maria has appropriated it as an empowered signifier of her own. In the novel, Maria does not have many sources of strength; the Corvette's signification of power and control, freedom and independence are not accidental. Presumably, this is the vehicle of Maria's choice, and it seems logical to conclude that she — as a former model — chooses an automobile that is both stylish and one that gives her a feeling that other objects do not. In the simplest terms, the Corvette seems to function as another *presence*, one that manifests an envelope of security and embodies power and control. Its ability to let Maria's "intentions" become movement, as in the accomplishment of her successful diagonal move across traffic, is powerful. Intriguingly, at one point Maria takes a television acting role, appearing in a series titled *Interstate 80*, which seems to be an allusion to *Route 66*, as if Didion is hinting at an association with the Corvette and the supposed freedom of the road that males enjoy (91–92).

Speaking of the "narrative technique" that Didion employs in the novel, critic David J. Geherin concludes that it resembles Eliot's "'a heap of broken images,' images of alienation and desolation ... the minutiae of everyday life joined in a mosaic of nothingness" (75). Critical interpretation of the novel varies from an ending where Maria is doomed to be institutionalized in a bleak, empty world, to a more hopeful, empowered Maria who has finally made up her mind to be active and take back her life. Writing about *Play It as It Lays* in the journal *Style* in 1990, Chip Rhodes calls the novel "one of the most astute — and troubling — literary investigations" of the "Hollywood-led culture industry" (132). Didion's book critiques "the en-gendering of mass culture" that other writers see as "a characteristic of modernism": mass culture is a "'feminine' discourse that functions as a convenient other for the sanctified, but beleaguered aesthetic discourse" based on "patriarchal, subject-object epistemology" (Rhodes 132). Maria, then, is caught up as a female "object" struggling to survive and, if possible, define herself as a "subject" in a culture of power that rarely, if ever, recognizes her humanity. Yet Maria should not be seen as entirely weak; her "passivity is a form of resistance as much as it is a sign of her psychic scars" (134). While Maria, as a woman, "has always been castrated ... she envies no phallus," and the novel is "best read as a 'postmodern tragedy,'" in the end "the 'nothing' [Maria describes] might well be something new entirely — something *subjective* and not *objective*" (original italics) (134, 132, and 135 respectively). In this interpretation, her last lines, "I know what 'nothing' means, and keep on playing.... Why not, I say?" are an affirmation of her *self* and an assertion of her power and control of that identity (Didion 214). Read this way, it seems that Maria may get both Kate and her Corvette back.

Analysis by female critics raises different points than those considered by males. In her essay "Freedom and Control," Marie T. Farr writes that the "automobile dominates modern America: it hints at our social status and our economic philosophy" (157). Historian Virginia Scharff, in her work *Taking the Wheel* (1991), says, "For nearly a century ... the auto has been identified with masculinity and male mobility, and women's right and ability to use cars has been disputed" (qtd. in Farr 157). The only time, the only space Maria has, that does not appear dominated by masculine influence is when she is alone, driving by herself except for the car, the Corvette itself. During that time, she has power, even though feminine power is "disputed" in the world Maria lives in. It is as if, for the hours they are together, Maria and her car are allied against the larger culture that would consume her. Either the Corvette is no longer gendered as masculine or, in a rare gap in its zone of control, the patriarchal system is vulnerable to having its own signifiers taken and used by those it would oppress. Feminist critic Marilyn French, in her book *Beyond Power* (1985), points out that "in Western society in this century," presumably in Didion's LA most especially, "the value of control has heightened dizzily, irrationally; there is increasing contempt for the 'feminine' elements of life; and there is an increasing awareness that the relations between the sexes are rooted in power, domination" (522). *Play It as It Lays* seems to be precisely this idea in action, acted out by Maria and the other characters, as if Didion had these lines in mind as she wrote. The struggle for power is also a fight for control; in the end, both are what act to define individual identity for men or women.

Farr writes that "contemporary American women novelists" have recognized "the power relations symbolized by the horseless carriage" (158). "To explore, critique, and reveal changes" in male/female relationships, female writers have "appropriated, adapted, and in some cases entirely inverted these previously male images so that power as control transforms itself" (Farr 158). This becomes what, "according to [literary historian] Judith Lowder Newton," can be called "autonomy, the power of being one's own person" and "self-definition or self-rule" (158 and qtd. in Farr 158). Didion may not take Maria so far as "self-definition and self-rule," but by the close of the novel, Maria does seem to understand what the "nothing" at the heart of the life of everyone she knows *is* and to be stronger for the realization. While the male relationship with the automobile may be "erotic" and possess "emotional complexity," a woman's bond with her car — especially a "potent" sports car like the Corvette — may be something slightly different (Farr 158). For women "actively seeking power," like Maria, "their skillful driving becomes a metaphor for self-control and autonomy" (159). If this is so, then the time Maria spends with her Corvette is very significant; those moments signify her desire to be free and independent, to take charge of her life. A woman's individual involvement with her automobile may be different than a man's with his car. How a man's Corvette reassures him of his masculine prowess is not the same as a woman's sensation of gaining control of her life through her Corvette.

Marilyn French writes that "men hate and fear women because they *must* control them, because control over women is essential to their self-definition" (original italics) (535). This is true in *Play It as It Lays* because Carter Lang and the majority of males — all of them at one time or another — seek to control, even to discipline and punish, the women they come into contact with. Maria is, most of the time, treated as "property" by the men she meets; she is valued for her image, her body, what she has between her legs more than any identity she possesses. Given the patriarchal masculine nature of Hollywood/Western society, there seems little direct escape from this. What exists for Maria is that daily quest to discover herself again, maybe really for the first time as an independent, adult, female human being. As Farr describes it, driving for women may become an "escape *from* someone or something [that] comes full circle into driving as escape *to* a mastery of self that makes continuing to live possible" (164).

Other female perspectives are also to be found. In her analysis of automobile culture, *Driving Women* (2007), Deborah Clarke states that the narrative of *Play It as It Lays* "situates the car [her Corvette] as Maria's anchor in the arid Hollywood landscape" and "Maria uses the car to forge a woman's — and a mother's — alternative to the sexist and masculinist California car culture" (93). For Maria the Corvette serves "almost as a retreat," and as it becomes extreme, "Maria's obsession with the automobile ... [begins] displacing human identity with automotive identity" (Clarke 93 and 94). The Corvette is like her home, a womb environment, a place she can temporarily escape to — even on the California freeway. Her automobile is, for Maria — the motherless woman and unhappy mother — a source of comfort; as Clarke describes it, "While the mother may not have become the car, she seems to have been replaced by it" as a source of security (94). In severe cases, the automobile — cars that signify power or freedom — do fulfill the role of "mothers," providing secure space for us to safely be who we are or wish to be. Certain cars, to certain people, are confirmation of a secure identity — a mother's love on wheels.

In her 1972 essay "The Women's Movement," also from *The White Album* (1979), Didion finds fault with a number of feminist ideas. She believes something vital is sometimes lost, a sense of being a woman, of living life as a female human being. Didion writes, "All one's actual apprehension of what it is like to be a woman, the irreconcilable difference of it — that sense of living one's deepest life underwater, that dark involvement with blood and birth and death — could now be declared invalid, unnecessary, *one never felt it at all*" (262). Didion is not, I think, denigrating the ideals of women or their movement, so much as she is arguing how they are seen or interpreted at a less critically thought out, even "popular," level. My point here is not that Maria Wyeth and her Corvette are feminist icons, but that the situation Maria is in resembles —figuratively and metaphorically— that of many American women of her time: they feel a need for security and identity, a place or space that they can call their own. Maria does have her Corvette, but what do other and less visible women have in a patriarchal world that values power more than feeling and Hollywood-style "deals" more than humanity? What Didion relates in her comments about the women's movement appears to be acted out by Maria and the other characters in the novel or depicted in Maria's narrative of her life.

Yet there is another *Play It as It Lays*. Didion and John Gregory Dunne, her novelist husband, cowrote the screenplay for the 1972 film of the same name, and Dominick Dunne, his brother, was coproducer. According to author Katie Mills, in addition to writing the movie, Didion exercised a measure of control over the cinematic version of her work that few, if any, other writers — male or female — achieve. She chose director Frank Perry — who had previously done *Diary of a Mad Housewife* (1970), among other films — to oversee how her novel was brought to the screen (Mills 151). This is Didion's sense of power and control — as in driving *her* Corvette — made real, at least to some degree. The female writer chose the male director of the film based on her book depicting the corrupting, sexist influence of Hollywood, and how the contemporary American/Western way of life looks upon women as things or objects. As Mills tells it, film critic Pauline Kael, writing in the *New Yorker*, said, "Perry hasn't found a 'visual equivalent' for the famished prose [of Didion's novel], but maybe this high-class-whore-house style of moviemaking is the *true* equivalent" (original brackets and italics) (qtd. in Mills 151). Didion herself had "an unusual amount of power for a woman in Hollywood," and this may have worked against the film's success (151). According to film scholar and critic David Thomson, the movie is "a disaster among literary adaptations, a disgrace to Joan Didion and Tuesday Weld [its star, in the role of Maria]" (676). More succinctly,

In Joan Didion's *Play It as It Lays* (1970) and director Frank Perry's 1972 film version, Maria Wyeth — actress, mother, and compulsive freeway driver — spends much of her time, or the best moments she knows, on the road in her Corvette. This image shows Maria (Tuesday Weld) stopped as a bemused state trooper (uncredited) speaks to her. The car is her alter ego, her place of safety and free-dom; the Stingray is a positive extension of the precious female identity she learns to cherish (Photofest).

Halliwell's Film Guide (1992) calls it a "with-it melodrama which audiences preferred to be without" (Walker 883).

The film's lack of success, at the box office and with reviewers, may be a sign of something more, however. As in the novel, Didion explicitly and implicitly critiques Hollywood and the film industry — in its masculine excesses and patriarchal way of doing business — holding up a mirror that many of the people involved could not have taken kindly. And former child actress, and perhaps a close parallel to Maria in real life, Tuesday Weld did earn a 1972 "Best Performance" award at the Venice Film Festival; the *New York Times* said her Maria character was "beautifully performed" (*Play It as It Lays*). In describing the film's reception and influence, Mills points out that much of the critical response was "gender-oriented rhetoric," spawned by how — apparently even today among some critics — the motion picture "affronts the ethos of critics championing" the New Hollywood style of film making (151). Maria's story may reflect a truer image than Hollywood still wishes to have presented of itself; the film may "break the unwritten rules" of the auteurist school of the film art and expose too much of the power structure and life inside Hollywood (152). Interestingly, "female automobility" was one of the "art film influences" that "Didion's cool parody" of the business pointed out most clearly (152).

The film is very close to the novel, but it does yield interesting variations. Maria's automobility is a major part of the action portrayed onscreen. Once the opening sequence of her walking through the grounds of the sanitarium ends, the film jumps abruptly to Maria behind the wheel of her yellow Corvette at high speed on a desolate stretch of road, shooting real bullets at highway signs that read "Welcome to California" with a snub-nosed .38 revolver (Perry). This is not part of the novel, yet it clearly and accurately captures Maria's feeling and state of mind; it is one of the frequently recollected images she calls to mind in flashbacks, along with the trashcan bearing the remains of her aborted child and the water running down the drain as the doctor washes his hands. All of these are painful images, but the speeding Corvette and the gunfire from inside are the only repeated image of Maria with any power to strike back, even if only at a highway sign. Maria, outside of her car, is less powerful, her attempts to respond to challenges or threats usually muted. As in Didion's own photograph, the Corvette adds an aura or appearance of power and strong identity. Maria does possess the ability to sharply comment on the words or expressions of others, but it is most often suppressed by the voices of those — males with power, the majority of the time — who can exert control over her, as Carter forces her to have the abortion by making clear that he will take custody of their daughter.

Another scene that is not in the novel is the curious few moments when Maria stops on the freeway to change the left front tire on her Corvette. It is uncertain to the audience if the tire is flat, or if Maria merely wishes to be involved with the car, to look after it almost as if it were a living thing, a child in need of her attention. Oddly enough, this recalls the scene in the institution where Kate resides when Maria talks to her of their future life together as she brushes the girl's hair. While Kate attacks another child with the hairbrush — Maria seems unable to stop her — the scene with the Corvette goes smoothly. A state trooper who stops and offers to help is surprised to have Maria tell him that she "likes it out here" and that she is comfortable changing the tire, since her father taught her how to be independent and self-reliant.

If changing a tire demonstrates control of the situation, and a woman handling it for herself is an unexpected sign of her strength and ability to look after herself, then the cinematic image of Maria doing this is developed in a different manner in artist Greg Hildebrandt's lithograph *Yellow Rose of Texas*. "Rose," the young woman in the work, is changing the left front wheel on her bright red, with contrasting white side "coves," 1956 Corvette. At first glance, women viewers would probably be offended by the pose Rose strikes. The inverted "V" of her legs points directly up to her pudenda and buttocks; her back seems to be arched as she pauses bent over the new tire in her white-gloved hands. One breast is posed in full profile, and her face turned to present an unself-conscious smile and a level, matter-of-fact gaze at the viewer. She has big blue eyes, but her face is not where the male gaze falls: her primary sexuality is on display. Her overall position may be womanly, but it is not ladylike. She is not embarrassed by the short yellow sundress blowing up to reveal her thighs and behind. If we read her face closely, what do we discover? No shame or concern, no haste to interrupt what she is doing. She is in control, not in need of assistance, like Maria on the freeway with her Corvette.

A male artist created the lithograph, so the perspective is masculine, yet does "the gaze" manipulate the female body, leer at the audience, and point to Rose's sex as its sole purpose? Is this so very different than how the males in Hollywood regard Maria? First of all, the image is from a collection of similar portraits of women in revealing poses, some more so and some less, called "American Beauties" done by the same artist (www.brothershildebrandt.com). All are in the style of forties or fifties pinup pictures as created by a range of male artists, and all are commercially available. Like Maria in the films made by Carter, are the women being exploited, or is this legitimate "art"?

The color scheme of the print is predominantly red, white, and blue: All-American colors to match the All-American Corvette. Presumably, Rose is the All-American girl. Her yellow dress gives the picture its title and serves to connect it with the song, and what state is more American than Texas? Some critics might object to this depiction from a feminist point of view; the female is presented as first and foremost a *body*, reminiscent of how one of Maria's admirers differentiated her from other women as "not a cunt." However, considering the image in context, comparing it to similar representations of women and automobiles, Rose is actually an example of a woman who possesses admirable qualities signified by the Corvette. She is another of the women found in literature, film, and/or popular culture who demonstrate or struggle to achieve the freedom and independence, or "mastery of self," that the fast, powerful automobile suggests. Unlike the women in most of Hildebrandt's other "American Beauties" lithographs, Rose is actively engaged in performing constructive work directly affecting her own well being, replacing the Corvette's flat tire. Also, she is alone and independent, not helpless without a man around. Rose is an object of desire, but not an "object" in a static or passive sense. As a woman, she is defining herself through *action*, and — unlike Maria until the end of the novel — in control of her situation and sexuality.

What we do not see at all in *Play It as It Lays*, the film, is what is least commented on in criticism of the novel: the actual violence toward women as almost routinely performed by men, *all men*, even Maria's closest thing to a friend, BZ — the producer/procurer behind Carter's successful career as a director. In the book, Didion makes it obvious that when persuasion or coercion fails, violence is not out of bounds. And, by and large, the women take it, seeming to accept that this is their lot in Hollywood life. Male anger, rage not necessarily at the woman, is a right or entitlement. Nothing protects the women, except Carlotta, who has so much wealth that she apparently "buys" and discards men at will — treating them like "women." Early one morning at BZ and Helene's house, Maria notices "a bruise" on Helene's "left cheekbone"; when BZ comes in, he and Helene argue, and BZ hits Helene in the face (Didion 163–164). When Maria screams, "Stop it," BZ looks at her and laughs (164). BZ may be under extreme duress, he may feel the "nothing" that he knows is getting the better of him, yet he is no kinder or gentler than any of the other men at this moment.

Frustration, anger, whatever the reason, women are the objects of abuse, verbal and physical. In their motel room out in the desert shooting Carter's latest film, Carter and Maria argue late at night. Finally, he tells her, "Well, *go* to sleep, cunt. Go to sleep. Die. Fucking vegetable" (185). Although he does not hit Maria, his words carry the force of a blow, and clearly — whether Carter cares for Maria or not — he is willing to be cruel, to abuse her, to call her "cunt" and "vegetable," and to wish her dead: not the conduct of someone who cares (185). Maria's automobility is, in part, a flight from this kind of treatment, but there is nowhere the Corvette can take her that makes a difference. The film omits these scenes and other incidents of violence toward women; perhaps this is more than was suitable or "marketable" in 1972, but Didion's inclusion of male domination of women through violence is another aspect of the Hollywood/American/Western culture that *Play It as It Lays* is about. Female empowerment through automobility is constrained because, as the final fact of the matter, the women seem to have no place else to go.

Or, maybe not. In the desert, left to herself while the film crew is away, Maria comes to know the woman who runs the hot, dismal town's coffee shop. At the woman's trailer, sand blows across her small, split-rail fenced-in yard; she takes a broom and sweeps it out, even as new sand drifts onto the concrete (Didion 198–199). Looked at critically, this scene is significant. The nameless woman, alone running her business in the almost extinct desert town, is like Sisyphus in Hades, forever doomed to roll his heavy stone up the hill, only to see it tumble down again. Yet she is, unlike Maria and the other women in this miserable Waste Land world of Hollywood and the late twentieth century, not quite so despairing and hopeless as the rest.

Her secret, if it is a kind of secret, is revealed in the question she asks Maria, "You ever make a decision?" (199). To which Maria replies, typically, "About what?" The other woman now relates that she made "my decision in '61 [eight or nine years ago in the time frame of the novel] at a meeting in Barstow[,] and I never shed one tear since." This is it, the one piece of human communication — from a female source, not a masculine, patriarchal one — that imparts true constructive advice to Maria. Her answer is, "No ... I never did that" (199). If there is "a secret" that Maria is given at any time that will benefit her, this is all it is: she must decide something for herself, not let herself be led or told or coerced, or simply drift into situations. Automobility, as defined earlier, is autonomy and mobility; the autonomy Maria has possessed in the past has never had direction, it has never really, truly been freedom and independence. What the Corvette always needed was for Maria to point its nose, and herself, toward some destination. By the end of the novel, which is also its beginning, Maria seems ready to do just that. In the film, for the first and only time, Maria breaks into a genuine smile with the words, "Why not, I say" (Didion 214). She indicates, by words and expression, a life and vitality she has not shown before.

The "Remedy for the Disorders of the Great Sympathetic Nervous System"

In a more optimistic world of greater possibilities, Brad Barkley's "quirky, emotionally resonant" novel *Alison's Automotive Repair Manual* (2003) tells the story of Alison Durst, a college lecturer and young widow who acquires her brother-in-law's decrepit 1976 Corvette and works through her husband's accidental death by restoring the car to life (Zaleski). As a woman, Alison is not expected to be a mechanic, to be knowledgeable enough to repair the Corvette. Yet such a challenge, to do what is not antic-ipated of her, is exactly what she desperately needs to do after two years of mourning. As one reviewer puts it, repair of the old Corvette becomes a metaphor for learning about "forgiveness and hope: the differences among facts, lies, and truth" (Kelm). Rehabilitating the Corvette is a process of turning her self-awareness outward again, of rebuilding her *self*, of Alison's reconstructing what Judith Butler, in *Bodies That Matter* (1993), refers to as "the signifier of identity" (220). The term suggests what may be a break with past iterations of established identity to allow for *agency*, the "being constituted in and by a signifier" that empowers one to either create a new self or release an old one (Butler 220).

Although a popular novel, not a literary work, *Alison's Automotive Repair Manual* shares central concerns with *Play It as It Lays*: like Maria Wyeth, Alison goes for drives alone in her Corvette with no destination in mind; like Maria, she seeks escape ... or, at a deeper level, attempts to assert control over herself and the life she has — overfull of those "lies, facts, and truth," like Maria's — which seems empty and without purpose. The driving itself, the sharing of motion and vitality with the car, is significant. The Corvette is, again, a source of *power*, not masculine except in its implicit connotation of freedom or an ability to transcend limitations or constraints. The Corvette fulfills a need, addresses a "wound" that Alison cannot treat in any other way. As R.D. Laing says, the "*presence*" of another — and the Corvette works as a *presence* for Alison — moves one toward "human *conduct*" (original italics) and actions become significant once more (Groth). However, where Maria fills the void of meaningless time, that existential emptiness of postmodern life, waiting to come across something that counters the "nothing applies" state of her life, Alison progressively makes herself and the old Corvette better. While she cannot make it new again, or forget her husband, she can make the car and herself functional, bring them back to the point where both perform as designed: the car drivable, Alison independent. When ready, Alison gives up the Corvette, both of them able to go their separate ways. While any material object, living thing, or motivating force *might* fill this role — the "signifier of power" that transforms someone or feeds a deepseated human need — the Corvette as a cultural symbol, an "icon" as Chevrolet proudly calls it, appears to possess a special, although not unique, virtue as an automobile: it carries an aura of freedom and purpose that the vast majority do not.

Cocteau's previously quoted statement about the automobile — "A car can massage organs no masseur can reach. It is the one remedy for the disorders of the great sympathetic nervous system" — expressing the notion that cars offer some form of healing or a sense of security that nothing else can, serves as the novel's epigraph (Barkley). Cocteau's words get at the heart of the fascination the Corvette has for many people, and not just Americans. If automobiles do allow us to contact a deeply emotive, psychological part of ourselves, then this is part of the reason Corvettes are dear to their owners and those who dream of possessing one. If Cocteau is right — and in light of the devotion Corvettes inspire, he must be — then the car reaches a place that aches or longs to be touched. As strange as it sounds, a machine — something composed of purely physical parts, like the human body — helps women and men deal with wounds that are more spiritual than physical and hurts that no human therapy quite touches. For a female driver, like Maria or Alison, this may be doubly true because women are usually only given access to themselves in ways that a masculine, patriarchal way of thinking approves of and that society too often wishes to dictate to them. In other words, a female Corvette owner becomes especially free: an image that may seem patriarchal, the Corvette, gives her access to freedom and power, and is doubly sweet for being her automobile and her freedom independent of any male influence.

The car in Barkley's novel calls to mind the William Stafford poem "Old Blue," discussed earlier (chapter 4, pages 40–43). The old Corvette, in need of attention, stored away unused and out of sight, is called upon for another journey, one to redeem the owner/driver, to take him/her away. In the novel and the poem, the Corvette is a signifier of some potency, an identity that bears with it power, freedom, and individuality. The car becomes not male or female, but an object or an identity that carries masculine attributes of strength, yet goes beyond them — in times more open and willing to generate reinterpretation than when the Corvette name originated — to become fluid in its gender identification and subject to feminine appropriation. Alison and the speaker in that poem, a presumed "male" voice, share an involvement with an old Corvette that makes the car not merely an automobile, but a "resignification" of power. This signifying in a new way, according to Butler, "marks the workings of an agency that is ... though *implicated* in the very relations of power [masculine, patriarchal culture] it seeks to rival ... not, as a consequence, reducible to those dominant forms" (241). In other words, the Corvette's image and identity allow the car and its mistress or master to break away from the masculine cultural associations and to create new ones for themselves. Or, as Maria says in the end, "why not" go on playing the game once one sees a new way to interpret the rules?

"Liberation, Mobility, and Selfhood"

For women, it is never easy. As Deborah Clarke writes, "The car often functions as the site that calls into question the issues of female agency, female power, and gender itself" (118). Outside forces, as "feminist geographers" Monu Domosh and Joni Seager contend, act against feminine interests: "The control of women's movement has long preoccupied governments, families, households, and individual men. It is hard to maintain patriarchal control over women if they have unfettered freedom of movement through space" (qtd. in Clarke, 119). This is part of the theme of Bobbie Ann Mason's novel *In Country* (1985), which takes place predominantly in the small town of Hopewell, Kentucky, in 1984. Samantha "Sam" Hughes, its seventeen-year-old main character, is in search of both her future and her past. Patriarchal ideology and elements surround her — her Vietnam veteran uncle, her pleasant but uninspiring boyfriend, her widowed and remarried mother who wants her to go to college — but Sam's own uncertainty about her destiny is the greatest concern. There is no direct, dominating influence, benevolent or otherwise, in her life. Unlike Maria Wyeth, Sam is free of entanglements with a bleak or threatening world; with the possibilities of "liberation, mobility, and selfhood" before her, what she wants most is to come to know herself (Clarke 118). This takes two forms: Sam wishes to learn all she can about her father, who was killed in Vietnam before she was born, and to acquire a physical freedom that matches how independent she feels in spirit.

Automobility for *In Country* is not so much an issue of escaping the forces that crush an individual woman's spirit or of redefining oneself as it is — amid the overwhelming environment of mass culture, peer involvement, and social pressure — of discovering where one comes from and what an empowered human being can choose to become, "a desire to break out of the restrictions" of the roles society sees for her (Blais 107). For a woman, especially a young female caught up in a world not designed for her benefit, gaining knowledge and making choices are difficult: genuine feminine agency is hard to come by.

One of the keys to Sam's dilemma is her need for a car. But automobile ownership is largely male; as she thinks of it, "Boys got cars for graduation, but girls usually had to buy their own cars because they were expected to get married — to guys with cars" (Mason 58). Young women — "girls" — are generally thought of in "traditional" roles (Blais 110). They are "protected and controlled," their freedom and independence discouraged, as one critic describes it, where young males are encouraged to be "macho and possessive" (111). The automobile that Sam eventually does acquire — from Tom, one of her uncle Emmett's Vietnam veteran buddies — is that sign of counterculture proletarian automobility, a rebuilt and rusty '73 VW convertible.

Yet there is a phantom Corvette in the novel, a suggestion of freedom and independence, and the mention of it echoes the invisible, but present ghost of Sam's father. Emmett's friend Pete once owned a red Corvette. As Pete describes the map of the county — "outlined in blue, with the towns in red" — tattooed on his chest, "that little red thing that looks like a ladybug is my old Corvette. My wife sold it while I was gone. It would be a classic now" (49). The missing or "lost" Corvette is something like Sam's father, a "classic" or significant absence for those who remember or wish to possess knowledge of the car or the man. Like the Corvette, Sam's father is never seen or heard from in the novel; all Sam has are his letters home and his journal, along with a single photograph of him in his U.S. Army uniform. The missing father, like the missing car, is something that might have been, but it no longer exists and must now be discovered indirectly. For Sam, the VW is her Corvette, her "freedom machine" — like Buz and Tod's fast, stylish roadster in *Route 66*. While the Bug proves unreliable on the long trip to Washington, D.C., to the Vietnam Veterans Memorial, it does get Sam, Emmett, and her paternal grandmother there. Sam's autonomy and mobility are limited by her lack of money and her dependence on her mother's credit card, but they are real and valuable qualities nonetheless.

The "lost" Corvette seems like an echo of absent or unknown identity, which is what Sam is struggling toward. Terry Berkson's memoir *Corvette Odyssey* (2004) also features a Corvette that is "missing," in his case the 1963 red Sting Ray stolen from him the day his son was born (chapter 8, page 85). In Berkson's story, recovering the stolen Corvette becomes an obsession, one that jeopardizes his relationship with his family. Like Sam, he searches to find a missing part of his identity. In both works, the Corvette, or its absence, is a metaphor for power or self-definition — while the car appears "masculine" in the guise of Berkson's writing, it is more a signifier of *self* or identity than an attribute of masculinity. The Corvette stands in for the phallus, the instrument or object of power — which is not necessarily male, as *power* itself has no gender. Figuratively, for the generation Sam's father and Uncle Emmett belong to, the experience of fighting the war in Vietnam appears like the stolen Corvette for Berkson: it frequently creates a void in their lives that they wrestle to fill. It is they, not the Corvette, that are "missing in action."

The gender of the individual may be an important factor; for Sam, being born female seems to almost automatically entitle her to "less" of an identity that males, through little or no effort of their own, get to enjoy. Nevertheless, in a way, the Vietnam experience for many veterans is a feminizing event; it robs them of part of their identities, leaving them without their metaphoric phallus or Corvette. They become emasculated in their psyches, like Jake Barnes in *The Sun Also Rises*, not completely male — or perhaps human, since gender is an undeniable part of our identity. Emmett's impotent friend Tom particularly demonstrates a "damaged" masculinity like Hemingway's Jake Barnes. The name or signifier "Corvette" does not mean just the material object, the automobile, but the sense of self or "potency" of identity that empowers both autonomy and mobility. "Corvette" stands for *me* or *you*, as we exist in our definition of self; the idea of the Corvette is the freedom or independence to be ourselves.

Sam achieves a measure of female automobility and takes steps toward becoming an aware and caring adult by the close of the novel. She also, according to Stephen N. doCarmo, performs what cultural critic John Fiske, author of *Understanding Popular Culture* (1989), calls "excorporation," the "'tearing' or disfigurement of a commodity in order to assert one's right and ability to remake it into one's own culture" (qtd. 589). Although it is not likely that Sam will come to possess a Corvette of her own, the personal independence and freedom to travel, which "America's sports car" signifies, does filter down to her through the old but nonetheless appealing VW. The Corvette's "aura" or power to signify is still shared by all automobiles — however much everyday use and bland, unexciting performance mute its voice — and Sam does "tear" some of this meaning away for herself once she is behind the wheel of the VW.

In a sense, the old Bug is a Corvette with its power to signify in sensual and overtly sexual ways "disfigured" by its age, lack of speed, and "cuteness" rather than aggressive styling. The female ability to "excorporate" masculine cultural symbols is not often acknowledged, yet from the overwhelming mass of popular culture around her — Bruce Springsteen, the television series *M*A*S*H*, and old movies she has seen — Sam draws appropriate meanings

A VW Beetle convertible, much like this one, has a significant role in Norman Jewison's 1985 film adaptation of Bobbie Ann Mason's novel *In Country*. Sam, the daughter of a Vietnam War soldier who never lived to see her, is trapped by the life and opportunities open to her in a small, rural Kentucky town. As a restless young woman, she seeks knowledge of her father and a wider, richer life of her own. Limited as the VW seems, the freedom and mobility it signifies resemble the power that Corvettes possess (Hulton Archive/Archive Photos/Getty Images)

that are significant to her. But driving her own car is something new and more powerful than the other influences. As author Lesley Hazleton describes her earliest moments driving, in what might be a parallel to Sam's own voice, she recalls,

> I had the clearest vision, fully formed, of myself hurtling headlong down the road, laughing into the wind, heading into the long distance of my own life. For the first time, I had experienced power.... No, this was power plain and simple, in its purest form. ... And even then, I knew with absolute certainty that there was nothing at all plain and simple about it [45–46].

As a young woman speaking about the feel of driving, of real automobility — regardless of the car — this is what Sam experiences. And she uses it to further define herself and look for her father. *In Country* is about being young and female and coming to discover oneself; Sam's acquisition of automobility is part of this process. This "extension of female power beyond the female body" that Sam's VW grants her is real *power* (Bordo 109). Through their automobiles, Corvettes or lesser vehicles, "women have moved far beyond whatever sphere may have been constructed to constrain them"; "out there" in the world, women discover new possibilities, they reach for power through automobility (109).

The "Tuff," "Cool" Sting Ray

In contrast, S. E. Hinton's novel *The Outsiders* (1967) does offer a Corvette-driving female. "Cherry" Valance, nicknamed for her striking red hair, drives an apparently new mid-sixties Sting Ray. Cherry is a "Soc" girl, a cheerleader from a "Society" family, one with upper-middle-class money, maybe even more than that. Yet she is kind and sympathetic to the "Greaser" boys she meets, if they treat her with respect. As Ponyboy, the narrator with a feeling for language, even literature, describes it: "That Sting Ray was one tuff car. A bright red one. It was cool" (Hinton 127). There is not much higher praise than "one tuff car" and "cool" that any of the greasers know. And Cherry herself is both tuff and cool. She is not afraid of the Greasers whom she knows are not really "hoods" looking for trouble or wishing to do harm. Intuitively, she seems to understand, to have seriously thought about, how the world is divided into camps or classes. Cherry does not judge by appearances alone.

"Tuff" and "cool" together add up to a strength and sophistication that gives someone a broader perspective, and Cherry has this. To go along with her, the Sting Ray carries matching attributes. If someone else were driving it, some aggressive and superior Soc male, Ponyboy's description and admiration for the car might be different. He would find the Stingray to be threatening, as he does the blue Mustang that a number of the male Socs ride in when they come looking for trouble. However, in the context of Cherry's character, the Corvette is associated with her grace and sophisticated intent to see more than the majority of her social class are willing to observe. Her perspective is both worldly and female, so the young males — Soc and Greaser — find her attractive. Also, her Corvette, like her hair, is a vivid red — as in Prince's song about the seductive woman he meets — another suggestion of passion and sexuality. Red Corvettes dominate stories and visual media by default, as in the title of James Schefter's account of the development of the 1997–2004 C5, *All Corvettes Are Red* (1996). Cherry's Sting Ray complements both her social position and her desirability. She may be an object of desire, but she is an empowered and independent-minded young woman who thinks for herself and acts accordingly. Cherry is a strong female whose virtues are mirrored by her automobile.

Hinton does not focus on automobility in *The Outsiders*. In the novel, social differences and distinctions account for the problems that occur. It is social mobility, or the lack of it, that is central to *The Outsiders*. While the Greasers have cars of their own, they are not stylish machines, not new or possessing the latest technology. The year the book was published, 1967, was the time of the original Sting Rays, that "coolest" of the Corvettes, and Cherry's ownership fits with her affluent status. The Corvette is a signifier of her social position, and the car moves from a limited "masculine" signification toward that power to intensify the sexuality and/or sophisticated taste of its owner/driver, regardless of gender. The fact that the female author, Susan Eloise Hinton, looks at the Corvette through a male character only enhances how Cherry's beauty and personality and the Corvette's desirability become matched to each other.

In a 1967 interview, Hinton said that she wrote "from a boy's point of view" to add credibility to the narrative voice (qtd. in Gillespie 44). As in other works of fiction, the Corvette carries its ability to communicate an abundance of power, freedom and independence, and potent sexuality; it functions as both a ready and a fluid — able to move across contexts and assume different aspects — signifier according to the narrative context. Like other authors, male and female, Hinton uses the Corvette to quickly establish a character's attitude, power, and social position. Whether masculine or feminine, evil or good, the Corvette retains its distinctive identity. Females

in Corvettes are uniformly desirable, confident women "in charge" of themselves — or wish to appear so — both as "tuff" and as "cool" as any male
behind the wheel: the photo of young Joan Didion in her Corvette is only
a variation of this phenomenon; Maria Wyeth and Alison Durst are others.
The viewer's perspective may change, but this particular aspect of the
Corvette's image and its power to signify remain stable across its range of
signification. The gaze of the spectator, male or female, is the most telling
factor.

Chapter 13

The Female Gaze and New Identities

The Corvette takes on a transgressive gender role depending on how it is presented. At times the car appears to be a masculine signifier, enhancing the attractiveness and potency of its male driver. Yet the car sometimes seems to be female or takes the place of one: the Corvette itself becomes a love interest, a potential partner who replaces or rivals a human woman. In another, perhaps less anticipated transformation, a woman takes the wheel; she drives and owns the Corvette independent of any male presence. She and the Corvette — or a vehicle with similar, but lesser power to signify — are complete and self-sufficient; their sexuality is mutual, and their attraction enhances each other's allure. For a time at least, the woman and her Corvette own the road. The car is not, by necessity, a Corvette. But as we have seen, few other automobiles work so well. The Corvette and the woman become partners in identity without need of male influence or approval. They capture and hold the viewer's eye, remaining all the while free and independent. As women's self-awareness and automobility have increased, so has their ability to make themselves both active and visible, to men and each other.

The word "corvette," before there was any automobile by that name, was a nautical term for a small ocean-going vessel. Originally applied to merchant ships, it came to be used as a descriptive or "class" name for sailing ships larger than sloops but smaller than frigates. The actual word is French in origin — like the family name "Chevrolet" — which might have influenced its adoption ("Corvette"). According to the *Oxford English Dictionary Online*, the word's etymology is from the Latin *corbita*, "a slow-sailing ship of burden," related to the word *corbis* or "basket." More pertinently, the–"ette" ending is a diminutive-forming suffix that denotes smallness of size, as in "flechette" ("little arrow") or "cigarette" ("little cigar"). The suffix also denotes a feminine variation or female identity: "coquette" for "coquet," "a woman who uses arts to gain the admiration and affection of men" or "a woman who habitually trifles with the affections of men" ("Coquette"). In this form, the name "corvette" suggests a female identity; the ending matches the feminine of other, similar words. As a term first used in describing sailing vessels, and later variations on the small warship, it seems appropriate that the Corvette, the automobile, sometimes has a "feminine" allure. Yet it is never so simple as that; as we have seen, the Corvette mixes its genders, assuming first one aspect, then the other: embodying power, but also grace; performance, but style as well.

An editor at large for *Car and Driver* magazine recently wrote: "Women who drive Corvettes cause onlooking men to become aroused in a way that is actually fairly creepy" (Phillips 26). What he finds "fairly creepy" may be that women have appropriated the "male" gaze along with their Corvettes and now present images of authority and identity that are both arousing and unsettling. Perhaps men's unspoken assumption of patriarchal status, including personal and political domination, in Western culture feels threatened — as in Prince's "Little Red Corvette," when the man must "tame" the Corvette/female to assure himself of his "position" socially and sexually. To put it plainly, the female Corvette owner/driver has power at her control: she and the car share an almost irresistible aura of style and self-confidence.

Men acquaint the Corvette's image with desirable women. Country singer George Jones' song "The One I Loved Back Then (The Corvette Song)" (1985) plays out a variation on this theme. A young man, riding in his Corvette with his girlfriend, meets a middle-aged man who declares that "she" makes him think of "the one" he loved in the past. As the driver listens, he hears how "she" was designed for fun, to give pleasure (Jones). The song is about remembered desire and sensual pleasure. When offered the keys, the older man laughs, replying that the female passenger is what he meant, not the Corvette. The confusion, the merger of the two objects of desire — woman and automobile — occurs naturally in the mind of the driver and the listener. Sexual pleasure and the thrill of the Corvette's speed and performance are alike: sexuality and sensuality are unquestionably aspects of both cars and women.

This common male perception of the Corvette or of a desirable female assumes that either is something a man should be able to possess. If the car is masculine in its power, it appears feminine in how it attracts the eye and invites masculine appreciation. As Laura Mulvey describes the male gaze in her essay "Visual Pleasure and Narrative Cinema," a woman may be the "bearer of meaning, not [the] maker of meaning": women do not create signifiers, however much they may fulfill the role of one (part I A). Mulvey also claims that "mainstream film coded the erotic [view of women] into the language of the dominant patriarchal order," and the same rule applies in most, if not all, of the wider field of popular culture (part I B). The problem is not so such that women are found "erotic" — eroticism could suggest power and creative force — so much as it is the passive, "fixed in place" nature of their portrayal. Like the automobile, they seem to be things for men to collect or acquire for temporary use. Yet, as we know, if the woman's intelligence, beauty, or personality — or her Corvette — invites attention and gives her power and control at the same time, then she should be able to return the masculine, patriarchal gaze with one of her own.

Another song, much less widely known, Don Herman's "Corvette Cathy," places the woman behind the wheel. It begins with a revving engine as Cathy taunts "the boys" and dares them to race, then leaves the males to "eat her dust." Herman sings about how Corvette Cathy is the woman he wants, the one who knows "all" that it takes, presumably to drive a car and please a man. The driving drums, the fast pace, make it more like sixties rock and roll than contemporary country. Cathy and the singer's fascination for her are the song's reason for being. Her fast Corvette does not wait on any man; her decisions govern where and how fast she goes. Although the voice is of a male who indisputably desires Cathy, *she* is the one with power and control of the situation. The man/woman dynamic here is biased towards Cathy's ability to both attract and dismiss male attention at will. There is, although it remains underdeveloped, a "female gaze" at work. In the end, the singer rides with Cathy; the two reach a mutual understanding, yet she still drives. The woman retains her Corvette and independent nature; the man does not dominate or come to possess the Corvette. Cathy does *not* become a "representation [that] signifies castration [loss of potency and/or power]," as Mulvey describes is so often the case (part III Summary). This is a minor, relatively unknown song; however, other works with strong, independent females are to be found. When women, in search of freedom or themselves, take to the road, they often encounter resistance, danger, or hostility along the way. This can lead to controversy.

In *A Fine Romance: Five Ages of Film Feminism* (1995), feminist film critic Patricia Mellencamp writes of the motion picture *Thelma & Louise* (1991): "The film was an event. It triggered impassioned pro and con debates about women and men, women and violence, whether the film was feminist or not and what brand of feminism" (147). The "event" brought together feminism and automobility in what for many viewers, male and female, was controversial form. Mobility, independence, violence — toward and by women — and patriarchy were all to be found in the film's text and subtexts. The single most recognizable image is Thelma and Louise's car, a turquoise 1966 Ford Thunderbird convertible that director Ridley Scott, in his audio commentary, describes as the detail-obsessed Louise's "baby," her immaculate pride and joy. Within the film, the car closely associates with Thelma and Louise; it becomes a "female" space, a zone where they discover their own strengths and abilities. In the end, the two of them become more than softly and weakly "feminine" — as the majority of men define women — in its most limited, passive sense; in Mellencamp's opinion, "They leave femininity, rely on friendship, and achieve fearlessness" (117). Taking the Thunderbird "on the road," exposing its occupants to the world, is a step toward the "fearlessness" in women that patriarchal males seek to repress, if not exterminate. As described earlier (chapter 10, pages 112–114), the film presents the male and female gazes in conflict; the red Corvette belonging to Thelma's husband and Louise's turquoise T-bird come to signify opposing aspects of power and a struggle for female subjectivity.

As *Thelma & Louise* makes clear, the male gaze strives to dominate minority perspectives and alternative points of view; other "gazes" are not welcome. For women, the struggle against patriarchal culture takes place within that culture, yet detached from it. Women may acquire an automobility that hints at subjectivity, but it seems to exist only within the bounds of the patriarchal worldview. If the Corvette is usually a masculine signifier, a sign of male power, then the circumstances women endure must demand, on occasion, something to counteract it and offer an opposing name and image. In this film, we have Louise's Thunderbird: pristine, neat, and quietly unassuming in its beauty and understated power, a "female" counterpart to the Corvette. We know that in automotive history the Corvette and the T-bird were apparent rivals in the 1950s, and Louise's car stands as a point of difference, even departure, from Darryl's. The Corvette oozes what Darryl takes for virility and charm — he is mistaken about the car, because he is wrong about himself. The T-bird is prim and proper. In fact, Louise's car is so "cherry" at the beginning that it is suspiciously a sign of just how constrained and enclosed by the patriarchal system Thelma and Louise truly are. The masculine gaze is everywhere, yet "despite the dominance of patriarchal forms of culture ... these patriarchies cannot be fully understood ... without an attempt to interpret the causal role the 'female gaze' plays in their formation" (Goddard). The "gaze," male or female, is a tangible demonstration of the power to both present an image and control how it is perceived; as such, the film *Thelma & Louise* is a literal movement across the western United States — like many of the so-called "masculine" western motion pictures with macho male heroes — and also a figurative progress from male to female gaze.

However, as the film makes clear, the male gaze is intimately intertwined with the power and influence of patriarchal culture; confronting the masculine gaze invites the attention of patriarchal authority and the application of its power to crush opposition and destroy opposing points of view. Darryl's red Corvette is not a machine to be made fun of; the culture it is associated with does not look any more kindly on female resistance than it does any other. The Corvette is a reminder of the culture of masculine machines and the web of power that responds forcefully to challenges to its authority. The Corvette in *Thelma & Louise* both points to itself as a signifier of masculine power and implies the deceptiveness of the image that power wishes to sustain. The "male" Corvette is critiqued, if not interrogated, by the narrative of the movie and the actions of its female protagonists, women in search of subjectivity.

As the male gaze shifts from Thelma and Louise as objects — the "Kewpie dolls" that Harlan calls them in their China doll makeup (Louise) and Barbie-doll outfits (Thelma) — the women take on subject status, changing their physical aspects and the way in which they relate to men and the masculine system of machines — firearms, patrol cars, helicopters, radios, and television — and laws that seek to limit, define, and capture them. Scenes early in the film frequently depict the graceful T-bird surrounded by loud, aggressively suggestive, and masculine-appearing tractor-trailers. The patriarchal world is one of machines, or of living beings who behave according to their "programming" — while the women appear to gain power, it is always bounded by the surrounding and encroaching masculinist culture.

Near the end, in the desert out west, the Thelma/ Louise/Thunderbird trio destroy one of these male symbols — the one belonging to a particularly lewd, crude, and offensive male trucker — striking back at the male gaze. The women become, as the trucker shouts at them, "bitches from hell." While the Corvette is nowhere to be seen, the message towards its kind, macho male machines, is clearly one of opposition and defiance. But, like the women in *Route 66*, Thelma and Louise do not triumph: they do not escape, nor do they create a lasting "space" for female subjectivity. Convertibles, by their nature, suggest vulnerability along with freedom.

According to Kathleen McHugh, the use of the convertible "feminize[s] the story, pitting spectacle against mobility" (404). Much like Osteen's concept of "convertibility" in *film noir* as "openness" or vulnerability as well as an expression of freedom (chapter 2, pages 24–27), Scott's visual style in *Thelma & Louise* "frames" its female main characters, "with or within the car, either stopped or in motion.... The car becomes a prop for their bodies ... [in] an array of compelling poses.... The women's automobility is ultimately subordinated to their appearance" (McHugh 404). The "gaze" or the look of the film creates its narrative context, one that shifts as the story progresses. The T-bird and the conditional freedom it gives the two women become, or so it has been argued, signifiers of female assertiveness and freedom. Thelma and Louise travel from Arkansas to Arizona's Grand Canyon, and from subjugated feminine objects to independent female subjects of their own agency. They do not gain total freedom from patriarchal authority, but they do create a "space" where female autonomy and mobility are temporarily achieved.

Thelma and Louise's Thunderbird is the setting for much of the movie's action and, like the Corvette in *Route 66*, the car becomes an extension of the two main characters, if not a third. This automobility as "enhancement" of power and identity is not unique to a single film or novel; it is an occurrence that is — as we know — repeatedly found. For women, especially ones attacked by outside forces or confronted with a hostile masculine culture, the automobile offers what novelist Marge Piercy refers to in *Gone to Soldiers* (1987) as "a joy of extension, of becoming one with a fine and powerful machine that carried her [Bernice Coates'] senses beyond herself as it responded to her decisions, her will, her skill" (qtd. in Farr 163). The feeling is similar to what Maria apparently experiences in her Corvette, Alison in hers, and Sam in her VW. For Thelma and Louise, there are additional, ominous factors: they are fleeing a patriarchal culture in which violence toward women appears to be accepted and the masculine system of power seeks to punish females who act to defend or stand up for themselves. The characters move beyond the stereotypical patriarchal view of women, as articulated by pioneer film director D. W. Griffith: "Man is a moving animal. It isn't so with women" (qtd. in McHugh 393). What happens in the film is a movement from the male gaze that represents masculine domination to a female gaze that appropriates power and identity for itself.

In his essay "Looks Maketh the Man: The Female Gaze and the Construction of Masculinity" (2000), Kevin Goddard writes that "the dominant ideas about the male gaze emerging from the feminist movement are that any gaze that appropriates the other in its scope is by definition 'masculine'" (www.questia.com). If this is true, then women taking the gaze from men and assuming the power "to gaze" for themselves are behaving in what has most frequently been defined as a masculine fashion. The story of Thelma and Louise is the acquisition of the traditional male power to define by looking, which the women turn into viewing themselves truly for the first time, and being transformed as a result. The male/female gaze is based on "a hierarchy of power relations" that must be disrupted in order to permit the female gaze to function (Goddard). The contemporary Corvette, as "macho symbol," comes to be replaced by the classic Thunderbird as subversive and feminist signifier, yet the "power" itself remains the same, still essentially masculine, and the road is a place of danger and discovery. Thelma and Louise are not Dean and Sal, not just passing through on their way west. For them, the trip is both an adventure, a discovery of self, and a flight from the male culture that they can defy but not escape. As the creator of *Thelma & Louise*, Academy Award-winning screenwriter Callie Khouri comments, like Edna in Kate Chopin's novella *The Awakening* (1899), the characters come to realize their full identities as female human beings, but society and the culture they live in will not permit them to further utilize or develop their abilities (Khouri).

Over the course of the narrative, Thelma and Louise grow into what are variously termed "self-reliant, resilient," "outlaw," "bad girl," "defiant/deviant heroine[s]" (qtd. in Dobinson 101). Each of them "takes an autonomous role in the action or ... drives events" in the course of the story (Dobinson 101). The automobility the car offers makes *Thelma & Louise* a "road story" for women, one that provokes reactions on the part of the public and critics alike. Along the way to their eventual demise, much like western outlaws Butch and Sundance in *Butch Cassidy and the Sundance Kid* (1969), the two main characters come to possess and demonstrate to the audience a way of seeing from a woman's perspective, that "female gaze" which confronts and responds to its more usual, more culturally stereotyped male counterpart.

Unlike Didion's Maria Wyeth, who becomes active and determined only at the end of her story, Thelma and Louise are, once compelled by male arrogance and violence, willing to act when the circumstances around them — the male-centered culture and its power to entrap women or direct the course of their lives — create desperate situations. The significance of the film is to Khouri — a self-described feminist — how two women become their own agents of change and achieve their own identities: "If women become truly whole, completely who they are, true to themselves in every way, complete, self-determined, and self-defined, then the world might not be big enough to hold them, certainly not the way it is now" (Cook 188–189). The film is, in Khouri's words, "nothing more or less than an outlaw movie," one that follows "the structure of a classic outlaw movie" (188 and 182). It is not unlike the *film noir* road picture *Gun Crazy* (1949) in its world of cars and guns and a wild flight from the law (chapter 2, page 25–26), except that both characters are female and act in ways normally reserved for potent, aggressive male figures. If "the male gaze" is the perspective of masculine, patriarchal culture, then "the female gaze"—even if it is "masculine" in its appropriation of power—is a threat to the established systems of meaning and order. A female gaze, women seeing themselves and each other according to their own standards of belief, is a powerful force that challenges all other authority. Women like these acquire signifiers, like the Corvette, for their own purposes.

The connections that women make with Corvettes—or other machines that signify in a like fashion—are no less complex than male relationships with automobiles. In fact, given the roles society assigns women and how patriarchal culture comes to regard them as objects of desire, mere "vessels" or recipients of male power, the Corvette would appear especially significant in how women relate to it and use the car and its image to achieve their own ends. Real women, not just fictional characters, drive Corvettes. Prominent women depicted in media who have recognizable names or faces, such as Joan Didion, own or drive Corvettes. The cars become, again, extensions of the women's personalities; more than this, a material object or machine—Corvette or not—often acts as an enhancement or reflection of the individual woman's own *body* or conception of herself, making her feel more attractive, in control, and powerful/potent in a world (at least a society) that seldom recognizes female autonomy or self-determination. The Corvette as "body" does not replace the female's physical self in its sexuality or strength, but does serve to augment mobility in space, that "male" quality women value as much as or more than men, and the effect—the emotional value of possessing the stylish, powerful machine—makes a woman (like a man) *feel* more "in charge" and able to accomplish her own goals and act on her desires.

Although Judith Butler does not mention Corvettes or automobility in *Bodies that Matter*, her critical and philosophical analysis of the constructedness and meaning of "gender," she describes "the body," male or female, as a site of meaning and power; its "materiality" is "rethought as the effect of power, as power's most productive effect" (2). And the body is a gendered construct, the result of social attitudes and forces that make biological males and females into "men" and "women." For those — frequently female, but not necessarily so — who are "abject," life represents "'unlivable' or 'uninhabitable' zones of social life ... populated by those who do not enjoy the status of the subject" (Butler 7). This lack of *subject* status raises what Butler calls "the question of *identification*" (original italics), leaving an individual existence circumscribed or limited in "its own claim to autonomy and to life" (3). Lives like this offer us the examples of real women who have sought *subject* status, power, and *identification* through the use of the Corvette as both tangible material object, a signifier of power, and sexual image.

One of these women involved with the Corvette is Traci Lords, the one-time underage pornographic film star who has gone on to become a legitimate actress, musical performer, and author. According to her book *Traci Lords: Underneath It All* (2003), she once owned "a black '67 Corvette" that she paid for with her $5,000 check for appearing as the *Penthouse* magazine "Pet of the Month" in September 1984 (Lords 80 and 84). Lords writes that "the speed and the power of that car both scared and excited me" (80). Later in the book, she calls the car "my beautiful black Vette" and refers to "my Vette" as "she," as if the car shares a female identity with her (102). In fact, Lords' Vette seems to be her alter ego, in a sense a better, stronger, more confident version of the fifteen-year-old Traci Lords who is beginning an unwanted career in the adult movie industry. For Lords, her Corvette is a sign of power; more importantly, once she became comfortable driving it, the car appears to offer some security and sense of control over her own life. When it is destroyed by her reckless boyfriend, she has "no idea what to do next" and misses her "dream car" (102). Today, from how she appears, Lords is a mature, self-confident woman, comfortable in a quieter sexuality.

Yet for the late-adolescent runaway from an abusive home, the 1967 Sting Ray had to be an "adult" possession. Moreover, owning and driving it marked her passage into a presumed adulthood that — although sexually active and a "performer" in blue movies — empowered *her* with what she looked upon as adult womanhood and greater authority over herself. Lords was, as an underage porn "star," one of those "abject" people that Butler describes, someone whose social status was questionable — she had no bank account or credit cards and was "employed" in an industry regarded as, at the time, little better than prostitution. There was little, if any, *subjectivity* in her life. The Corvette was a source of "agency" for her, if only in how the car made her feel. Lords was only valued for her body and her sexuality, as the stereotypical female always has been. The Sting Ray, as her "dream car" and a "she" outside herself, served as means of "negotiation of sexual difference [being "female" and therefore "Other" in the overtly masculine-run and profit-oriented adult film business]," and controlling the Corvette made her less one of those "figures of unmasterable passion," either woman or beast, than her "acting roles" allowed her to express (Butler 29 and 43). As an object and an image, the car gave Lords a sense of security; the Corvette's "aura" of power and success shielded her own vulnerability. Lords was, like Maria Wyeth, caught up in an industry whose leaders were uniformly male, and their view of women closely matched that of the manipulative directors, conniving producers, and egocentric "stars" Maria often worked with.

At the other extreme, the seemingly opposite end of an evolution of a career in media, is Vicky Vette, a Norwegian-born, Canadian-raised, now forty-four-year-old blonde who became a pornographic film star in her mid to late 30s. According to an interview on the Adult Video News (AVN) website, she took "Vette" as her stage name because she found classic Corvettes to be shapely and sexy, and the name Vette thus suited her appearance and her image ("Vicky Vette"). For Vette, the Corvette image is one she has appropriated in order to promote herself. Arguably, she has used the car's image to achieve some measure of Butler's "status of the subject," that "claim to autonomy and to life" desired by anyone who has been marginalized or denied subjectivity in a patriarchal culture (Butler 3).

Looking at Vette's official website, www.vickyathome.com, her black 2003 Corvette convertible moves across the screen trailing an invitation to go further inside and see what she has to offer. Among other things is a picture of Vicky posed provocatively and revealingly in front of her Corvette, along with other, perhaps less mentionable, associates in a variety of outfits and poses (Vette, "Tour"). The selected images of Vette included here make it clear how she portrays herself: confidently female, flirtatious, and openly sexually desirable. She, her female body, her sexuality, are the subject that unifies all the onscreen images. Looking at the pictures, one is not so much aroused as impressed (or disgusted) at how far a woman can go in the process of self-commoditization and marketing — the website is more like Chevrolet's Corvette site, or other online "products for sale," than it is pornography.

If young Traci Lords lacked "agency of the subject" in her dealings with the California porn industry, then Vicky Vette's singular accomplishment is the "mastery of self" that Butler describes (7). A number of photos show a smiling, laughing Vicky exposing her breasts, admittedly surgically augmented, to the camera in a range of public places. If this is female autonomy, it is reached by catering to the male gaze, making the masculine desire for a woman's body a component of the empowered and controlling female gaze. The "Corvette" name serves the cause of a sexually liberated adult female attracting attention to herself by the manipulation of masculine weakness to her own advantage. Unlike many of the fictional women who select Corvettes to empower themselves, Vette directly connects her body and sexuality to the object of the gaze status that minimizes female identity in others, reaching for power by twisting masculine desire back upon itself, exercising female control of the male subject. As Butler writes, Vicky Vette has performed one of those "unanticipated reappropriations of a given work in areas for which it was never consciously intended" (19). Heterosexual male culture becomes a playing field for female sexuality and the female body on display, yet unlike Didion's Maria, the woman in this case directs her own performance and reaps the rewards, money and attention.

Vette links her name to the Corvette to convey a sensual image even when her own face and figure are not displayed. To her the name suggests the "curvy and voluptuous" qualities she remembers seeing in the Corvettes of the 1970s, and she blatantly, if not shamelessly, markets these same attributes in herself (Vette "My Biography"). As a sexual performer and film star, an image of desirability and erotic, eye-catching style or shape is her reason for being. Not only that, but as a female Corvette owner, there is that aura of power and independence as well. For Vicky, the Corvette is apparently all about the image she has of herself and shares with her fans and clients: her website offers a number of photographs and other items for online sale. The Corvette's image, to Vicky Vette, adds to her own physical and sexual appeal, giving her a useful and playful name that her admirers already know and can now connect to her desirability as a mature, sexually active, sensual female. The "official" GM/Chevrolet crossed flags Corvette logo is not found on "Vicky at Home," perhaps understandably.

If we think of Maria Wyeth as the fictional equivalent of, or metaphoric parallel to, Lords and Vette, does her Corvette's "diagonal move" across traffic suggest, in a sense, transgressing boundaries or limits that the masculine or indifferent world puts upon all females? For Lords, her Sting Ray was her only real possession of significant value at the time; it was her own action, exposing her desirable young female body, that earned the money to purchase it. For Vette, the car is confirmation of her success and an image of her continued desirability, that ongoing status as a contemporary MILF (Mother I'd Love to Fornicate with) name and face found in the adult film/video market. In a wider sense, do real and fictional women use the

Corvette to achieve some level of status and freedom? Do they, like Thelma and Louise, become the self-determined, assertive "bitches" in a car — that term now often used for women who disobey masculine/patriarchal standards of female behavior while thinking and acting for themselves — that men in books, films, and real life seem to expect? Perhaps, as feminist Z. Isiling Nataf says, "Being a bitch or being bad is unavoidable in transgressing the feminine constraints of the social order" (64). The ground between submissive, compliant "good girl" Kewpie dolls and "bitches from hell" appears to be quite narrow, and a woman who wishes to drive her Corvette may be transformed from one to "the Other" if she, like the Vicki from *Route 66* in the 1960s (chapter 7, pages 72–73), seeks too much freedom and subjectivity.

From what we have seen, men are "traditionally" thought of as having "an implicit heterosexual relationship" with their cars (Kelso 266). And when a woman owns a particularly fast, powerful machine, such as a Corvette, it is presumed that she takes on what might at one time have been thought of as "masculine" characteristics: independence of body and mind (Traci Lords), active if not aggressive sexuality (Vicky Vette), and an implicit ability to think and act for herself (Maria Wyeth, Cherry Valance, Alison Durst, Thelma and Louise). The female takes on a powerful role, what I will call a "phallic female" — for want of a better term — who performs in a way that creates for the Corvette a different type of identity and image than as an emblem of masculinity. The woman Corvette owner/driver creates a gender identity that may not be distinctly male or female (the car no longer has a specific gender image) for the machine itself, and the Corvette's "aura" and image come to serve a variable gender identity that offers an attractive "self" to the viewer while maintaining the driver's own independent identity. The Corvette can be male or female depending on what the owner/driver looks for and finds in it. It is not so much the male/female identity as much as it is the quality of the identity that the Corvette's image lets the person behind the wheel perform. It is performative power in action.

Chapter 14

Empowered Women and the "Resignified" Corvette

How, then, do we describe an empowered, self-sufficient, free, and independent woman? As we have seen, the word "bitch" is sometimes used — particularly by men who resent females who take active roles or speak their minds with little regard for the "niceties" of feminine conduct or the accepted performance standards and restrictions placed upon women. Female identity, like its male counterpart, is rooted in the words and images we use to depict its characteristics and behaviors. If automobility is regarded as one of the expected qualities of masculinity, how do we categorize or name women who maximize their potential abilities, who show "phallic confidence combined with female allure," and become — as Callie Khouri calls them — "complete, self-determined, and self-defined" (Bordo 171)?

Women owning and operating Corvettes, females who "link" themselves to the car's tangible physical power and presence along with its image of autonomy and mobility, are not necessarily phallic females, yet some are. Women who possess the phallus, that intangible quality of power and authority, sometimes present "male" behaviors, acting in ways or exhibiting interests, strengths, and actions most often characteristic of the most masculine of men. Ellen Ripley, the central character portrayed by Sigourney Weaver in the *Aliens* film series — *Alien* (1979), *Aliens* (1986), *Aliens³* (1992), and *Alien Resurrection* (1997) — has been described as embodying "traditional nurturant femininity alongside breathtaking macho prowess and control," becoming the "archetypal phallic mother," a woman able to deal equally well with deadly weapons, complex machines, and horrific monsters, mastering each of them with heroic "masculine" will and determination (Bordo 173 and Burston 6–7). She is not "butch" or lesbian; her sexual orientation is actively heterosexual — demonstrating neither saintly celibacy nor promis-

158

cuous submissiveness. Ripley possesses what feminist critic Marilyn Frye calls "full citizenship, full humanity," while *not* "disclaiming responsibility" for her actions ("Necessity" 991). Minority females may also exhibit "phallic female" behavior. Pam Grier as the revenge-seeking young black woman in *Coffy* (1973), one of her blaxploitation film roles, and the customized black Corvette-driving, karate mistress, CIA agent Tamara Dobson in *Cleopatra Jones* (1973) present aggressive, strong, "take-charge" action-oriented females who are unafraid of violence or men in pursuit of their goals. White and black females take on power and responsibility as they find necessary.

What these women possess — the qualities that Thelma and Louise grow into and came to represent in the minds of many women — are a sense of self and the ability to direct their own actions independent of any male influence. The Corvette, that "macho symbol," or Thunderbird is an outward sign of their autonomy and mobility, a signifier of what has all too frequently been conceived of as the "masculine virtues" of independence and freedom. Phallic females push the limits of this envelope, becoming aggressively active and often acquiring the tools of phallic masculinity: big guns and fast cars that give them power equal or superior to that of the male figures they meet. These women do not take on

Ellen Ripley (Sigourney Weaver) takes action against the creatures that threaten her and those she cares for — such as Newt (Carrie Henn) — in James Cameron's *Aliens* (1986). Powerful females — with automobiles, weapons, and machines of all kinds — are attractive to both male and female audiences. Ripley is one of the females who show their ferocious nature in film, demonstrating that "masculinity" is not only a male quality (Photofest).

the "female masculinity"—the male appearance or personae—that Judith Halberstam acquaints with an extreme of female power and identity, but they do reject "feminine" weakness and dependency. In *Aliens* (1986), when Vasquez, the Latina female Colonial Marine, is asked by a male fellow squad member if she has "ever been mistaken for a man," she instantly replies, "No, have you?" This tone is phallic female, able to confront masculine ego and willing to be as strong, as tough as that ego assumes it may be.

If patriarchy is "the monism that passes for a man/woman dualism," then women are actually not just struggling for recognition against an oppressive system, but in fact are at war with negation of their identity and subjectivity (Frye 997). Outside the phallogocentric domain's narrow definition of "woman," there is only the fringe area of "Other" and the absolute

Federal agent Cleopatra Jones (Tamara Dobson) fights crime and corruption with karate, guns, and her customized black Stingray. As a black exploitation film with a female hero, director Jack Starrett's *Cleopatra Jones* (1973) was not unique—Pam Grier's *Coffy* (1973) was a contemporary—but the pairing of the active, attractive woman and the Corvette added that image of power, affluence, and style to the film's fight sequences, car chases, and "action" content (Photofest).

negative of being nothing at all. Male representations of the female are, most likely, going to be flawed and generic at best. If "the sexual specificities of the female body are translated as absence," according to authors Bray and Colebrook, then acquiring the phallus — authority over the self, or subjectivity — is, at least in part, a struggle for the body to be recognized as more than an object of the male gaze (40). The earlier citation, that "women who drive Corvettes cause onlooking men to become aroused in a way that is actually fairly creepy" (chapter 13, page 147), then takes on more meaning: the Corvette either looks like it has no driver at all (an unlikely absence), or the woman is empowered, "arousing" because of her potency/female appropriation of masculinity that men discover to be both sexually stimulating and upsetting to their conceptions of gender. In this case, the woman is behaving in a "phallic" manner, taking power that the male — the would-be Corvette owner/driver — senses is an assumption of his role, his place of automobility.

Following what Rosi Braidotti and "some other feminists" conceive of as "the vital necessity of thinking-through-the-body and of establishing the corporeal grounds of intelligence," the Corvette as "extension" of the female body is an assertion of identity by women (Bray 46). Driving a Corvette is not just driving any automobile; the car's image, its physical power, and its associations with affluence and sexuality make it a statement about one's self, a signifier with multiple meanings depending on the audience. If women are "disembodied" by patriarchal culture, reduced to mere physical objects, it comes as little surprise that this loss of body/self is "strongly aligned with alienation" and that reason and rationality are "masculinized," leaving female human beings with little where else to go (Bray 48). Physical freedom and independence through automobility is a way to reclaim female identity, even control of women's own bodies, by means of the machines that males have assumed to be their tickets to selfhood and subjectivity. The Corvette, then, is one of American women's ideal choices because of all the strengths and virtues the car brings with it as object and as image. By driving a Corvette, a woman asserts her *identity*, an "effect of difference" that emphasizes "the body's positivity" (54 and 58). In aspiring to "phallic" status, women seek to escape being "loaded down with the seriousness of ideological meaning and sexual history" associated with phallic masculinity while taking advantage of "the contingent, floating nature of the phallus" that gives them all those sought after traits: independence, self-determination, and identity (Beckman 186 and 189).

For men, the Corvette appears to be an object to be desired and or possessed, like a beautiful woman, the "red Corvette" lady Prince lusts after, for example. However, although the car's power and its "potent" image make it appear masculine, in modern times the autonomy and mobility it offers are open to anyone who can afford to possess a Corvette or make sufficient claim to one. For women, the issue is not the Corvette as *object*, it is more a statement of *self*, like a stylish piece of jewelry or outfit of *haute couture*. It is a manifestation of positive identity in a world that all too often equates personhood with masculinity. Although the Corvette still has the early, primitive automobile's seductive, alluring combination of freedom and independence, most of today's vehicles seem more like machines produced simply to be acquired and driven, sometimes statements of style or social position, yet never with an equivalent measure of meaning given to the first remarkable horseless carriages. The Corvette still embodies that "spirit" of the open road along with an aura of power, speed, and exclusivity that both men and women find desirable; the car feeds their egos and bolsters their hearts and gonads.

If the Corvette is "macho" and a phallic symbol of male desire, the power to gaze upon and control others, then for men it serves as ego enhancement and carries a cachet of sexual prowess. Yet to women it is more of an assurance of controlling one's own life, one's own body and the desires it has — to not be at the mercy of quite so much patriarchal authority — or to turn that male gaze and power back on itself by taking a symbol of masculinity and making it signify additional things: what Butler calls *resignification*. The Corvette is a signifier of *romance*, idealized or personal views of one's self or place in the world, and of *power*, the agency that gives a man or woman identity and sets one apart from the common or ordinary — it is a car that stands out with a minimum of pretentious "look-at-me" social posturing and a maximum assertiveness of individual power and control.

Chapter 15

Dreams, Romance, and the "Endless" Corvette

In the case of Man Martin's novel *Days of the Endless Corvette* (2007), the Corvette and a woman are both the objects of a young man's desire. Earl Mulvaney, a nerdy but gifted teenage mechanic in rural Georgia in 1973, is in love with Ellen Raley, the redheaded girl across the street. They are fond of one another and date briefly, but she is — quite unknowingly — pregnant with the child of another young man, the son of the local and successful plumbing contractor. Ellen marries the other guy, but Earl continues to love her over the years; in a sense, the sweetest stage of their relationship, the "courtship," never ends (Martin interview). The Corvette, an original "creamy white" and "luscious red" — "like a red velvet cake" — 1953 belonging to the owner of the town's used-car lot, gives the book its title and serves as the other component of Earl's dream, a car with an identity of its own (Martin 40). The Corvette is usually referred to as "she" and is a thing of beauty that "gleamed like a pearl" after Earl begins to maintain and repair her (40). The Corvette needs "constant attention, like a woman," and Earl's love for Ellen is, in part, sublimated into affection for and devotion to it (Martin 42 and interview). The Corvette is really not a "what" in the novel so much as a "who," waiting for the right man to come along.

Ellen and the Corvette together come to embody Earl's passion for life; as the novel says, "The car was half the reason Earl was out; Ellen Raley was the other half" (Martin 4). After observing his skill with automobiles, the car-lot owner hires Earl and asks him to see if he can make the old Corvette run again. Earl, hopelessly but silently in love with Ellen, does so, but in the process a visionary idea comes to him: as he repairs and maintains the Corvette, Earl collects the "spare parts" from it, as he does from other automobiles, and in time — over an indeterminate period — Earl will construct

163

a new Corvette of his own, and then ... once two Corvettes exist, others should follow (43). As in his ongoing romance with Ellen, he is confident of success and has faith that life has a way of rewarding those with patience and persistence. According to Man Martin, Earl's character appears to be the "empty center" of *Days of the Endless Corvette*; while patient and remarkably skilled with cars, he is an odd combination of dim wittedness and a calm, accepting, and tranquil nature (interview).

Writing about the "masculinity" of "technology and modernity," Deborah Clarke observes that "the symbol of the car unsettles this gendering, for the automobile is both phallic symbol and female object" (46). *Days of the Endless Corvette* seems to do just this: the Corvette Earl works on and drives appears to be a phallic symbol — the masculinity of its owner and his successful business and place in the community — yet it is also an object of Earl's affection, a surrogate for Ellen perhaps, or a parallel "romance" between man and machine. And Earl's identity, that "soft" or easy masculinity he possesses, fits with what is described as "the fragility of male identity and privilege in an increasingly technologized culture" (46). While the Corvette may signify power or affluence to most male onlookers, for Earl the car seems to be a feminine object, a source or site of intimate involvement and personal care. The Corvette itself is part of the "romance" of the novel, that atmosphere of affection and possibility found in "tall tales."

Earl is like one of those "abject," outside people — often female but not limited to women — that Butler describes: he seems to have little going for him, and yet in the book, he is charming, winning the reader over, leading us through funny, sad, and improbable situations and events with an eccentric, Faulknerian quality that gives the entire novel a feeling of folklore, of a "tall tale" told in modern times (Martin interview). The Mulvaney character is not a patriarchal male; he does not work his way through the world by means of strength of will or masculine aggressiveness. He is strangely quiet, not the male persona one usually acquaints with Corvettes, yet he is someone who pursues a lifelong dream and carries a romantic view of the world that sustains him. If the Corvette is a "sex symbol" in the world of automobiles, Earl is the dreamer who aspires to it, one who forms a relationship with the car that parallels his connection to Ellen, the woman he loves (interview). What the Corvette signifies to the world at large is transformed in the novel into an almost ethereal romance between a man and a woman: they live in sight of one another, but their "intimacy" comes through the books they read and the continuing evolution of this "Endless

Corvette," a collection of parts that accumulates over the years, growing into something that may or may not take the shape of another 1953 Corvette.

The novel is a romance of the imagination; in point of fact, we know that no such thing as Earl's dream is logically possible. Spare parts do not become, in our normal, rational world, a real and complete automobile. Just as Earl's love for Ellen is apparently hopeless, so his dream of building a classic Corvette from excess and leftover parts is foolish. But that is precisely the nature of the "endless" Corvette; it is a parallel to Earl's faithful love for Ellen. In the course of the novel, we see that love borne out: as a volunteer firefighter, Earl saves Ellen's little girl, continues building his stock of parts for the Corvette, and becomes close friends with Troy, Ellen's husband. And he and Ellen do have a "romance" of a kind: through the Great Books collection at the local public library, they exchange notes or comments on life and literature. And Earl increases his collection of parts, forming what some townspeople see as the chassis of another 1953 Corvette. The Corvette and Ellen are the loves of Earl's life.

In truth, there are three Corvettes in the story. One is the real Corvette that Earl works on and drives occasionally. The second exists only as a stack of components that, over time, comes to acquire a life and vitality of its own in the hearts and minds of people who appreciate Earl's dream. This intangible object, merely a fanciful image to those who share something like Earl's view of the world, is the "third" Corvette. These three aspects of the "Corvette" are what the car has come to represent in the more general sense of the car's actual existence in our "real" world. It is a real, physical thing, an automobile constructed of plastic and steel. The Corvette is also an emotionally evocative image for many individuals, one that conveys a variety of meanings, as explained thus far. And finally, the Corvette is — to those who buy into a "dream" or way of thinking — an imagined "thing," a legend or icon that exists most powerfully in the thoughts and feelings of its faithful fans and followers. In describing why a Corvette appears in the novel, Martin says that this "sublimated love" for Ellen "had to be an American sports car," which — if we recall Zora Arkus-Duntov's comments that sports cars exist because of human emotion, not reason (Introduction, page 4) — makes perfect sense (Martin interview). *Days of the Endless Corvette* captures something of the car's essence in its fictionalized world where romance and dreams do count for something. The Corvette's continuing appeal is a consequence of its "dream car" image, and this is especially meaningful for those individuals who have traditionally had a less tangible position and power in the outside world; this includes — most emphatically — women who either look at Corvettes with hope and longing or use them to assert their own self-image.

Earl's love for Ellen and his dream of a Corvette are likenesses or images of what we find in our imaginations. The Corvette is not a rival for Earl's affections; it is a manifestation or signifier of the strength of his dream of eventual closeness with the woman he continues to love. The endless Corvette is an instrument that unites two people in a dream that is outside the reality of their real lives. That, in a sense, is part of the human need that Corvette automobiles answer: while real machines, they are vehicles that help make our fantasies and dreams real, if only as physical, material signs of what we have inside. Cocteau's words — "A car can massage organs no masseur can reach. It is the one remedy for the disorders of the great sympathetic nervous system" — holds true for Earl in the novel and for many Corvette owners in what we choose to call "real life." The idea of happiness with Ellen and the imaginary Corvette are the parts of Earl's internal life that give him meaning and purpose, valuable qualities in any place or time. These are virtues that the Corvette has come to suggest in both men and women, once they come to understand themselves and are willing to act, to take on the "power" the car offers.

Summary

Now, looking back to *Play It as It Lays*, we see that Maria Wyeth possesses some of the qualities of real women, such as Traci Lords and Vicky Vette, as well as other fictional characters, who are or become involved with Corvettes. She is desperate and desires real, positive control of her life; put upon by the male establishment and its conception of women, Maria struggles to define herself and discover a stable identity. Owning and driving her Corvette in part fulfills those needs, if only while she is at the wheel. "Why a Corvette?" is answered if one considers the car's reputation for style, power, and appeal to both men and women. Also, Corvettes of all descriptions are normally not inexpensive automobiles, so having one carries with it the cachet of a degree of "success," of having "made it" in contemporary American society. Yet while the sense of control Maria feels while driving her Corvette gives her temporary release and escape, she must stop sometime, and it is clear that real, lasting freedom is much harder to obtain. The Corvette is a moving image and not easy to hold onto. Freedom and independence are themselves performative qualities, processes of renewal, not absolutes or states of being.

In an attempt to put it simply, the male/female image the Corvette now has is dependent on the image women and men have of themselves as they own and drive it, and the emotions and identity invested in the car and their own self-identity. Women Corvette owners and drivers have power if they will take the car and make it perform to suit their needs. If the Corvette image transgresses boundaries, it does so with the ability to take them with it. The car is a physical body and an image; the two are not readily separable. The Corvette has a name of its own that men and women utilize to strengthen or enhance their identities. Sometimes, we need a machine to discover who we really are, or to make ourselves appear as we would like to be seen. The Corvette is an image car — a fast, powerful machine — and something of a sex toy as well, exciting men and women with its promise of thrills. The car promises a bit of danger to go with its romance, and people swoon over it on occasion.

Writing about modern sexuality, Edward R. O'Neill says, "The choice between subject and object leaves out the third possibility for identification so tantalizingly inscribed in the structure of fantasy that Freud outlined" (14). He then cites Jean Laplanche's analysis, which suggests that a given fantasy of subject and object often "contains three terms, not two: the subject, the object, and the *action itself*" (original italics) (14). Automobile ownership and driving is, in our time, not a male or female activity. While we may all too often fall back on "traditional" modes of thinking, our feelings and our fantasies are at emotive and creative levels freer to act and form new concepts that do not have to obey earlier sets of gender concepts. The Corvette, along with other cultural artifacts, is no longer purely governed by the ideas of the past. If the Corvette were a style and design that dated back to an earlier century, it would be more limited in its image; on the other hand, if it had come into being later in the twentieth or early in the twenty-first centuries, it would perhaps be "freer" of gender and cultural associations. As it stands, the Corvette is rooted in the past but fluid in its ability to signify.

Today the Corvette does not project precisely the "iconic" image that General Motors and Chevrolet market it as possessing. Over fifty years of history and cultural interpretation in music, film, print, and all other media have given it a more vital and complex image than its designers and engineers can control. As Swedish anthropologist Ulf Mellstrom writes about the process of anthropomorphizing automobiles, "Machines may also evoke emotions that can be compared with the kinds of emotions other social relations evoke and are constituted by. Certain machines become dear objects and are transformed into subjects receiving tender care as well as frustrated emotions" (471). I would contend that for Corvette owners, drivers, and enthusiasts — women as well as men — this is what has happened, and it all goes on independently of what the corporate mentality of the car's masters may think. Mellstrom goes on to say, following another anthropologist's line of reasoning, "Artefacts and machines [those like the Corvette] become partible bits of people that in themselves symbolically transform and are being transformed in the interaction with others" (472). Corvettes are machines, material objects, yet also — for those devoted to them — parts of themselves. Especially for women who may wish to be "empowered" and project a "potent" identity, the Corvette may be the perfect automobile.

Another critic writes that "the automobile played a crucial role in shaping the modernist tensions between the machine and the body; it both displaced and displayed the body, replacing some bodily functions yet demanding bodily skill" (Clarke 46–47). The automobile, with the Corvette as an outstanding example, has come to represent "both masculine and feminine power" (47). "More than any other machine," the car is "anthropomorphized in American culture, generally functioning as both extension of the self [for women, Maria Wyeth and others] and treasured companion [for men, Buz and Tod in *Route 66*, among many], both subject to human control yet often seeming to possess a mind of its own" (Clarke 47). It should come as no surprise that women have appropriated a vehicle so capable of signifying such a wide range of qualities and abilities. Power is one of the crucial aspects of identity in patriarchal culture, and the Corvette carries with it that "aura" of potency and success that is most valuable. It may not always be subtle, but the Corvette is a complex signifier worth investigation.

PART IV

The Corvette as Art:
The Expressive Image

Chapter 16

Images with Power

The automobile exists as a material object, a real physical presence, in a world composed not just of physical things, but also "images," thoughts and ideas that are *real*— possess power and express meaning — yet are not necessarily tangible and material. Depictions in visual media, the written or spoken language, and seemingly solid objects may all create images with a power to signify ideas greater than the simple, physical thing they draw their appearance from. Works of art and literary descriptions may take the form of or borrow the name and outward aspects of the physical world: machines, living beings, locations, or people. Yet art is not limited to the world of solid objects or three-dimensional space; images can be purely abstract forms, things that exist only as ideas or concepts. These shapes, pictures, or forms are works of creative or interpretative "art" that serve to represent ideas or convey "meanings" outside or beyond themselves. Things sometimes function in the creative arts in order to convey "meaning."

Automobiles can do this; the Corvette, as a machine and a name with associative power and material existence, is already the subject of numerous photographs, as well as being used in a variety of creative contexts to suggest a range of ideas, as we have already seen. The form of automobiles themselves, their "beauty" and clarity of style, is the subject of intense artistic attention: stylists and designers work as artists utilizing steel or plastic to create dynamic, exciting shapes with an eye towards aesthetic value. And, at least to appropriately educated tastes, the automobile works "to convey both masculine and feminine imagery" in ways that render it "a unique object," a "modern hermaphrodite" that "appeals equally to men and women" (Marsh 201). For most men the car is "a phallic extension" and "a mistress to covet"; for the majority of women, the car is "an object of adoration and a reflection of their own sexuality" (201). Automobiles — the

Corvette presents itself as an outstanding example — have always possessed what the critics Marsh and Collett, in *Driving Passion* (1986), refer to as an "expressive function" that reaches beyond their physical and mechanistic existence (206). Our contemporary society and consumer culture view cars — stylish, powerful cars like the Corvette, in particular — not "merely" as objects designed to provide transportation, but as tangible images of what we wish to say about ourselves. Automobility itself is the tip of the iceberg of what we have come to get from our automobiles, those dear, intimate machines. What began with running down the road has accelerated, gaining strength all the while, and become more than simply going places.

In global — no longer just Western — culture, automobility and the car's expressive function have become dominant, frequently masculine, ideas. Yet, as we have seen, women and minorities have also come to take advantage of the image the car presents and what it signifies. Very few people's lives remain completely untouched by either automobiles or the effect they have on human consciousness. Cars seem to be everywhere, especially in media. Yet over the course of the last hundred years, the independence of spirit and freedom to move the automobile represents have been superceded by the car's ability to express our own humanity. Owning and driving a car like the Corvette are now performative acts; we "act out" the image the car has come to signify, and that dominates all practical or logical considerations.

The automobile and what it signifies is a surface that hides our human need to express feelings and emotions, to give ourselves the power to signify, at least indirectly. Cars are, or have been transformed into, the cultural arti-fact of the age we now live in, and increasingly the ideology of the auto-mobile now spreads across the earth, like a song of vanity and desire all men and women sometimes hear.

Automobiles are the signifiers of our emotional states and the images we have of ourselves. The car is, in modern times, what Roland Barthes describes in his essay "La nouvelle Citroën" ("The New Citroën" [The Cit-roen DS 19]) from his book *Mythologies* (1972) as "*l'équivalent assez exact des grandes cathédrales gothiques*" ("the rather exact equivalent of the great gothic cathedrals"): it is "*une grande création d'époque, conçue passionnément ... consommée dans son image, sinon dans son usage, par un peuple entier qui s'approprie en elle un objet parfaitement magique*" ("a great creation of the age, passionately conceived ... consumed in its image, if not in its use, by a whole people who appropriate it as a perfectly magical object") ("La nou-velle Citroën" online and *Mythologies* 88). A certain car, one that possesses "style" or expresses "passion," appears "*d'abord comme un objet superlatif*" ("firstly as a superlative object"), "*une transformation de la vie en matière (la matière est bien plus magique que la vie)*" ("a transformation of life into material (the material is much more magical than life)"). As Barthes says, the automobile as an object has become something more than a physical thing; it is something "*visitée avec une application intense, amoureuse ... la grande phase tactile de la découverte, le moment où le merveilleux visuel va subir l'assaut raisonnant du toucher*" ("visited with an intense, amorous application ... a great tactile stage of discovery, the moment when the marvelous visual is going to undergo the reasoning assault of touch") ("La nouvelle Citroën" online and *Mythologies* 90). Cars are, on occasion and in special cases, more like works of expressive, creative art than machines of motion — they can "transport" us in different ways. Corvettes, and other automobiles that excite the imagination, do this; the automotive experience is both physical motion and an affair of the heart.

British philosopher and aesthetician Richard Wollheim, in his analytical work on the nature of art *Art and Its Objects* (1980), writes of an apparent "incompatibility of property between works of art and physical objects" and that this comes from the "representational properties of works of art" (12). Stated more concisely, representational art is not as simple as it seems, a picture or painting of a "thing" is not necessarily a "work of art." The "expressive properties" of an object are valuable, although this "value" may be difficult to describe and/or determine (Wollheim 12). The issue is "how can anything purely physical be expressive?" (22). This is part of the problem with defining a work of art; if we dismiss representations of real, tangible things, what are we left with? And its corollary, "What is art if its 'representations' are only 'objects'?" seems to leave material things, such as automobiles, outside the domain of art (22). What Wollheim is after is a practical theory of art that allows for works of representational art — which is to say, tangible goods, objects drawn from everyday life — to be fit subjects of artistic study. The Corvette, as an object and as a representation, is found in works that appear to be art, so his points of inquiry apply to them as well as more major, accepted works.

It is the ability to present ideas in a contextual form that has meaning not just read into it, but suggested by its content and associations that gives an image real significance and artistic meaning. Wollheim says that "whether we can attribute specific expressive properties to physical objects solely on the basis of what is given [what they have to suggest]" is an important question (56). In terms of an automobile, we should ask what does or can the car suggest outside of itself that might permit its depiction to become a work of art? To some extent, the earlier chapters have already answered this — concepts and conceits of masculinity and the female gaze are both regularly found in or in the vicinity of the Corvette — but now we are attempting to tie these ideas together, to get at both the idea and the power that the image of the automobile — through the Corvette — exerts *on* or *in* both people and creative works.

"Works of art" are, as a partial definition, what John Dewey termed, "refined and intensified forms of experience" (qtd. in Wollheim 100). While this is incomplete and less than comprehensive, it does point the way toward art and the automobile as connected, if not related subjects. The *Oxford English Dictionary* (OED) online defines "art" as "the expression or application of creative skill and imagination, typically in a visual form such as painting, drawing, or sculpture, producing works to be appreciated for their beauty or emotional power. Also: such works themselves considered collectively" ("art"). If automobiles can be thought of as "rolling sculpture" or "architecture on wheels," then some definition of art may apply. At *Art Encyclopedia*'s online glossary page, ArtLex.com, "art" is described as, "for numerous reasons, the most difficult word to define without starting endless argument!" (artencyclopedia.com and artlex.com). Art, according to these sources, "involves a degree of human involvement" implying "made by humans instead of nature"; art is "artificial," and "more useful" definitions might be found in the field of "aesthetics" ("art"). Bearing this in mind, looking at certain representations of the automobile as art seems possible, if not certain.

For now, the image of the Corvette does seem to possess "iconic," if not "artistic" qualities. Wollheim writes that for an object "certain very general principles ... have historically been advanced concerning the essential characteristics of a work of art": it must be "enduring," "apprehended by the 'theoretical' senses of sight and hearing," "exhibit internal differentiation," and "not be inherently valuable" (110). The Corvette, as a material object and a signifier, meets the qualifications of all but the last of these. As to that, as a successful corporate product for sale in the marketplace of a global capitalist economy, it would seem to have earned the right to be considered an exception to that rule. If "apropos both of artistic creativity and of aesthetic understanding," a "particular view in the psychology of art" can be endorsed, then we can — in another partial definition of "art" — consider it to be "the manufacture of certain artifacts which are conceived of and valued, by artist and spectator alike, as preeminently independent and self-subsistent objects" (Wollheim 129). It may be then, in the right circumstances, an automobile such as the Corvette may become, in its image and depiction, a work of art.

A mass-produced commodity's image may move from popular or mass culture towards high culture if it endures long enough, attracts a significant following, and takes on established meanings. In this chapter, the Chevrolet Corvette — manifested in a variety of instances in mass and popular culture — is described in terms of how the car's image has become meaningful in an artistic sense. This image has evolved through media, not necessarily as "America's only sports car" — the "icon" its owners and enthusiasts believe it to be — but as a signifier carrying connotations of style, power, and desire. The signified "Corvette" now has all of these suggested meanings. The resulting Corvette image is the sum total of its physical being and accumulated wealth of attributed qualities: sensual design, seductive allure, and high performance.

The Corvette's image began with the actual car, but took on meanings that are today aspects of the total being of six generations, more than fifty years, and over 1.5 million cars ("Milestone"). The associated ideas and values developed over time, growing and changing as years passed and connotations developed. From the Corvette's origin as a stylish roadster through its evolution into the powerful Sting Ray and acquisition of ever more material and sexual overtones as a symbol of American culture, the car has come to be both a physical presence and an image with a variety of interpretations. In this part of the book we consider how the Corvette's image is not just masculine or feminine, but one of its own, an identity including but not limited to reflections of gender. Two stages in this continuing evolution are the image's use in advertising and appropriation by serious art. In these places too, the car has become subject to interpretation: as static or kinetic art, the automobile is presented as an object of sculptural value, even beauty in it most aesthetic sense.

Modern automobiles are complex structures composed of lesser machines and devices that are organized into systems in order to accomplish one overriding practical goal: human mobility. They are mechanistic bodies, imbued with shape and color to suit our perceptions. However, we interpret their designs in different ways, and the majority of the time, our personal automobiles come to signify our own individual attributes and styles, to be extensions of our humanity, reflections of ourselves. They are texts we willingly read for what they mean and say about us. An automotive design, as Barthes says, often becomes "*une grande création*" ("a great creation"), "*un objet parfaitement magique*" ("a perfectly magical object") that we consume "*dans son image, sinon dans son usage*" ("in its image, if not in its use"); sometimes, cars are works of art ("La nouvelle Citroën" online and *Mythologies* 88).

Although, as we have seen, the Corvette appears as a sensual, even seductive image in literary works, we will not be considering literature here so much as "artistic" works that bring together the fields of automotive culture and artistic creation. The Corvette is already found in many literary texts, but how it can be discovered in visual arts, including the omnipresent power of advertising that shapes so much of our modern world, is a bit different. The Corvette is a signifier, one with a special, if not unique, presence in automobile and general contemporary culture; just how far its aura and personality extend is the open question.

As works such as paintings and photographs, along with advertising in visual media — print, television, and motion pictures — demonstrate, we read into the forms of automobiles what we are able to discover based on our notions of pleasing shapes that appeal to our sensibilities. Cars are not just "things"; they are sensual forms, suggestive images. Visual media give us cars that act performatively; they behave like characters in a story or act and embody emotions much as human beings do. Advertising often imposes a narrative upon the article it presents, endowing the object or commodity with some form of identity, even a subjectivity that renders it more than an item for sale. In a like manner, the film *Corvette Summer* (1978) makes a Corvette into a signifier of youthful sexuality and freedom, yet the car also becomes an icon, an example of style and excess to be imitated. Product stylists and critics of design, such as Raymond Loewy, write of automobiles as works created by people dedicated to the merger of art and engineering. And in the works of Dana Forrester and other artists, automobiles — frequently Corvettes — are the subjects of carefully posed images, juxtaposing the car with backgrounds and locations, just as portrait art depicts human subjects.

Given our need to analyze and critique the physical world for its emotional qualities, we often take our automobiles to be statements of grace and power, sexuality and affluence. These analyses are frequently emotive and critically meaningful. One vehicle that serves as an excellent example and has carried significant appeal for most of its long life is the Corvette, first coming into being more than half a century ago and growing and changing with the times. The Corvette is only a car, but its image is much more than the material object. Automotive art takes advantage of the Corvette's appearance and its history, making it the subject of innumerable pictures of all kinds. The power of these are in all of the Corvette's associations, how it reflects back to us a great deal of how we think and feel. This is what we value images for, their ability to meaningfully give back to us the ideas and emotions we invest in them. Our cars — at least some of them — are agents of transformation or images of ourselves transformed.

Chapter 17

The Corvette as Concept: The Automobile as "Art"

When we speak of "concepts," we make reference to no less than two distinct areas that pertain, if not influence and act upon, the automobile's pretensions to artistic status. While millions of cars may be suppressed symbols of automobility, lost in the space of everyday life and a capitalist, consumerist culture, there remain a few specific examples that stand out. In the automotive world, concepts are drawings, models, and — in often dramatic, even shockingly original cases — visually striking cars with stunning paint and innovative physical shapes. In form these "show cars" may resemble current models, yet they are often incredibly different cars from what normal eyes are accustomed to seeing. In the sense of Dewey's "refined and intensified forms of experience," these "concept cars" come close to being art; they are valued for their style and how they express emotion, vitality, and even practical functionality in new ways, shapes, and forms. Some of them, those most promising of success in the marketplace, become real automobiles.

In 2003, the fiftieth anniversary of the Corvette's first production, the Italian automotive design house Italdesign, Italdesign-Giugario S.p.A., well known for its work on BMWs, Maseratis, and other stylish European makes, produced a one-of-a-kind car called the "Moray," a futuristic, bubble-topped, curvaceous shape that was photographed with the appropriately beautiful female human model and displayed at various major auto shows after debuting at the Geneva Motor Show, perhaps the biggest and brightest of the European car shows ("Moray"). As a concept, the Moray served several purposes: it demonstrated Italdesign's ability to fashion sensual shapes that packaged sound engineering design, it confirmed the maker's skill at crafting both an exterior and interior that were stylish and functional, and it showed that designers Giorgetto and Fabrizio Giugario were in touch with both European and American automotive history while looking forward to new forms and technology. The Italian show car was also a Corvette, a tribute to the brand's fifty years of style and performance.

The car was described in one report as "an elegant extreme" that carried "a pure profile," possessing a "sinuous contour line," with "the unmistakable look of the Corvette grill" ("2003 Italdesign Corvette"). The Giugarios stated that, in creating the Moray: "We vowed to honor the rhetorical principles that dictated the American muscle-car of excellence era: simplicity and pragmatism, handlasting [hand in hand] with the hedonist concept of sportiness evolving through the restraints of time" ("Moray"). The car was a vivid, eye-catching red; in publicity stills, the Moray poses like a fashion model in front of a red, white, and blue background that emphasizes its shape and color while acknowledging its American origin. While on tour in the United States, the car became a vibrant, lustrous blue that mimicked the Corvette Mako Shark show cars of the past ("First Drive"). The Moray is an attempt to craft a new variation on an enduring image, the Corvette's notoriety in the automotive world. The car is also an homage that honors a cultural object's history, a stylization of an existing form that draws out its attributes while projecting them forward, giving the finished work both a historical context and a glimpse of the future.

The Corvette Moray is like a work of art in these qualities; its expressiveness and intent are not so different from the images of famous places and people that seek to capture their spirit or comment upon them by portraying them in new and perceptive ways, like Andy Warhol's red-tinged image of Marilyn Monroe that — in one artistic analysis — casts her in the light of fame and publicity (Dilworth 254). Even the name "Moray" possesses a connection to the many concept-car Corvettes that have drawn attention to themselves and the car's image of exciting shape and form: with the names of sea creatures, like Sting Ray, Mako Shark I and II, Manta Ray, Tiger Shark, and the flying car sounding Aero- and Astrovette have all been concept Corvettes that stressed the car's looks and design features over and above the Corvette's nature as a high-performance automobile ("Corvette Concept Cars"). In fact, the 1997–2004 C5-based Moray does prefigure the design and appearance of the next generation C6 Corvette; the nose and tail treatments of the Moray concept are amazingly close to the actual "new" Corvette that debuted two years later. The concept car as art is not an unreasonable stretch in the world of automotive culture. The car as icon, or signifier, lends itself to reinterpretation, even reification, if its image — the stamp of identity its existence has given it — has the qualities of style and staying power in the mind of the viewing and driving public.

In his essay "The Automobile In Art" from *Automobile and Culture* (1984), published in conjunction with the Museum of Contemporary Art, Los Angeles, art historian Gerald Silk writes,

> The automobile, one of the great modern inventions, has become a major attraction in museums of history, technology, and transportation; as objects of potential beauty and aesthetic significance, motorcars are exhibited in the design sections of art museums. But as imagery and subject matter in works of art, the automobile appeared in museums and galleries long before the cars themselves were put on display [27].

The concept car, where art and the automobile meet as artistic design, takes place in this kind of in-between world. Part art and part performative and promotional display, concept cars — and many Corvettes have been and continue to be — are hybrids of consumerism and creative, three-dimensional art. The newest and latest Corvette concept, Bertone of Italy's Mantide (Mantis) show car, eclipses the Moray in its stylistic flourishes. Much like a human celebrity famed for being famous, the Mantide can be found on the web and in print, yet it is also a technically advanced, fully functional automobile, a work of art that works. In the words of one auto enthusiast who in 2009 drove the car from Manhattan to Los Angeles — a trip oddly evocative of the *Route 66* Corvette's journey from New York out into the world of real life America — the Mantide is "among the world's most desirable supercars," equal in style, sophistication, and performance with any Ferrari or other expensive, exotic automobile (Liu 69).

According to Silk, early in the twentieth century, European artist Francis Picabia visited America and was inspired to write: "It flashed on me that the genius of the modern world is in machinery and that through machinery art ought to find its most vivid expression" (qtd. 77). In Picabia's work, machines as art became a motif, an analogy for humanity. Cars and car parts are metaphors, "object-portraits ... [that] represent human psychology and behavior" (Silk 79). Picabia writes: "The machine has become more than a mere adjunct of life. It is really part of human life ... perhaps the very soul. In seeking forms through which to interpret ideas or by which to expose human characteristics I have come at length upon the form which appears most brilliantly plastic and fraught with symbolism" (qtd. in Silk 79). What this says is very like what automotive art does and what the concept car, in its best iterations, manages to convey: humanity's own qualities become visible through the machines it invents and uses to depict itself. As

Silk makes clear in his analytical, comprehensive essay, art and the automobile have from the early twentieth century onward *together* served an expressive function for humanity. "As long as the car is with us," he writes, "providing emotional experiences ... and altering perception, art will comment on and be influenced by this most inspirational of modern inventions" (169).

The other "concept" that resonates with the automobile and art is conceptual art, a field founded in the 1960s that seeks new definitions of art, ones not bounded by conventional representations in painting, sculpture, or other "established" forms. Conceptual art is not about traditional forms of art; in the words of artist/essayist Sol Lewitt: "Three-dimension art of any kind is a physical fact. This physicality is its most obvious and expressive content. Conceptual art is made to engage the mind of the viewer rather than his eye or emotions" (214). Conceptual art is about *ideas*, not the "physicality" of a work. The application of conceptual ideas to concept cars or automobiles in general then is a tricky business. If we take the emotional content — as well as "the colour, surface, texture[,] and shape" — away from a car, what then do we have (Lewitt 214)? The answer, the image and identity of the Corvette, is what is left. Since we know how long a history the car has, how many times it has signified freedom and independence along with other ideas, we may be able to see the Corvette as a suitable subject for conceptual art. And it seems, all contemporary art is now, at least in part, conceptual.

From the conceptual perspective, it is the idea about the subject that matters, how the "work" — whatever it may be — can be used to present a meaningful image to the public. If we recall Warhol's red-faced Marilyn, then we see how the images of people or objects can be used to comment on their fame or the causes, political or social, associated with the person or object. In this conceptual sense, anything could be, potentially, the beginning for a work of conceptual art. If the Corvette were a new model, or if its name lacked recognition, then it might not have the idea content to be "conceptual"; as it stands, automobiles *en masse* would only be generic subjects for art, dependent on the interpretation and ability of the artist. On the other hand, the Corvette's established image and its cultural identity make it, like Marilyn, a face and figure that the public mind knows and carries associated meanings for. These meanings are fit sites for artistic interpretation and presentation, places where the public's knowledge and the artist's perception may meet. When a context for art exists and the artist's ability to render a subject, representational — like an automobile — or not, produces a suitable product, then a work of art may come into being. It could be that, given the right time and place, an object which possesses the right attributes can be used to convey artistic ideas, the ideas that conceptual art values over subject and content.

Writer/critic Peter Osborne, in his book *Conceptual Art* (2002) — itself a "conceptual" work in how it alters the expected forms, typography and format of published works — writes that the new field of art was "a revolution ... in the perception and practice of art" that "redefined [it] as the vehicle for ideas" (no page number). The advent of conceptual art was "a major turning-point in contemporary art" Osborne (preface). For automobiles — as Silk said, "the most inspirational of modern inventions" — conceptual art has led to more representations and interpretations, rendering the role and significance of the car in modern society more open to question and critical thought. Yet conceptual art itself is the subject of harsh criticism by experts in parallel, if not the same, fields. No less than Gilles Deleuze and Félix Guattari believe conceptual art "dematerializes sensation [the feeling or emotional content of art] by banalising it" (Zepke 157). Conceptual art "allows for a 'generalisation' of materials," "transforms sensation into [reproducible] 'information,'" and neutralizes "art's ontological status by making sensation depend on the 'opinion' of the viewer" — all of these "dematerializing" agents work against the best or most valuable functioning of a work of art (158). According to Stephen Zepke, in its making "anything" into art, Deleuze and Guattari find conceptual art to be empty or hollow; art's distinctive ability to present meaningful concepts and sensations becomes merely "information" (159).

Are the Corvette and its image "art" in the popular culture sense? The answer would be "yes," because we see it depicted as such in diverse forms and in a wide range of popular sources. But these are, by and large, commodity products, no more than disposable goods. Some images of the Corvette, the best quality photographs, look like art, but they lack a context and a meaning outside of the image and identity of the Corvette itself; they are, as Deleuze and Guattari describe it, "information" deprived of the "sensation and concept" that make for real or "high" art. To be art in the more serious and cultural sense, the Corvette and its image must do more than signify an automobile; it must be presented in a way that creates Dewey's "intensity" and conveys what the *OED* refers to as "beauty or emotional power." For general consumption, the Corvette may be "art" in the everyday, common sense of the word, stuff that people readily consume and identify with, but at this level it lacks the ability to signify complex ideas.

On the most popular, publicly available level, the Corvette as "art" — a work of limited aesthetic value that captures the thoughts and feelings of the audience without advancing the meaning or context of the signified subject — is most clearly represented through its depiction in a "car movie," in this case *Corvette Summer* (1978), directed by Matthew Robbins. The film speaks to what should be a teenage, but often lingering over into adulthood, search for identity — the "discovery" or transformation" of self that medieval alchemists and modern artists seek to discover. Like many 1970s films, *Corvette Summer* is about young people on a quest for love and adventure; however, the significant difference here is that the centerpiece of this film is a wildly customized mid–'70s Corvette. In the motion picture, after the once wrecked, then newly reborn Stingray is stolen, the high school senior who worked hardest rebuilding the car sets out to recover it. As the paperback novel, "a fiberglass romance" based on the film script, says: "Dantley was a typical 18-year-old American boy. He loved cars. Vanessa was a prime specimen of the new breed of liberated young woman. She loved freedom. Just one thing could have brought these two together" (Drew front and back covers). The "one thing" is the wildly styled Corvette Stingray, an eye-grabbing visual presence in the film and source of controversy among Corvette enthusiasts. Like a work of conceptual art, one outrageous or thought-provoking, it attracted attention to itself, even could be seen — among automobile buffs and car customizers — as "making a statement" about cars as popular art and stylistic expression.

Instead of the clean, elegant style that Sting Rays were known for, the curvaceous design of the 1968–1982 C3 was altered by the added features of what came to be called "the *Corvette Summer* car." According to automotive historian Jerry Heasley, "the Corvette used in the movie has achieved near cult status" and influenced custom automobiles of all kinds for years afterwards (265). The Corvette image as a desirable, sensual object has regularly been enhanced by appearances in motion pictures, television, and music. *Corvette Summer* gave the Corvette image an outrageous quality in a time when automobiles were becoming more utilitarian; the daring styling of the '50s and '60s had yielded to the heavy bumpers and the other safety features of newer cars. The film offered a love story for its intended youthful audience, and if the Corvette could not be a speed machine, then perhaps it still could be a love machine or a work of automotive sculpture, admittedly one of questionable taste. The movie affirmed the Corvette as a representation of freedom and independence when a charismatic image was needed most.

Annie Potts (standing) and Mark Hamill (sitting on car) co-starred in Matthew Robbins' *Corvette Summer* (1978), a youth-oriented romance: guy loses Corvette, girl finds guy, guy and girl together save Stingray equals happy ending. The Corvette itself combined a range of customized features that made it either a styling revelation or an exercise in the most extreme of automotive taste and bodywork. The "*Corvette Summer* car" is one of the most recognized movie cars, an icon of outlandish styling (Photofest).

Although he never had input into its engineering or advertising, Raymond Loewy and his ideas regarding the forms given items of all kinds — from immense locomotive engines to desktop adding machines — should be included in a discussion of the Corvette and its existence as a material good, an automobile, and as an image. French-born and educated, Loewy came to the United States in 1919 and soon became a leader in the then-developing and evolving field of "industrial design." In equal parts material design and industrial art, the field encompasses a sense of "style" and suitability of shape and form for manufactured goods that, it could truthfully be said, have come to influence almost, if not all, consumer products. Industrial design seems to be a practical middle ground between purely commercial products and designs that aspire to something artistic, objects with lasting beauty and purpose.

Loewy writes, in *Never Leave Well Enough Alone* (1951), that "function alone does not necessarily generate beauty[,] and it seems that there can be no beauty without order" (210). This most resembles what in physics is thought of as "elegance," the beauty of something rationally consistent, structured and orderly, not physically "beautiful," but with a sense of proportion — even a "style" of mathematical symmetry — that makes it both functional and an object of admiration. As far as automobile expertise, Loewy's firm designed innovative, forward-looking cars, such as the 1953 Studebaker Starliner, a sleek, cleanly designed car featured — along with the original Corvette — on the "Sporty Cars" commemorative stamp series in 2005. Loewy's emphasis on tasteful designs for all products was influential in the 1950s and 1960s; the 1957 French Citroen DS 19, the "*Déesse*" or "Goddess" design that led Roland Barthes to reflect on the significance of automobiles in the twentieth century, was a variation on Loewy's work (Zumbrunn 26). What Barthes found in the Citroen DS was the style that was coming into being in the late 1950s; the success of the contemporary sports car in post–World War II Europe and America would influence General Motors, leading to the development of the Corvette.

What Loewy saw as most important, greater even than functionality, was that "simplicity is the deciding factor in the aesthetic equation," and "beauty" was achieved through "function and simplification" (Loewy 210). The first Corvette models were this motto in action; although stylish, they were in reality simple cars: in the early years, the style of the car spoke more about the Corvette's image and ambition than its performance. Loewy believed in the logic of the MAYA (Most Advanced Yet Acceptable) school of design, and in the early Corvettes this was carried through (278). If there were flaws in Loewy's thinking, they were not clear to the American automobile-buying public; Loewy wrote that "the automobile that makes the best instant impression is the one that looks alive ... charged with speed and motion even at rest" (310). If the Corvette has enjoyed a long life and endured challenges by time and circumstance, it is in part due to how the car as a material object demonstrated style and performance and the growing and changing Corvette image following Loewy's principles. The Corvette may be a pop-culture work of art that aspires to high art status, but it has remained relatively simple and straightforward over the years. The car delivers speed and performance in an affordable package; it has also clearly expressed an assertive, not understated or subtle, American style.

If the Corvette was not always "artistic" in its looks or handling, it never wavered in its American identity: once the Corvette was fast and powerful, it abstained from the need for European pseudo-sophistication. The

Corvette as art may never escape from its American identity, and its approach to interpreting the sports car mystique, which it sought to borrow from Europe, stresses an image of *power* over *refinement*: this is today's argument regarding the Corvette and the Porsche 911, the balance of two virtues essential to the modern sports car. The power the Corvette demonstrates in its physical being carries over to its image and reputation; what the car does for its fans and those others who consume it is a combination of how the Corvette is portrayed and what people see in it. Maybe the Corvette image is art in that the conception of it presents a complicated set of images and associations that cannot be easily unraveled, perhaps not at all.

Chapter 18

The Corvette Image in Advertising and Media: Beyond *Route 66*

The television series *Route 66* is unquestionably a major contribution to the image that the Corvette possesses. As one researcher states, "*Route 66* was the first of several television series over the decades that would make *a single automobile* the centerpiece of the series" (original italics) (Scott 147–148). The Chevrolet Corvette was becoming a successful, although not outstanding, money-making product for General Motors by the time that the show debuted in 1960: however, the series gave the Corvette that "image," that essential cachet that the car has never lost, regardless of the changes in its cost or appearance. In media, most especially in automobile advertising, the Corvette has always played some kind of role, yet the car itself acquired much of its "personality" and name recognition through *Route 66*. According to one automotive historian, the show created more of an image for the Corvette "in the consciousness of America ... than any advertisement or marketing campaign" (Burton, *Corvette* 43). While the Corvette may be an "object," its portrayal in print and visual media continues to endow it with a measure of subjectivity as well; the car is not an individual artifact, but an ongoing series of images spread over a landscape of the last fifty years.

Television is, by and large, a medium of disposable images; they come and go rapidly. Few register in the mind longer than a momentary thought. It is, overall, what is now recognized as a component of popular culture — or its artistic equivalent, "pop art" — not fine art or high drama, but the art of the popular and the readily available. In spite of their rapidly passing nature and interchangeable characters and forms, a few television shows do present images that linger or take hold and persist. The various Corvettes in *Route 66* did this, forming a continuous image over the years, as if it were one single automobile, not a succession of new Corvettes. In a like manner, pop art — even examples that have crossed over and become accepted as high art — play with this sense of how an image lasts in the thoughts of its viewers, how it may acquire or be given "meaning" outside of a commodity's market identity. Pop art as a phenomenon embraces the ideas and images of popular culture — especially advertising in all its manifestations — and transforms them in new ways, creating a contemporary form of art distinctly a product of the twentieth century.

The outstanding instance would be Andy Warhol's work. As one of the leading figures in pop art, Warhol "used common everyday objects to portray elements of popular culture, primarily images in advertising and television" ("Art History"). Whatever the image might be, it was subject to artistic appropriation that parallels the social and cultural appropriation of the Corvette and its image, for their own purposes, by women and minority males. Pop art looks to popular culture as a source of celebrities and cultural objects to embody its observations of "growing materialism and con-sumerism in society" ("Art History"). Rather than "art," in the narrowest sense, being defined by its supposed "sophisticated and elite nature," accord-ing to the World Wide Arts Resources website, "Pop art shattered the divide between the commercial arts and the fine arts." Warhol and other pop artists felt free to create representational images that the public could perceive, not as blatantly critical of contemporary life, but "challenging the [established artistic] concept of the unique art work" (Livingstone).

While the automobile in general, and the Corvette specifically, are not known to appear in Warhol's work, images of Marilyn Monroe, Elvis Presley, and objects such as "Coca-Cola bottles and tins [cans] of Campbell's Soup" are quite prominent (Livingstone). The relationship between pop art and commercial advertising seems to be not so much parasitic as symbiotic. While ads strove to promote goods and services in a competitive market economy, pop art took the signifying images of these commodities and, cre-atively, turned them back towards the buying public as what David Burnett, curator of international art at the Brisbane, Australia, Gallery of Modern Art, calls "not an attack, rather a questioning of elitism in art and in life" (Saint Martin). The Corvette and its image, as the focus of advertising in any and all media over the course of the last fifty years, certainly would be fit subjects for pop art, yet not too many examples are to be found. Sources like Koolart-USA — which offers humorous, flattering caricatures of all mod-els of automobiles — exist, but it may be that the Corvette image and the car are oddly positioned socially and culturally: the car is expensive, and relatively few are built each year, yet the six generations are widely seen, and many Americans who are not wealthy or noticeably affluent are pleased to own Corvettes.* As a commodity with a well-known face and image, the Corvette is a "celebrity commodity," a pop art kind of subject that can both be parodied as social or cultural commentary, or looked at as reflecting values that have been commercially appropriated but remain strongly American in their worth and virtue — that freedom and independence, among other characteristics, we never deny as our birthright.

Corvettes appear significantly in various advertisements, and frequently the car is a device, a means of suggesting something else. According to *Advertising Age* magazine, General Motors/Chevrolet did not feel the need to advertise the Corvette on television from 1984 to 1997; print ads still appeared, but apparently the car's image was so well known that it did not need to be seen on the nation's most prominent medium — how far the Corvette had come since *Route 66* (Halliday 3). Yet in 1997, when the new, re-engineered and restyled C5 Corvette first came on the scene, Chevrolet spent an untold amount promoting the latest incarnation. The percentage devoted to the Corvette is unspecified, but GM's "total media spending" for the year was $321 million (Endicott 44). Presumably, as the "halo car" whose light shines on the rest of the product line, the Corvette was heavily promoted, and the new C5 was a marketing and sales success.

Writing in *A Sense of Things* (2003), Bill Brown describes a combination of "idealism" about objects, as in the writings of psychologist Mark Baldwin, and "materialism," as thought of by "Objectivist poet" Louis Zukofsky, that is to be found in objects (1). In many cases this yields a "physical presence" that "is inseparable from its metaphysical past" (Brown 1). The Corvette brings this with it when it appears. While the physical presence is an apparent fact about most tangible goods in the marketplace, that "metaphysical

---

*Websites such as WallWerks and Automotive Art Gallery have a wide range of pictures, not just of Corvettes, but of many desirable cars of times past. Automotive Art Gallery carries no less than ten different artists who paint Corvettes, and prices range from a low of $20 to over $400. Koolart-USA's website has humorous and flattering caricatures of well-known automobiles available as prints, t-shirts, and a variety of other products; Corvettes of all kinds are plentiful, most with huge engines or enormous tires. Enthusiast publications include *Corvette Enthusiast*, *Corvette Fever*, *Corvette Magazine* [the best and most serious], and General Motors and Chevrolet's own *Corvette Quarterly*. Most states, and many individual cities, have Corvette clubs with newsletters of their own. The National Corvette Restorers Society website, www.ncrs.com, offers a wealth of information for owners and prospective members. Finally, the National Corvette Museum in Bowling Green, KY, publishes *America's Sports Car*, the official museum newsletter.

past" and even a hypothetical present for the consumer is often what drives sales and gives an object a marketable quality. For the Corvette, the advertising done by Chevrolet to get and keep the car in the minds of the consuming public, the factory and independent teams involved in racing, and the automobile enthusiast press all combined to generate publicity. The majority of Corvette ads are typical of corporate advertising, yet some of them do suggest more; sometimes narratives are employed in combination with colorful, attention-grabbing photography to enhance the Corvette's role as what GM calls "America's only sports car."

Chevrolet has advertised the Corvette in a variety of intriguing ways that relate to women, and it is important to keep in mind that what occurs in the marketplace can be culturally significant. As Brown writes, "Our relation to things cannot be explained by the cultural logic of capitalism" (5–6). Also, objects are "texts" that "describe and enact an imaginative possession of things" (4). In the 1966 Corvette print ad, "The Day She Flew the Coupe," a husband and wife own a new 4-speed, 425-hp Corvette Sting Ray coupe that he is concerned is "too much for a woman to handle" and will "teach her to drive some weekend" (Stern 104). Her response is to one day hide the keys, leaving him to take "public transportation" to work while she yields to the "temptation ... [that] was overpowering" after a week of owning the car. She drives it "as smoothly as he." The Corvette is not "hard to drive"; more to the contrary, she is knowledgeable and capable, "upshifting and downshifting" with skill as she heads "off for the hills." The photo of the Corvette and the woman dominates the print portion of the ad underneath it.

In the photograph, the red Corvette coupe is posed near the top of the frame, claiming its own territory. The woman, dressed in what appears to be a sleek, fashionable sixties outfit, poses with her feet in a running woodland stream, eating a peach: she is totally calm, self-assured, and confident. Neither she nor the Sting Ray alone dominate; they seem to be a duality, both partaking of that sense of self that the husband sees in the Corvette as "a big hairy [that is to say, masculine and powerful] sports car" but does not recognize in the woman's identity (Stern 104). This is not exactly feminism via Corvette advertising, but the woman is the driver and co-owner of this Corvette, and she claims her rightful authority and privilege. The Corvette attracts her acquisitive, discerning "female gaze"— it could be that she sees herself in the Corvette — and it becomes an object that expresses what Brown calls "the congealed facts [the need for women to satisfy their own desires] and fantasies [the male and female wish for power and escape from the constraints society forces on them]" that often exist below the cultural and personal surface (4).

Looking at it a different way, the Corvette is a luscious apple red; it is positioned in a woodsy setting, near a clear-running stream. The woman to the right poses with the peach to her lips; she has an exotic look, slender and attractive. Although her face is not fully visible, she looks through the camera, seeming to make eye contact with the viewer. Like the wife in the Viagra commercial next to be discussed (chapter 4, pages 191–193), her feet pass through the running water, and that look is inviting. The ad looks like Eve in the Garden of Eden having already eaten the forbidden fruit, and she is posing a question to the observer, "Won't you have some of this too?" The apple in question is the Corvette, the irresistible that she has now experienced, but also herself: there are two desirable, tempting sources of pleasure, the powerful automobile and the sultry woman who has come to an understanding with it. So the ad suggests female independence and sensual/sexual temptation all rolled into one. It feeds the fantasy, while it promotes the purchase and consumption of the automobile. The Corvette image is made available to the woman, but it is linked to a desirability that bridges any gap in gender appeal. And the woman and the Corvette are both empowered without the aid of or the need for male intervention. The difference between this and porn star Vicky Vette with her Corvette, is that Vette promotes an easy, blatant sexuality, where the Corvette ad does more with the ideas of independence and temptation wound around each other.

Similar use of the Corvette image occurs in a recent Viagra television commercial. The ad begins with a handsome middle-aged man washing his classic, early sixties Corvette — a cool, sharp blue over white with gleaming chrome — while his wife (presumably she is his wife) watches from a lounge chair in the yard of their comfortable home. He soaps the car, which already looks immaculately clean, while the camera roams over its, or should I say "her," shapely body. So far this should be sexual enough; the car has his attention, and as his hands caress her, there is a suggestion of real intimacy, a significant relationship exists here — man and his machine, made for each other. Then ... the slender, attractive wife, dark-haired with just a little gray, crosses the yard, passes one of her bare feet through the arc of water put out by the sprinkler, and — with an inviting backward glance and her hips swaying — disappears into the house. The husband looks at the open door, then at the unfinished, soapy Corvette. He makes a face, obviously torn in his desire for both, then — inspired by passion — moves the sprinkler to complete rinsing the car and, not wasting any time, goes into the house and closes the door behind him. The rest is left to the imagination.

It would seem here that the two desires, or duality of sexual objects, present a choice many men must make in the face of temptation. The woman and the Corvette beckon; the image of one meets the image of the other, and neither physical presence can be scorned or ignored. As sociologist Max Weber states, "Culture will come when people touch things with love and see them with a penetrating eye" (qtd. in Brown 12). Through objects with some aesthetic and/or emotive value, perhaps like the Corvette, we come to see what Brown terms aesthetic "beauty"— Santayana's "pleasure regarded as the quality of a thing"— and "an element of sensation" that becomes "the quality of a thing" (qtd. 26). In this case, the Corvette may not be "art" in an absolute sense, but objects do possess beauty in the eye of the beholder, and this can be "reified pleasure, emphasizing less the quality of the feeling, more the quality (the thingness) of its apparent source" (Brown 26).

As the voice-over describes the benefits and appropriate cautions that go with Viagra, the water plays over the Corvette. We never see the man and woman again. Surely, of course, we know where they are and what they are doing. What I would point out here is that the commercial brings out the juxtaposition of the male and female and the Corvette. First of all, the car is a sign of his masculinity and attractiveness. The Corvette is pristine and perfect, a "cherry"— that is to say an unspoiled or virgin — example of a classic automobile. It seems strange that a guy who has this would need something more to boost his masculinity. But also consider the wife. She is, as presented, something of a trophy herself. Although the woman, the man, and the Corvette all appear to be of similar ages, each is well preserved, fit and quite attractive. The way the woman moves, the look she gives him, the motion of her toes through the stream of water, are all like the Corvette: alluring, mature, and inviting. The commercial is loaded with sexual suggestion: sensual shapes, seductive surfaces, and a moment of golden opportunity for pleasurable intimacy. The only choice, for the man, is with whom or what.

The wife and the Corvette have real "physical presence." It's the man's choice between them, and on the face of it, this seems to be about male potency and the desire a man can arouse in a woman. But it's a Viagra commercial for a male audience or for women who want their male companion to be virile and capable. So, in a sense, it is the woman and the Corvette that have the power here; there is an unspoken "metaphysical past" in the dramatic context. They may be rivals, yet each of them is the object of a male desire that may require chemical enhancement. The question is, as the voice says, "will you be ready?" If you as a man are not, then won't your woman and your Corvette go unfulfilled? The woman and the Corvette are positioned not really so much against each other as they are on the same side, the one that the man has to be empowered — capable in fact or metaphorically — to behave like a man should be (that is to say, *potently*) in order to satisfy. Each must be, in this case, "showered" with his affection; each is an object that has significance.

The wife and the Corvette echo each other's sensual and sexual appeal, and it is their mutual desirability that drives the little drama. Viagra makes a number of their videos available online at www.viagra.com, but this appears to be the only one that links sex, a woman, and a Corvette, or a car of any kind. In the commercial, the woman does not help wash the Corvette, and there is no suggestion as to whom it belongs; we read into it that it is a male possession, yet perhaps it is hers, not his. While the Corvette rivals the woman for the man's attention, like a mistress or some other woman, *it* or *she* is also a signifier of his male potency, as if the car — which might be thought of as female — possessed power in a masculine way. The car seems to move across gender lines depending on how we shift our perspective. For female Corvette owners, the image, on occasion, presents itself a bit differently. It emboldens or empowers their sexuality and identity. Corvettes give women *power*.

Other Corvette ads offer similar, if tamer, positionings of the woman and car. A 1964 Corvette Sting Ray promotion features what seems to be a photographer's set full of items: a racing helmet, binoculars, a map, a chess set, travel luggage, and so on ("1964 Chevrolet Corvette Sting Ray Coupe"). As we can see, all of them relate directly or indirectly to the Stingray posed on the right side of the photo, and they reflect an active, even adventurous lifestyle — a Corvette style of living. What is more interesting are the two people in the ad. Just to the left of center a man is posed, one foot on a curious chrome turtle footstool. He is dressed in what might be called the elegant, sophisticated playboy style of the early 1960s: jacket, sweater, tie, and so on. From a male vantage point we might conclude that the Stingray is his car, and it matches his style of dress. Yet a few feet away from him a blonde woman sits on the floor with her legs folded lotus style. She is posed thoughtfully, one hand to her chin, as if surveying the "room" and its contents. What can we make of this scene? Is "he" the owner, the possessor of all these things, the Sting Ray and the attractive blonde included? Or is "she" the one who owns him as well as the Corvette? Who is empowered and in charge here?

Since it is 1964 we are tempted to say the playboy lifestyle rules male consciousness — "playboy" in this case meaning Hugh Hefner and the magazine with that name. This is a man looking over his possessions, the woman among them. His head is higher than hers, he is dressed more formally, and "he" is a man — the typical, expected master of material things. Yet I think this is not what is going on. The woman is at the center, which is often the position of power, and she is equally composed and self-assured. The two of them are separate, not touching, not together, so this does not appear to be a couple — one of them is the "owner" of these articles and the focus of the ad.

A second version of the photo shows almost the same scene, the same possessions and the same two people. The man is shifted slightly, but his pose is much the same; he is static and has not moved. In this alternate view, the woman is lying on the floor, belly down. She is in the foreground

The E Type Jaguars or XKEs, produced from 1961 to 1975, are one of the outstanding automotive designs of modern times. Rivals to contemporary Corvettes, the Jags possessed European virtues and sleek aerodynamic forms. While the 396 and 427 Sting Rays had more power, the XKEs were stylish, good-handling cars. The contrast between the two pointed out different design philosophies east and west of the Atlantic; both remain desirable high-performance vehicles (James Jackson/Hulton Archive/Getty Images).

of the man, and seems to be playing chess with herself, and to be enjoying it. Her mouth is open, she is laughing. Looking from picture to picture, the woman is the one who shifts position, and she is the one who is active. She is either at the center of the first photograph or engaged in an activity — playing chess usually being thought of as a "thinking man's game" — in the second. Both photos may have been used in publicity for the Corvette in 1964; the GM PhotoStore website does not provide any information. But placing the two side by side, it seems that in the case of the Corvette Sting Ray, female owners or drivers are being solicited and encouraged. Since the Corvette's market competition of that time was primarily presupposedly "sophisticated" European sports cars, the Jaguar XKE being the best known and most remembered, a certain egalitarian approach to presenting the Corvette to the public might be expected. Some prospective Corvette buyers are going to be women with the means and the taste to look for automobiles that suit their style of living as well as their interest in power and performance. Taken together, these ads show us a female Corvette owner. The man is, based on what I see, one of the accouterments of her life; his style fits with her vision of the world, and *her* Corvette reflects her knowledge and control of her own circumstances.

Although often taken as a "male" kind of automobile — fast and powerful, that "big and hairy" of the 1966 ad — the Corvette also has appeal to thoughtful and cultivated tastes, as might be found in educated or independent women as well as men. In that sense a Corvette does transgress to some degree: it crosses the gender line and lines of class distinction. The Corvette is positioned by its designers and marketers, General Motors and Chevrolet, as both powerful and sophisticated, a balance of new-world assertiveness and old-world refinement. The car also comes to have personal associations given who wants one and what his or her desires happen to be directed towards. The car and a woman might occupy a similar place for some men, *or* her Corvette and a man could be the objects of a woman's desire.

Television and motion pictures continue to use the Corvette image to convey sensuality, if not sexuality. In NBC's 1986 television series *Stingray*, "Ray," a mysterious man without a past, appears in an immaculately beautiful black Corvette Sting Ray — reminiscent of the Corvette in the Viagra ad — to come to people's aid and then disappears, only asking in return that they repay the favor once, without question, when called upon. The car is memorable: it was an impossibly deep, lustrous black, like the *Kiss Me Deadly* Corvette (chapter 2, pages 21–24). Although the Sting Ray generation of C2 Corvettes ceased production in 1967, the car in *Stingray* is unmistakably a Corvette, and the episodes — more than in *Route 66* — do seem to act like stylized promotions of the Corvette image. The association of the Corvette with an adventurous life, with someone youthful, attractive, and actively engaged in pursuing his own way in the world is *very* similar to *Route 66*. The Lone Ranger returns in a young, handsome guise, but his mission, helping those in need, is still the same. The romance implicit in *Route 66* becomes more predictable, but still palatable and agreeably packaged for a television audience.

Although the automotive star of *Stingray* is only seen on the relatively small television screen, the way the Sting Ray is lovingly photographed and the look of the car demand that the viewer's eyes linger on it. Because the black coupe appears most often at night, light causes sensual reflections off the hood, fenders, and roof: the car itself is an object of desire without any necessary connection to a human male or female. It is an aesthetically pleasing form, and it might again be asked if an automobile — this Corvette in particular — can be rendered as art. To an extent this idea is recognized because *Stingray* won an Emmy award in 1987 for "Outstanding Graphic and Title Design," and the title sequence mainly consists of various images of the car moving in fields of light and shadow that accentuate its sinuous, graceful shape ("Awards for 'Stingray'"). The sleek image the black coupe presents is stylish and cool; it creates visual excitement and an aura of fantasy. But part of the Corvette image *is* the fantasy that began with *Route 66*. As shape or presence, the car's persona promises escape or reward; it carries with it a feeling of romance and adventure, yet with an aura of aggressiveness and sensual pleasure.

It might be argued, right here with the example of *Stingray* standing in for other instances of Corvettes in television and film, that the Corvette's six images, those recognizably American "faces" that the car possesses, are not unlike the images Andy Warhol and other pop artists present in their work. Like Marilyn or Elvis, the car has a distinct face and form, also — like a celebrity — it has an image and a reputation that many in the public cherish or hold dear. The *Stingray* images of the car are about the Corvette, it is true, but they are also, as the Emmy award attests, something of a "work of art," admittedly a graphic design sized and styled for the television screen. The response to them comes from us, the viewer who has been seduced.

Finally, we should look at the 2005 Corvette commercial "A Boy's Dream," directed by Guy Ritchie ("Corvette 2005"). As viewing reveals, the advertisement is presented in the form of a music video featuring the

Rolling Stones' "Jumping Jack Flash," surely a "cool" song that asserts the Corvette's dynamic energy, individualistic nature, and adventurous spirit. As one of the debut ads for the newly renovated 2005 Corvette, the ad is flashy and quick moving. The scenes of the red Corvette coupe — and we have seen red Corvettes before — soaring over the school playground, past the classroom windows as the adolescent male at the wheel waves to his classmates, and then heads into New York City, speeding along, accelerating, even flying again when he desires, are as the caption tells us, a dream, a fantasy. The schoolroom scene calls to mind the brief moment in *Geronimo's Bones* when the two half-white/American Indian boys ride past the school of the pretty white girl running away with them: they wish to be seen in the red Corvette Sting Ray — the "sight [signifier] of freedom" — want other boys and girls to look at them and dream of being who they are and having the freedom and independence that they appear to enjoy (Nasdijj 158). As said before, the Corvette is both a real automobile and a vehicle of fantasy, and the "fantasy" aspects of the Corvette's image are just as powerful as the reality of the car. The car makes promises that seem irresistible.

Perhaps most importantly, as the car becomes airborne one last time, in mid-flight the boy passes a new silver 2005 Corvette convertible headed in the opposite direction. In a slow motion instant, he makes eye contact with the cute dark-haired teenage girl piloting it, and she winks at him. What more could he, and we, ask for? All this speed and power and the promise of something more as well. Freedom, independence, and sex, too! Who could ask for more?

It should be stressed here that he is not meeting the girl in *his* fantasy or she dreaming of *him*. What the commercial means to tell us, and sell us on the idea of, is how the Corvette provides the dream, the wish fulfillment for *each* of them: the boy and the girl are meeting where Corvettes make flights of imagination possible, they are "crossing over" or transgressing into each other's dream. She, the female "other" to his masculine, phallocentric self, also possesses the ability to escape and is just as empowered as he is; what Brown calls "the congealed facts [the power of the Corvette]" and the "fantasies [that youthful and gender-defying wish for power]" make the commercial feel both enticing — speed and sex, the car and the girl — and at the same time pleasurably dangerous (4). As the desirable, mature woman giving her husband that "come-with-me" look and the pubescent girl in the flying Corvette convertible winking at the boy demonstrate for us, the Corvette is not actually a rival for man's affections. Instead, the Corvette enhances the sexuality and authority of whoever possesses it; the car becomes part of—an enabling, sexy, powerful extension of—individual identity.

As these examples illustrate, advertising and media play a major role in the promotion of the Corvette's image and the maintenance of the car's image. However, we should be aware that enthusiasm for the Corvette is not unduly based on television commercials or printed articles and photographs. The image of the car exists more in the mind of the public, in their taste for a car that presents a high standard of performance while embodying stylistic cues in a pleasing form. To say it another way, the Corvette and its image are *performative* in that the car is represented as a thing that does something to define itself; the car caters to our *habitus*, it feels our desires.

The Corvette passes gender and moves on into the realm of allowing the individual to create an identity of his or her own. The message appears to be that the Corvette is for both men and women; the car gives females the same thrill that it does males. If the action and the freedom are the same for both, then the Corvette is reaching across genders to bring them together in a place where identity is assured and independence is granted. The "A Boy's Dream" and other Corvette advertisements' purpose may, on the surface, look like the promotion of patriarchal, heteronormative masculinity, but they propel the Corvette forward in the direction of powerful females as well: it is the image of the car that dominates, not the male or female gaze. The Corvette is a "dream car," the magic carpet powered by imagination; it soars with the passion of those who aspire to its seductive image.

What we should realize by now is how advertising and art have become so intertwined that it is difficult to separate the two in modern life. "Art" as a general term seems applicable to almost anywhere the appellation will stick, and the best advertising and the most evocative art are not far apart in what they communicate to us. Pop art, in its best moments, does what the best, most "artistic" advertising does: it enhances images, uses them to convey an idea or an emotion, and leaves the viewer with an impression that lingers — words or pictures that stick in mind and are memorable. In what we see and hear in advertising media today, the ads and the pop art seem to merge: doing such similar things leads to a convergence of evolution. The Corvette and its image are significant examples of this phenomenon in action.

Chapter 19

The Art of Design:
The Fashionable Corvette

The sixth generation or C6 Corvette debuted in 2005. By many automotive journalist and enthusiast accounts, it is the best, fastest, most-refined
Corvette ever built and returns the car to where it once was, a level of styling
and performance in a single package that only the 1965–1967 Sting Rays
match or exceed. The latest Corvettes exhibit that "gut-level, visceral
appeal," "promise of speed," and "power ... [as] the end-all attraction" that
are the key, even core characteristics of the car (Healey online). Their speed,
a top end of 186 m.p.h., and power, 400 b.h.p. at 6000 r.p.m., would seem
to be enough to please all but the most extremely demanding (Webster 50).
Yet it is not just these qualities that define the Corvette in modern times.

Automotive design critic and author Robert Cumberford, who worked
as a designer on the first-generation Corvette, writes that in the years 1919–
1939 — a time of incredible stylistic experimentation and evocative designs —
automobile bodies were "more closely related to clothing" than either
architecture or sculpture (Zumbrunn 9). Auto bodies then had the cachet
of the latest fashions; on fine, expensive cars, the bodies were tailored like
chic clothing to the chassis of an elite manufacturer, such as Packard, Daim-
ler, Bugatti, or Duesenberg (10). This time did not last, but the aura of high
fashion had been added to the automobile's overall character, at least near
the pinnacle of the car market. After World War II, cars as individualized
"works of stylistic art" began to merge with the demands of mass industrial
production, and automotive styling became even more important than before
to the buying public. By the time the Corvette was conceived in the early
1950s, a sports car had to have *style*.

Power and style are substantive reasons that the Corvette endures, either
as a material object, an image, or as a work of art. In the area of "style,"

automobiles are comparable to other consumer goods; they must be attractive in the eyes of those who would purchase them. In her book *Changing Cultures* (1992), Mica Nava writes, "Consumerism is far more than just economic activity: it is also about dreams and consolation, communication and confrontation, image and identity" (167). What we have seen the Corvette do as an expression of automobility — stand for the strengths and qualities the car's owners would prefer to see in themselves — the car also does in a personal sense: it gives people a lifestyle as well. To flourish in a consumerist society, the Corvette has had to make a fashion statement, like the clothing Cumberford speaks of that reflects the taste — Pierre Bourdieu's *habitus* — of its owners. Style is a sense of art expressed as fashion; it involves the driver/wearer's ego as much as his/her pocketbook.

Writing of the fashion industry and clothing design in *Fashion, Desire and Anxiety* (2001), Rebecca Arnold claims, "The web of meanings and emotions that attaches both to products and the images that are used to entice the consumer has great impact in western culture, where identity is so often judged by appearance" (3). I would argue that both statements apply to the Corvette. The car, over the course of fifty years, has done just what Nava and Arnold describe — it has taken on a role in dreams, communication, and identity like few other products and almost no other vehicle. The automobile's role in modern society and the wealth of meanings these machines now have are perhaps more telling about us than any other device of modern technology. The Corvette is not the only car, but it is the American car that performs this role the best and to the greatest degree.

The chief designer of the sixth generation Corvette, Tom Peters, said that he thought of the C6's style or form as "a Coke bottle designed by Picasso" ("North American International Auto Show 2004"). The Coca-Cola bottle is a specific product design, sculpted for the express purpose of containing a beverage that fancies itself as the best in its field: a consumer good of the highest order. However, the attribution of it to Picasso makes it appear to be a work of art. As in the duality of aspectual and subject-matter content that John Dilworth proposes best describes the working of representational art (chapter 20, pages 213–214), we are struck with two meanings at once. The Corvette is a premium-priced but affordable commodity marketed to a wide, diverse group of global consumers, yet it also has fashionable and artistic pretensions; it aspires to be thought of as expressive of human desires and emotions while making a declaration of its own subjective identity — the design seeks to do two things at once.

If a building can be a work of architectural art and a practical home for human beings, like Frank Lloyd Wright's Fallingwater, then the Corvette should be capable of performing a similar automotive function — becoming a piece of rolling sculpture or "automotive architecture" while providing practical utility as functional transportation. In the case of the Corvette, we are not dealing with a single form, a fixed shape, but one that has evolved through six generations, taking design cues from one series and giving them new life in a contemporary form. Corvettes are a continuing line of work, a sequence of objects that all have the same subject or theme.

Art critic F. David Martin writes that sculpture involves "touch-space," real three-dimensional physical space, through "more direct associations of mass and volume" than painting does (47). Again, the idea of "associations" or contextual relationships comes to be a part of art, of the connection between the human observer/subject and the work being experienced. The Corvette, not as a single car, but as the continuation of an image, of a particular subjective identity, carries with it the connotation of success and/or power, but with a feeling of being "in touch" with one's self, of being connected with others not just through the car but by sharing an attitude and lifestyle that is reminiscent of a fashion statement. The image the Corvette carries is always embodied in its most current manifestation, the cars that are in production *now*, but the image itself is not the car, not the material object, but all the pertinent associations — many different, some contradictory — that the Corvette image has come to bear. This is what Corvette fandom comes to be devoted to, the intangible image. The car is only the host body, like the "familiar" a witch's companion spirit inhabits.

The design of the Corvette evokes a range of emotions. If we think of the car as sculpture, the mass of an automobile may create a pleasing, even startling impression. If the form it takes shapes material in a way that is pleasing to the eye and the touch, then it does approach aesthetic "art." In point of fact, the automobile is made to be touched and interacted with; its volume is one that we occupy, where we develop a sense of intimacy. The Corvette is not just a pleasing exterior, it is also an enclosing, enveloping space where we become a functional part of the mechanism. The car takes us inside, absorbing our body into its own. As a friend of mine says, "Would you get naked with this car?" Automobiles become intimate objects; touching, holding is part of their purpose, and driving can be an aesthetic as well as an erotic function. The "feel," as well as the "look" of a car, becomes important. In this sense, a car can be a work of art and a commodity at the same time. Martin writes of how sculpture "includes its material body when it is perceived," and most importantly, that "the forces of a sculpture ... activate the surrounding space" (49). The material object, then, projects itself into the space around it to make an impression, and the most stylish Corvettes, the 1963–1967 C2 Sting Rays and the latest C6 models, certainly do this well.

To carry the idea of space still further, the automobile is not just a surface, it is a truly three-dimensional space. In 1951, when Manhattan's Museum of Modern Art displayed a select group of automobiles as works of art, it referred to the cars as "hollow rolling sculpture" ("Hollow Rolling Sculpture" online). The automobiles presented — "five European and three U.S. models" — were described by the curator, Arthur Drexler, in terms of their "excellence as works of art" (online). The space around a well-designed automobile may be "activated," but so is the interior of a sufficiently artful model, the Corvette Moray and the Bertone Mantide, for example (chapter 17, page 180). Automobiles, then, can expose a human viewer to a surrounded-by-"art" experience once one enters the car. The textures and shapes of the body can be intensified or counteracted by the emotive response to the interior. The automobile adds layers of physical stimulation; a car that excites the onlooker can also offer tactile thrills when touched. A car like the Corvette, composed of sensuous external curves and surfaces, also presents an internal environment that engages the senses of anyone who looks at or sits in the car.

Art critic George S. Bolge says that painting and sculpture may combine to form "a third art form in which the work becomes primarily an 'object in space'" (55). He is not speaking of automobiles, yet the terminology is suitable. As objects that are designed to move through space while occupied and to be pleasing to the eye and touch, Corvettes are very much like works of rolling sculpture. We perceive ourselves in and around automobiles as part of our daily experience; they are part of our social environment, so we form attitudes of "style" toward them. As a "third art form," automobiles impress us, perhaps not always consciously, with a sense of style, or *taste*, which reflects our own ways of thinking and feeling.

Author and art critic Rudolf Arnheim writes that "dynamic forces issue from three-dimensional objects such as works of sculpture and spread through the surrounding space" much like Martin's "activated" space (319). These forces are "expressive vectors" that, while not normally perceived, are part of "the aesthetic attitude" a viewer must switch to in order to have an "art experience" (319). If one's aesthetic sense is activated for sculpture, and the automobile is accepted as a "work of art," then the best of automobile designs and their embodiment in material form become objects in artistic space, as Bolge would describe them. This is what happens for people who are caught up in the Corvette image as a work of art. It carries the connotations of style, power, and desire — for sexual and sensual experience or for confirmation of identity — for individuals who are attuned to automobiles as objects of beauty and are able to perceive the "expressive forces" that the image of a particular car, the American Corvette, carries with it. The image is not one that comes into being immediately; for the Corvette (and a very few other automobiles), it is the consequence of decades of perception by the public and portrayal in media of all kinds. *Route 66* remains one of the foundations of the Corvette's images and identity. Even if the series has been off the air for a half century, the image it bestowed on the Corvette has persisted, growing and becoming more complex over time.

Chapter 20

The Corvette as Art:
Examples and Theories

The idea of the Corvette itself as a "work of art" is a concept that has come increasingly popular over time. One of the most recent and obvious developments is the U.S. Postal Service's issuance in August 2005 of the "America on the Move: 50s Sporty Cars" series of stamps. Of the five cars depicted, only one is still in production — the Chevrolet Corvette. The particular Corvette honored is the original 1953 white roadster, but it is the Corvette name and image that are celebrated — like the youthful Elvis Presley, who was honored several years ago. And the Corvette lives on in more representations now than ever before. A Google search of the Internet yields over seven million results for the words "Chevrolet Corvette"; a search for the name "Corvette" gets more than 21.7 million of all kinds. The car is, like a historical figure or a contemporary celebrity, a point of interest: the "Corvette" is not just a car anymore, it is a cult figure, a well-known image.

As Michael L. Berger points out in *The Automobile in American History and Culture* (2001), the Corvette is "America's first true contemporary 'sports car' with anything approaching decent longevity," and it "began as a model and now really is a marque in its own right" (162). The sports car and "brand" identities are part of what goes to make the Corvette image a thing greater than simply the tangible car itself, and more than a machine existing as an assemblage of human-engineered and assembled parts. The Corvette may be an "it," but so are most meaningful representations of human emotions or ideas. Historian Marshall Fishwick says, "Icons do objectify [the] deep mythological structure of reality, revealing basic needs which go from age to age, media to media, generation to generation" (qtd. in Scott 209). Bill Brown writes that Karl Marx makes a "repeated point" that "the personification of things and reification ... of persons" leads to a world where "sensuous things appear social, enjoying a relation to one another irrespective of any human relation" (114). If the Corvette is often "personified," then it is enmeshed in a web of relationships with the six different generations of itself and with the people — real and fictional — who have become involved with it. As an object, it has acquired an autonomy and potency that makes it a successful commodity and an "icon" in the way that its image is used. And scholarly research by Michele Motichka and Phillip J. Scott has indicated that the Corvette — like famous objects such as creative works — has an "identity" all its own (chapter 3, pages 31–34).

If the Corvette is not an "icon" in that its image has come to have an existence above and beyond the material object itself, then why has the car's "image" taken on such a life of its own? If we search "Corvette image," the Google search engine comes up with 5.7 million references; not all of these may be the automobile known as the Corvette, but the name does seem to have strong recognition as a "brand" or an image, much like famous people. In comparison, a celebrity such as "The King," Elvis, gets 19.7 million results, Madonna 66.8, and Barack Obama — the current president — 71.5 (online search conducted 15 January 2010). If "image" is any measure of fame or influence, then late entertainer Michael Jackson is the most outstanding with 125 million results to be found. In terms of cars, Porsche's 911 series — a rival in the sports car field noted for its performance and expensive, refined nature — gets similar numbers to the Corvette, and the 911 family appeals to a narrower, more elitist, more affluent market segment than the Corvette, as the Jaguar XKE did in its day. It seems that the Corvette image is both a part of the car and an extension of it. We recognize the image of past Corvettes in the present machine, yet what Brown called the "metaphysical" part of the car is also instrumental in drawing attention to it, and this helps keep its image alive in both the past and present models: the machine is more than a material object, it exists in relationship to the humans who know its name and reputation. It may, in the best and most suitable circumstances, be a "work of art."

In describing the attraction the Corvette has for people, particularly those interested in art or in cars as works of art, professional watercolorist Dana Forrester — the owner of four Corvettes, a 1965 Sting Ray, a 1994 Callaway, a 1998 Indy Pace Car, and a 2003 Z06 — reminds us that "art" means "different things to different people" (interview). Speaking for himself, Forrester says the Corvette, in the form of the 1963–1967 Sting Rays, first caught his eye because of its physical form (interview). While others might have seen the Corvette's "artistic merit" in the thrill of driving one or the power of the machine, it was the shape of these "mid-year" cars — what enthusiasts often describe as the most outstanding Corvette design — that most intrigued him. According to his website, he first painted the car in 1989, and "always loved Corvettes in general, but the lines of the Sting Ray coupe made the car seem like sculpture as well as a sports car" (Forrester). As one of the few painters to be elected to membership in both the American and the National Watercolor Societies, Forrester began by composing portraits of "brick buildings and advertising art, studying related areas of plate glass window reflections, neon signs, and commercial waterfronts," specializing in what one "aficionado" calls "vestige billboards" (Forrester "The World of" 4, and Troesser).

While the popularity of the Corvette made it attractive as a potential subject, and automobiles in general intrigued him, Forrester's art took him into other areas: images of commercial advertising on older buildings, watercolor portraits of images fast disappearing from the American landscape (interview). While this interest in the popular and the commercial seemed to suggest pop art as a profession — according to how that field is defined — Forrester's established fondness for the Corvette drew him back, and automobiles, the Corvette as a special subject, came later. Sting Rays and other Corvettes "crept into" his work after his attention returned to cars after becoming an established watercolor artist. This renewed interest in the Corvette gave him "a new direction," which eventually led to designing a special option and appearance package called "the Milestone Corvette" for the 2003 and 2004 model years (interview).

Forrester is a successful and recognized commercial artist, a graduate of Truman State University in art education. As a graduate workshop instructor, guest lecturer, and artist in residence, he has taught others the process and the techniques of watercolor painting. He is also author of *Against the Wall: The Architectural and Automotive Art of Dana Forrester* (2003) and did the illustrations for automotive executive Jim Wangers' memoir, *Glory Days: When Horsepower and Passion Ruled Detroit* (1998). Among his honors are the President's Award from the National Corvette Restorers Society (NCRS), the Strathmore Paper and William Church Osborne Awards from both the American and the National Watercolor Societies, and many more. His original work has been exhibited at the National Corvette Museum in Bowling Green, Kentucky; the Butler Institute of American Art; the Rochester Art Center in Rochester, Minnesota; as well as the Alabama, Louisiana, and Southern Watercolor Society Exhibitions, among others. His lithographs are also found in private collections, such as the Yellow

Freight Collection, Wichita Art Museum, the Butler Museum and Institute of American Art, the Hallmark Cards Collection, and the Bloomington Gold Collection ("Dana Forrester").

While Forrester is widely known for his work on Corvettes and other automobiles, his initial intent was not automotive in nature; the architectural renderings came first. He desired to "combine design-oriented composition ... [with] an extremely detailed technique" to produce distinctive works ("Dana Forrester" Pacific Car Art). Forrester's paintings are representations of objects in settings created or styled to put forward his ideas and impressions. Although his style might be considered modern, the content of his pictures has elements of postmodern style in his assemblage of images that reflect and comment upon one another. In Forrester's own view, his work "is a study in realism with abstract composition, not a study of a nostalgic subject" (Pacific Car Art). The positions of the cars, the majority of them Corvettes, and other objects suggest meaning and imply ideas about both the vehicle(s) in the foreground and the surrounding environment; through this, a tension or emphasis is created in the paintings.

As to the cars he depicts in his work, Forrester believes that the Corvette's popularity accounts for much of the demand for his paintings (interview). *Route 66* gave the Corvette a "romantic" appeal and established the car as a different kind of vehicle in the minds of the public. Additionally, car enthusiasts find "great meaning" in owning a high performance automobile that also affords them a high measure of luxury and convenience; the Corvette makes a "statement of personality" and conveys a sense of "style" to most Americans (interview). Forrester points out that many of what others have called "the Corvette faithful" hold the car — not a particular year or model, but its image and lineage in general — in "reverence," suggesting both affection and respect. The persistent image of the car comes from all of these factors; the Corvette, like the word "art," means different — but significant — things to different people.

One particular Forrester lithograph, *Concrete Heaven*, which appears on the cover of this book, depicts a red '67 Sting Ray convertible parked in front of a Ted Drewes' Frozen Custard stand on a Missouri section of Route 66 (Forrester). The car is a 427 big block with chrome side exhausts, black sport stripe, and Red Line tires on aluminum wheels. Ted Drewes' is a chain of frozen custard stands in the St. Louis area, where Corvettes were initially built, and of course, Route 66 is the transcontinental highway that gave its name to the television series. The work, then, has a number of meanings; it is an image of a particular car in a specific place, on a road

Accomplished watercolor artist and Corvette enthusiast Dana Forrester paints scenes of our American culture: buildings, walls, and public places that capture the national spirit of freedom and enjoyment of life. Among his favorite subjects are Corvettes, all six generations: exquisitely rendered automobiles in settings that create a context of meaningful images. Of these, one of the best is *Concrete Heaven*, a red 1967 427 convertible posed on Route 66 in St. Louis (Dana Forrester).

with special significance, yet it is also that "sensuous thing" that Marx referred to, a powerful automobile on a "mythological" road that invites dreams of romance. "Concrete Heaven" is a special dish of frozen custard, but also refers to the Route 66 highway, or the experience of driving what is one of the most desirable Corvettes down the road. The image of the Sting Ray, the "Coolest Car," is juxtaposed with other images of local and national culture to create an overall depiction of American popular culture.* Forrester's work centers on the Corvette and creates a web of connections between it and its environment: the Corvette never exists in isolation; the nature of the car calls forth a context of its own — this is that "aura" of identity that gives the car its distinctive image and power to signify.

In 1990, according to reporter Josh Dean in the May 9, 2005, *New York*

---

*A number of Forrester's works are collected in his book, *Against the Wall: The Architectural and Automotive Art of Dana Forrester* (2003). Several of his Corvette lithographs are on display, and for sale, at the National Corvette Museum. More are available through his website.

Magazine, "pop artist" Peter Max bought a collection of thirty-six Corvettes — one from each model year from 1953 through 1989 — all at once for just under $500,000 (online). These cars had been part of a contest sponsored by cable television channel VH-1, and the winner received not one, but all of them (Dean online). Max's intent was to paint the cars as works of rolling art, the "Peter Max Corvettes." As of early 2010, the cars were still waiting, sitting unused and uncared for in a basement garage in Prospect Heights, Brooklyn. Reportedly, the comment, "No one loves these 'Vettes'" has been written in the dust that coats one of the three dozen seemingly orphaned cars. Why is this so, if the Corvette image is so well known and the cars represent potential works by a recognized and successful popular artist?

The primary reason may come from Max himself. As he has said, "I'm not a car guy. I never drive" (Dean online). Although he had initial enthusiasm for the project — thirty-six cars painted all colors of the rainbow, "the biggest PR [public relations] dream I've ever had" — Max's lack of love for the Corvettes kept the idea from execution (Dean). In the sense of appreciating automobiles as things of interest, even objects of beauty, the Corvette image never touched Max the way it has others. He does not partake in the consumption of its image sufficiently to make the transition from the car itself to the Corvette image as art that the sensibilities of other artists — often "car guys" with a passion for motor vehicles — allow them to make. This points to the idea of the *habitus*, the inborn or culturally developed interest in an object or subject.

Writing in his work of sociological theory and research *Distinction: A Social Critique of the Judgement of Taste*, French sociologist Pierre Bourdieu says that "judgement never gives the image of the object autonomy with respect to the object of the image" (42). As I interpret this statement, we cannot separate the image of a material object, in this case the Corvette, from the viewer, the person who looks at and responds to what the Corvette name (the signifier) and the associated meanings (the signified) carry with them. The Corvette image may or may not be a work of art, depending on how an individual views it and on the context in which the car is placed. Bourdieu goes on to say, "Objects, even industrial products, are not objective in the ordinary sense of the word, i.e., independent of the interest and tastes of those who perceive them, and they do not impose the self-evidence of a universal unanimously approved meaning" (100). The stylistic or artistic status of the Corvette, image or automobile, will then depend on the *habitus*, the complex totality of an individual's thinking and responding, his or her consciousness and unconscious mind. To appreciate an automobile as art, to see a car as embodying real *style*, one must think of it as an object of aesthetic value.

Another Corvette artist is Norwegian Idar Andorsen. Although, like Dana Forrester, he paints other subjects, Andorsen admits to a special affection for Corvettes and began producing Corvette and other automotive art in 1993 (LaEnvi 34–35). In an interview with Michael LaEnvi, Andorsen says, "Corvettes and other classic cars are one of my greatest interests[,] and I'm a member of the 'Corvette Club Norway'" (34). His website features no less than twenty-two different images of Corvettes, six of them 1963–1967 Sting Rays and seven 1968–1979 C3s (Andorsen). On his homepage Andorsen writes, "In my main [mind] the Corvette is not only a sports car, it is also an artwork. I think that is what inspiring [inspires] me to create new artworks — oil paintings where the original artwork is the motive." From what the website shows, many of these are "portraits" in the classic sense, carefully posed paintings of individual subjects, not mass-produced works for a general public. The paintings create images of the Corvette that add an ethereal quality to the actual cars; they are idolized, if not idealized — much like the appearance of the Corvette in the television series *Stingray* (chapter 18, pages 195–196). Andorsen's Corvettes have a glamorous, idyllic "look" to them, like soft-focus photographs or landscapes of unworldly beauty. They are the "magical" or "superlative" objects that Barthes describes (chapter 16, page 172–173), and the artist and the viewer's attention wish to linger upon them.

Andorsen's preferred medium is oil paint on canvas, and his works reflect "America's most classic bodies of automotive design" (LaEnvi 34). Unlike Forrester, Andorsen says he has "no formal art education"; he began painting in 1971, and since then his work has focused on boats, houses, and nature scenes (34). But his passion is cars, Corvettes in particular. It is perhaps telling to compare commercial artist Idar Andorsen and pop artist and entrepreneur Peter Max: the one self-taught in his approach to art, but moved by a desire to create and a love for his favorite subject, Corvette automobiles, and the other, much more successful, even rich and famous, who can afford to spend almost $500,000 on thirty-six Corvettes yet lacks the emotion to care for the cars and has come to feel little potential thrill in working with them, "transforming" the Corvettes into works of art. What is the difference in the one, Andorsen, who feels a devotion to "two of the passions in my life," and Max, who says, "I'm not a car guy" (LaEnvi 36 and Dean online)?

When Pierre Bourdieu says that "objects ... are not objective," he implicitly states the subjective nature of taste (100). The signifying value of objects is not "independent of the interest and tastes of those who perceive them," and neither Corvettes, nor any other material object, possess "a universal unanimously approved meaning" (100). With Andorsen and Max as examples, we can see the truth of Bourdieu's judgment. Even in the field of art, among what we might acknowledge as "cultivated" or at least intensely interested individual minds, there is little predicting what will or will not be perceived in a given way. Signification — the domain where sign, signifier, and signified meet — is not an absolute realm; automobiles, or their images, may have artistic value and be powerful signifiers to those who have the ability or taste to sense them as such, but not everyone will. While I make a sound case for the Corvette and its image as having artistic merit, I cannot definitively prove it so; I am counting on my own *habitus* and that of my audience to permit the perception to occur. Andorsen and Max have different perspectives; while I agree with the position and taste of one, I must recognize the indifference or neutrality of the other. The Corvette could be art if our thinking grants it permission and the evidence can be found sufficiently convincing. The thinking and perceiving of the individual are the final determining factors.

How an artist positions an object and the selection of its surroundings, not just the material items but the suggested and implied *associations*— to use feminist technology studies author Wendy Faulkner's term — is perhaps the key element in the creation of the automobile as "art" (online 2). By careful choice of place and related images, the material object's image — the Corvette automobile or some other "thing"— is granted the context that creates meaning, and "meaning" through context is an essential component of representational art. While the lines of a Corvette or other sports car, the pleasing shape, the suggestion of power and speed of the machine — as the Italian Futurists stressed — are all important, the structuring of a context for a "thing" that is a popular commodity seems to be the crucial determiner of artistic status. The Corvette image offers sufficient associations and cultural/historic complexity to make it a suitable subject for artistic depiction. As a "thing," the Corvette has enough cultural capital to be meaningful. When Barthes said that we "consume an image," he was speaking of how we see the Corvette: even those who are not automotive enthusiasts, who are not in thrall to a powerful engine or the rush of speed, know what a Corvette is and have at least some faint inkling of the freedom and independence — not to mention the sexuality — that the car has come to signify.

One objection, perhaps the principal one, to the "Corvette as Art" hypothesis would be the car's own success and the million plus "copies" and variations that now exist. The number of Corvettes produced and the long life span of the car have, to a degree, diluted any significance or exclusivity that the car might have ever possessed. It is, to some perceptions, simply too much of a commodity to demonstrate an "artistic" aspect. Most Corvettes, as marketable items in a consumer culture, do have the "inherent value" that Wollheim specified (chapter 16, page 174) as a negative characteristic that works against work of art status; indeed, it is an object's status as a manufactured good, a commodity that can simply be purchased with money, that may raise objections to it being considered a suitable artistic subject. Exceptional, unique, or very limited series works are most likely to be taken as art in the real, serious sense of the word. For just any object, a large number of copies are simple reproductions of a not-so-special image: they are not necessarily "art" in any sense of the word. As Walter Benjamin writes in "The Work of Art in the Age of Mechanical Reproduction" (1936), the "quality of the presence"—perhaps not unlike what R. D. Laing also used *presence* to signify in a psychological sense (chapter 12, page 128)—of the work of art is "always depreciated" when mechanical reproduction makes possible numerous and ready copies. Benjamin says,

> In the case of the art object, a most sensitive nucleus—namely its authenticity—is interfered with.... The authenticity of the thing is the essence of all that is transmissible from its beginning, ranging from its substantive duration to its testimony to the history which it has experienced.... What is really jeopardized ... is the authority of the object [online].

Without a doubt, the Corvette name and image seem vulnerable to this criticism, despite their longevity and the widespread appropriation of both in popular media and creative works.

Yet given the Corvette's rather "limited series" production when set against the total number of automobiles of all kinds that populate — or some might say threaten — the world today, it does resemble the signed and numbered copies of a photograph or print that artists such as Dana Forrester sell to a selective public. While "the authority" of the Corvette as a material object may be compromised by the sheer number of reproductions available, the Corvette image — even as an emblem of masculine aggression, female assertiveness, and passionate sexuality — appears to demonstrate an ongoing authority that is not so easily affected. The Corvette itself and the car's image seem to exist in an in-between, twilight, or even transgressive area of automotive culture: the car has both fame and a history, yet its total production is much less than other significant vehicles, such as the Ford Model T or the original Volkswagen Beetle. The various models, styles, and generations of the Corvette are significantly different and diverse in their power, efficiency, and technology ... enough so to be completely different cars. However, they all share a Corvette-ness, a carefully crafted identity. This is not a gendered, human selfhood, but the "identity" of an object that is inseparable from its image, as a famous work is known for being what it is, not just the qualities it possesses. For instance, if we think of Leonardo da Vinci's *La Gioconda*, the famous *Mona Lisa*, we also may call to mind *L.H.O.O.Q.*, a homophone in French for "she has a hot ass," Marcel Duchamp's moustache-and-goatee-wearing imitation; the object and its image have such strong identification that we cannot fail to make connections and associations. This "personhood of objects" for the Corvette came about in part through the advertising and publicity efforts of General Motors, the car's parent and creator, at the time the largest and most powerful corporation on Earth, and from an enthusiast public, but it was the car itself and the image it acquired and developed that perpetuated the Corvette's name and identity. The Corvette has survived and prospered because of how it appeals to the desires of American automobile lovers, how people buy into the material object and its image.

More theoretically but relatedly, John Dilworth, in his essay "A Double Content Theory of Artistic Representation," from *The Journal of Aesthetics and Art Criticism* (2005), presents a dualistic idea of how real works of art, those with true artistic merit, possess and demonstrate two levels of representation. On the surface, to the discerning eye, a representational work — the image of a tangible object — presents an obvious "aspectual" content, with "expressive, stylistic, medium-related, formal, and intentional factors," but these alone are not sufficient to account for the quality of "specifically *artistic*" artworks (Dilworth 249). As Forrester's *Concrete Heaven* is immediately perceived to be about the 1967 427 Sting Ray, an audience with an appreciation of and affection for Corvettes would at first focus *here*, perhaps dwelling on the "expressive" qualities of the car while not seeing the "subject-matter" content, the broader context of the work. Dilworth contends that "artistic meaning outruns any standard view of representational content"; like the woman in the "Day She Flew the Coupe" advertisement cited earlier (chapter 18, pages 190–191), this red Sting Ray is posed in a meaningful setting that carefully positions lesser objects to create a wider overall subject-matter content (249). This content requires "a higher level interpretation or decoding during the perceptual process" that is characteristic of what

Wollheim and others intuitively think of as the "twofoldedness" of the perception of artworks (249 and 250). The material object Corvette, or at least its image, may assume an artistic role if its context is appropriate and well crafted.

For the work entitled *Concrete Heaven*, the subject content is not just the stylish, powerful Corvette Sting Ray, but the "coolness" of the location and the delectability of the frozen dessert; the romantic associations and possibilities of Route 66; the subtle American red, white, and blue colors that point to the Corvette and stress the nature and origin of the car. Overall, the subject-matter content of a work of art is complex and not always quickly arrived at without knowledge of the particular subject and experience in interpreting a given style or set of artistic values. The "simultaneous perception of both kinds of content," aspectual and subject-matter, opens new ways of seeing (Dilworth 250). This "double content" perception, if we utilize it properly, may allow for what Richard Wollheim calls "the enrichment of the context" both of art and our awareness of how things may be perceived as works of art (Wollheim 152). And this, I believe, is much like the approach we have followed here in tracing the reasons for the Corvette's continued existence and popularity.

According to Dilworth, "The stylistic content itself provides only an encoded form of information about the relevant subject matter" (252). If we look at the Corvette correctly, we should now be able see much of its aspectual content, as discussed thus far, and be working toward that "higher-level" subject content, which is harder to achieve but may give us a more complete sense of why the object and its image have both flourished and lasted so long. What we have done over these chapters is to break some of the "encoding" of a signifying object, and along the way gain some insight into how that particular device, the Corvette, works as a signifier of so many diverse ideas that call for criticism. In a number of creative works, we have seen examples of a strong, desirable expressiveness and the use of the Corvette's image to evoke and enhance both meaning and ideas. Looking at the Corvette as art, as an object *and* an image, has enabled us to look back over what we have covered and tie much of it together.

Summary

In a 1977 interview, author/critic/intellectual Susan Sontag said, "Among other things, art is an instrument of pleasure — and one doesn't have *that* much pleasure in life" (Sontag 7). While we may analyze the appeal of the Corvette and argue the position it and its image have in relation to art, there is no denying that the Corvette gives pleasure to many human beings. Some own and drive it, others depict it in words or pictures, but all of them receive pleasure of various kinds from, as Barthes would remind us, "consuming" it. The question of the Corvette as art has not been settled here, but we do know that automobiles are serious subjects of real works of art.

Although it makes no direct statement about the Corvette's nature as art, there does exist a serious, critical organization that takes a position on the automobile and art. The Automotive Fine Arts Society (AFAS, website: www.autoartgallery.com/afas) sponsors exhibits and sales of automotive art; its two big events — held at the Pebble Beach, California, and the Amelia Island, Florida, concours events — are well-attended, upper-crust affairs where people of means and cultivated automotive tastes gather to exhibit their possessions, the cars that give them pleasure (Wilson). While, as *Autoweek* magazine editor Kevin Wilson writes, membership in this society is relatively small and elite, only thirty artists, the range of art itself includes paintings and sculpture of diverse forms. And non–AFAS artists also work with cars as art; any search of the Internet turns up Corvette "art" amid a wealth of automotive works of all kinds, some critically rewarding and many more that are pleasurable sources of affordable fun, but not serious collecting.

All the images that the Corvette brings together — not just the car itself but its many representations and depictions — make it an exceptional instance of how mass, popular, and high culture combine in a consumer-driven society. Meanings are created intentionally, through advertising, for example, yet the society and people generate interpretations through songs, television series, and films that amplify and even transcend what may be intended. The comprehensive image of an object or person changes over time, and its potential impact and acceptance as possessing artistic merit may do the same. Elvis postage stamps and Andy Warhol prints of Marilyn Monroe can be art that both evokes and plays with the image as signifier and the identity as signified. Images of a given automobile can function in a like manner; their form refers to the vehicle itself, yet their meaning or sign is part of a complex association. The Corvette image is an icon of the American automobile and a reflection of American culture; like that culture, the image is sometimes imperfect and yet in other instances artistic.

Images of the automobile, most especially the Corvette, may be high culture to an audience of automotive enthusiasts because of its power to suggest meanings that — to borrow Sontag's idea about pleasure — answer needs of individual psyches and desires in people's hearts. The cars themselves may come and go; however, their images are mutable but not mortal. High culture status may be fleeting in our present time when status itself is fluid and "culture" becomes more and more difficult to define as it evolves in a multitude of forms, some of them new and never seen before. Nevertheless, like the images of famous celebrities and prized works of art that are now icons beyond themselves, the Corvette will most likely be with us for a long time: its ability to reflect and express what we project onto and into it persists. As Marsh and Collett stress in *Driving Passion*, the expressiveness of an image may exceed and outlive the tangible objects that give rise to it. Human needs determine artistic status; and art, except in its most extreme conceptual forms, is a product of both the intellect and emotions, just like sports cars. Some of us have a *habitus* for cars that attract our attention: the Corvette is one of them.

Yet the images of six generations that the Corvette encompasses do not work in a static formulation. The history of the car has been dynamic and continues to be. The associations of the name "Corvette" and how the "real car" carries an aura of seductive power are now inseparable. Identity, sexual desirability, horsepower, and the suggestion of thrills and excitement are all caught up in an image developed over half a century. Automotive historian Michael Lamm writes that "timeless designs look as beautiful and fresh today as they did when new" (Thompson 13). If art offers us designs that are "timeless," then maybe our question should be *not* "is the Corvette art?" *but* "what about this car and its image is beautiful enough to last and remain beautiful?" In his survey of six successful automobile designers — "renowned" graduates of the Art Center, a prestigious college of automotive design — Lamm discovered that the 1963–1967 Corvette Sting Ray was the only American car selected that fulfilled the criteria of "timeless" and lasting beauty (13). In time, perhaps another American car will be included in a new version of the same list. Most likely, it will be another Corvette.

Conclusion: The Corvette, Image and Object

A material object has a physical existence, yet we may all too quickly accept objects as merely things — items with little, if any, significance beyond our momentary use or attention paid to them. However, when a "thing" acquires some significance, or when it reoccurs often enough, it may break through our conscious glossing over of the material world and begin to be appreciated for all the meanings and associations it possesses. This is not exactly what has happened during the writing of this study. No sudden insights were gained. Rather than realize that an automobile is a signifier all at once, I came to the idea slowly. The Corvette seemed to be an interesting object — cars interest me, as do literature, film, and a host of other things. But the Corvette has come to feel like a *textual* subject: as a material object, it is utilized in a wide range of media and presents an attractive physical being, but — as it has slowly occurred to me — the car is more than a tangible thing, its image is much more than the automobile itself, and this goes beyond just being a cool, fast, car that I wish I could afford to own and drive. The Corvette, and many other objects of similar rich, densely nuanced background, respond to critical analysis and the application of theory, yielding ideas and impressions that touch on a number of areas.

Where we began with images of the Corvette, a material object that suggests a sense of power, potency, and sexuality, we end up at much the same place. Coincidental to be sure, but less so than one should suspect. The Corvette has been transformed over the course of a half century into a protean form; it touches desires common to both men and women and raises issues of masculinity, female identity, and the nature of patriarchal authority. What we have tried to look at more closely is how the Corvette image has really empowered women just as much as men, except that the signs of this have been less plentiful for women and have taken time to evolve. *Route 66* (1960–1965) gave us the seemingly appropriate union of men, machine, and automobility that suggests the homosocial, phallogocentric view of humanity that is perpetuated in *The Right Stuff* (1979). Yet if we recall how in *Play It as It Lays* (1970) Maria Wyeth made a satisfying, empowering diagonal move across traffic and Prince's "Little Red Corvette" (1982) lady parked in a way that claimed her own space, we should see how the Corvette has opened an area for itself where gender matters less and taking charge of the moment, as the woman in Hildebrandt's *Yellow Rose of Texas* painting has done, is of more importance to the Corvette owner and driver than the identity the outside world presumes.

To me, with my interest in automobiles and mechanical things, and my years of looking at and educating myself about them, the Corvette image and the physical car *do* represent a work of artistic creation in the case of several Corvettes but not all. For another person, a car may just be a car, no one automobile that much more than the other, and his or her taste in "art" will not allow certain objects to be considered. Thusly, I argue that for myself—in keeping with Bourdieu's *habitus*—some automobiles are works of art, yet this does not hold true for other people. If the 1963–1967 Corvette Sting Rays are not objects of beauty, their images stylish and pleasing, then the onlooker's understanding and experience do not grant the perception. Yet I would have to add, if one examines objects and images closely, over time an appreciation may come into being, and what those with more practiced eyes are able to discern may be clear at last.

The Corvette possesses an expressive quality for some people, much as a song, a poem, a painting, or a photograph might for someone else. It is not the physical car so much, although the material and sensual nature of the car is part of it, as it is the image of the car that is present in the plastic and steel. The fact that automobiles are made to be touched and cared for — intimate relationships can form in those private moments — makes them different from other machines. At least for some of us, automobile/human relationships are passionate and long lasting. Corvettes are special cases, machines with a history and a provenance lacking in lesser vehicles.

Writing of the "Machine Aesthetic" of the early twentieth century, architectural critic and author Reyner Banham describes a movement to see aesthetic ideas in machines, one special case being the automobile, and the struggle of engineering and architecture to discover the beauty and/or elegance of mechanisms designed to achieve motion and carry human passengers (44–47). In American literature after 1900 — Lewis' *Free Air* (1919), for instance — we see the automobile emerge, not merely as a curiosity or expensive toy of the well to do but as practical, affordable transportation for the mass of Americans. By the Dust Bowl Era and the Great Depression, cars had become what they represent for the Joads in Steinbeck's *The Grapes of Wrath* (1939), an essential part of the family, one upon which their continued survival depends. In the postwar years and afterward, the automobile was the preferred mode of transportation for the bulk of America; as Kerouac depicts it in *On the Road* (1957), the road *is* life and automotive travel is the truest means of discovering oneself as an individual with a mind, heart, and soul.

The opening page of *Cars: Freedom, Style, Sex, Power, Motion, Colour, Everything* (2008) states that "the car is the most cherished and admired of all contemporary objects, and car design is one of the distinctive, even defining, art forms of the twenty-first century" (n. pag.). As British design and culture critic Stephen Bayley writes, "Great cars [those described in *Cars*] are, with pop and the media, our age's singular contribution to cultural history"; "Nothing ... has more passion, expertise and cunning put into its design. This is a book about cars as purely magical objects" (11). Bayley paraphrases Barthes' comments about automobiles, but it is true that cars are remarkable creations, if not in fact, then in how they have come to be the icons and signifiers of so much of our contemporary technology and culture. In Part I, we looked at material objects and cultural criticism and found that automobiles demonstrate a wealth of associations and interpretations that no other objects in our time quite match. In the Corvette we find not the only, but the best and most American of these superlative creations: no other car has been incarnated six — soon to be seven — times and put in so many appearances in creative and cultural works of all kinds, novels, films, songs. No other name has fifty years of history to draw upon; while other "brands" or "marques" have similar longevity, none of them is a single model bearing one name for all its history — not even Ferrari or Porsche have a car with so much time to acquire the power to signify.

The question I began with was why this car, among so many, has persisted as a name and an image. If we do not have an answer by now, we do have certain clear reasons. First, the Corvette has become, from a not-too-promising start, a successful product in a market that stresses competition and survival of— if not the fittest — then those with the most personality and appeal to an often fickle buying public. The Corvette is General Motors and Chevrolet's "halo car," the one name and model that sets a standard for performance, style, technology, or whatever the market may demand. A large portion of the Corvette's success is due to the identity the car has, its status as a celebrity in the automotive world: it has a notoriety and fame that exceeds the million and a half examples that exist. This is the second reason it persists.

The Corvette came into being with a distinctively American style — small tailfins, chrome trim, an aggressively toothed grill — mixed with European sports car characteristics. More than that, starting with the addition of the V-8 engine in 1955, it took on the mantle of America's fastest, most powerful automobile, a claim the Corvette has seldom, if ever, relinquished. As it developed poise and power, the Corvette found what Bayley calls "the essence of a brand," that is to say, the car took on its *identity* (30). Or, as French philosopher Gilbert Simondon writes in *Du Mode d'Existence des Objets Techniques* (On the Mode of Existence of Technical Objects) (1958), "Artifacts evolve using themselves as the point of departure: they contain the conditions for their own future development. The structure of the object moves to match the future conditions in which it will be employed" (qtd. in Bayley 30). Where other automobiles, some with outstanding style or impressive power, eventually stagnated and were dropped from the public mind and mass production, the Corvette followed the strict Darwinian demands of the marketplace and continually evolved, yet it never ceased being what it always has been, a material object and image defined by the name Corvette.

When Tom Wolfe described the culture of the automobile among young 1960s Americans in *The Kandy-Kolored Tangerine-Flake Streamline Baby* (1964), he wrote, "I don't have to dwell on the point that cars mean more to these kids than architecture did in Europe's great formal century, say 1750 to 1850. They are freedom, style, sex, power, motion, color — everything is right there" (78). From what we have seen, this sounds like an expression of the patriarchal nature of American society at that time. Power was, for many Americans, derived from the apparent success of their social systems and their technology, and the automobile represented both. As we know, "the righteous stuff" astronauts were, in the majority, Corvette enthusiasts; the technology, the speed and power of the cars, were a statement of confidence in the American way of doing things. That it was predominantly a masculine way of looking at the world, through the antagonisms of the Cold War, seemed natural at the time. As the sixties and seventies wore on, as the Space Race — in Wolfe's *The Right Stuff* (1979) — and the Vietnam War — in Mason's *In Country* (1985) — and demands of a changing social order called into doubt the precepts of unquestioned masculinist ways of thinking, the automobile itself became an object of criticism.

Although the Corvette reached what may be the peak of its power and style in the Sting Rays of 1963–1967, the masculine persona of the car remained a performative thing, a social construct, and women — along with men of minority background and alternative ways of thinking — appropriated the Corvette for their own purposes, letting it signify *their* power and assert a different, more individual *identity*. The car's image changed with the times, giving people what they wanted or needed. As a signifier, the Corvette is consistent — representing power and style — but fluid, taking on new associations as it moves through time and culture changes. Physically, the Corvette design adapts to the demands of the automotive market; in its image, small changes occur over time, not altering the car's essential nature, but adding to it, evoking new, sometimes subtle qualities. The Corvette always suggests sex, but it speaks of technology as well: no longer does the Corvette exist as an object with a single focus, in the present moment, its image possesses depth, even complexity.

The Corvette stays the same, but its signifying value — its *power*— has become more open to interpretation; the car and its image have been embraced by "others" in American society. As Maria discovers in *Play It as It Lays* (1970), her Corvette is the best, most powerful extension of herself that she has available. Although her life is constrained and, at least on the surface, controlled by males and their institutions, she does have the power to achieve some measure of authority over herself, but the Corvette is where it happens first. For women and men whose access to power is limited or directed into vain or self-destructive courses, taking the wheel of a car that signifies power or affluence, such as a Corvette, is a tangible source of empowerment. On film, African American males achieve success and reward themselves with Corvettes or similar machines. In 1929, the French designer and critic Le Corbusier noted the need to fortify one's self through an automobile: "Cars, cars, fast, fast! One is seized, filled with enthusiasm, with joy ... the joy of power. The simple and naïve pleasure of being in the midst of power, of strength" (qtd. in Bayley 12). This pleasure through power, the embrace of the Corvette to signify authority, is another reason for the Corvette's continued success and popularity: the car feeds our egos and makes us feel that rarest of experiences — as Sontag called it: *pleasure*— through the experience of power at our command, even if the Corvette is only ours in the imagination.

If the arguments for the Corvette and its image on the basis of automobility and its manifestations through literature and film are not convincing, then the case for the car as art will appear less so, at least to someone who is not an automotive enthusiast. Bayley writes that the subject of car as art, while not impossible, remains "elusive" (11). Others are more certain: designer, critic, and journalist Robert Cumberford states unequivocally that "many cars, although certainly not all, are works of art in the purest sense, representing perhaps the defining physical art of the past hundred years" (Zumbrunn 8). We also know that cars have been, and are now, exhibited as works of art; in fact, "the first production car in New York's Museum of Modern Art" is the Corvette's chief European rival (as in Jan and Dean's "Dead Man's Curve")—and a design similar in form, if not in philosophy, to the Sting Ray—the 1961 E-Type (XKE) Jaguar, a "sublime work of art," according to Stephen Bayley (210).

Co-founder of the Gateway Colorado Automobile Museum, car collector, and creator of the Discovery Channel John S. Hendricks says that his "sense of the aesthetic was abruptly awakened by the glistening curves of the 1958 Corvette that literally roared into my life" (Stein 7). Hendricks believes that the cars in his collection "represent America's century-long quest for 'performing art' in vehicles that allow us to undertake our personal journeys of discovery," which returns us thematically to *Free Air, The Grapes of Wrath*, and *On the Road,* if not *Play It as It Lays* and *In Country* (9). The Corvette is not found in every, or perhaps even many works of literary or visual art, but the theme of automobility that the Corvette embodies more than any other automobile now with us is so distinctly American that the Corvette's image is inseparably bound to those national ideals of freedom and mobility that are part of American art.

In *Driving Passion* (1986) Marsh and Collette showed me the primacy of the "expressive function" in the persistence of the Corvette. While they do not pursue it as a particular and excellent example, the ability of the Corvette to express and to be looked on as expressing the emotions of—as Barthes would say—"those who consume its image" was one of the significant discoveries that I made: I knew it all along but was not critically aware of the idea's real power until I read it elsewhere. The power of the automobile—Corvette automobiles more than the rest—to express ideas is, as Marsh and Collette say, just as much a reason for their existence as their value as transportation, and in the future may be their unique and special function. Mills' *The Road and the Rebel* (2006) confirmed my ideas about automobility and broke it down into autonomy and mobility, useful distinctions I have capitalized on in these pages. Still, if I have not made the case sufficiently yet, I contend that part of the Corvette's special virtue is how this one line of cars has come to stand, more than any other, for the freedom and independence that automobility has given us for over a century.

In *The American Design Adventure* (1988), Arthur J. Pulos quotes an unknown American author: "We are born in haste ... we make a fortune at a stroke, and lose it in the same manner ... in the twinkling of an eye. Our body is a locomotive ... our soul, a high-pressure engine ... and death overtakes us like a flash of lightning" (394). Although this was written in 1839, the images it creates call to mind the speed of our contemporary world, and the references to "engine" and "overtake" make me think of a fast car, not a steam locomotive. If I separated the essence of the Corvette too far from its speed, how fast the car can go, then that was an error. A Corvette is a Corvette in its urgent need to go fast. The cars convey a sense of life in their speed; they are dynamic — limited in time and space to be sure — yet the Corvette expresses a fundamental truth in the name's evocation and the car's image of *speed*. In writing about his philosophy of automobile design, Harley Earl, GM's first head of Art and Color, which became the Styling Section, says that his goal is to create "a vehicle with its own character, purpose[,] and individuality" (Earl 18). The 1953 Corvette, only three hundred produced, is — in one critic's words — "a shameless display of sexual suggestiveness," surely setting the stage for all the sexuality the Corvette would carry for the half century to come, and the 1963 Sting Ray, the original and one-year only, "looked like a diagram of desire" (Bayley 118 and 254). Speed and sex, not what the SS in one concept car's name stood for, but close enough.

Arthur Drexler, of the Museum of Modern Art in New York City, said that cars have "interior spaces corresponding to an outer form ... but the designers' aesthetic purpose is to enclose the functioning parts of an automobile, as well as its passengers, in a package suggesting directed movement along the ground" (Bayley 8). In this balance between inside and outside and the "functioning" of its mechanical bits and pieces, we have the dynamic relationship a car has with itself. Corvettes managed to strike a delicate equilibrium between an excess of power on the one hand, the 1967 L88-engined Sting Rays, and an overabundance of styling to the point of kitsch on the other, the 1958 chrome-laden, scooped, and louvered Corvette. This was never easy, but the Corvette survived. In the mind of the public, most of them were beautiful to some degree — although not "art" as in high art; this is what the Corvette was and continues to be. Stephen Bayley says, perhaps too provocatively, that "car design has usurped the roles contemporary art has abandoned: the public learns about symbolism, form, about how light falls on objects, how details can articulate meaning from cars" (30). The Corvette is one of those automobiles.

In the final analysis, the Corvette and its image have survived and prospered because of a number of factors. The literary, cinematic, and artistic examples I have cited get at some of the truth as to why. The car was, most of the time, well designed; it grew into a fast, powerful machine that reflected American tastes; it reflected, early in its life, those prototypical American values of freedom and independence that we hold so dear. The Corvette was also sexy; it excited the eye and the heart, of both men and women. The best specimens of the Corvette line, yesterday and today, present speed and power in a relatively affordable form that no other car can match. This is all information gleaned from books and material about the Corvette — I wish I had one to give a more personal and penetrating critical analysis.

The Corvette also seems to have made a connection with people's bodies. Men and women appear to find that "extension of themselves" through the Corvette ... other cars too, but no one speaks of them so much as Corvette owners do. The Corvette image goes beyond the automobile itself. It hovers around and above the cars, communicating — silently, until the engines start — all this allure and history that over fifty years of racing and speeding, and sex, and customizing the Corvette has endowed them with.

The absolute and best description of the Corvette as a phenomenon — car and image — comes from the late Beverly Rae Kimes, automotive journalist and historian, in the book she edited, *Corvette: A Piece of the Action: Impressions of the Marque and the Mystique* (1977). Rather than cite history, specifications, or other information, she simply says, "The Corvette is more than mortal, more than animate, more than existential. The Corvette is ... well, a definition just won't do"; all I have done is try (8).

Works Cited

Abrams, J. J., director. *Star Trek*. Perf. Chris Pine, Leonard Nimoy. Paramount. 2009. Film.

Adams, C. Jama. "Respect and Reputation: The Construction of Masculinity in Poor African American Men." *Journal of African-American Studies*. 11, nos. 3/4 (2007): 157–172.

Aldrich, Robert, director. *Kiss Me Deadly*. Perf. Ralph Meeker, et al. United Artists. 1955. MGM Home Entertainment. 2001. DVD.

Alexie, Sherman. "When the Story Stolen Is Your Own." *Time*. 29 January 2006. Web. 15 June 2009.

Anderson, Sherwood. *Perhaps Women*. New York: Liveright, 1931.

Arnheim, Rudolf. "Notes on Seeing Sculpture." *The Journal of Aesthetics and Art Criticism*. 43, 3. 1984. 319-324.

Arnold, Rebecca. *Fashion, Desire and Anxiety: Image and Morality in the 20th Century*. New Brunswick: Rutgers University Press, 2001.

"Art." *Art Encyclopedia*. Web. 26 January 2010.

"Art." *Art Encyclopedia*. Glossary. Web. 26 January 2010.

"Art." 8. a. *Oxford English Dictionary Online*. Web. 26 January 2010.

"Art History: Pop Art (1958–1975)." *World Wide Art Resources*. Web. 5 February 2010.

Banham, Reyner. *Design by Choice*. Edited by Penny Sparke. London: Academy Editions, 1981.

Barbree, Jay. *"Live from Cape Canaveral": Covering the Space Race from Sputnik to Today*. New York: Smithsonian Books, 2007.

Barkley, Brad. *Alison's Automotive Repair Manual*. New York: St. Martin's, 2003.

Barthes, Roland. *Mythologies*. Translated by Annette Lavers. New York: Farrar, Straus and Giroux, 1972.

_____. "La Nouvelle Citroën." *Citroënët*. Web. 20 January 2010. <http:www.citroenet. org.uk/passenger-cars/michelin/ds/32.html>.

Bayley, Stephen. *Cars: Freedom, Style, Sex, Power, Motion, Colour, Everything*. London: Conran Octopus, 2008.

Beckman, Karen. "The Archive, the Phallus, and the Future." *Camera Obscura*. 22, no. 1 (2007): 186–193.

Benjamin, Walter. "The Work of Art in the Age of Mechanical Reproduction." 1936. Web. 17 January 2010. <http://www.markists.org/reference/subject/philosophy/works/ ge/benjamin.htm>.

Berger, Michael L. *The Automobile in American History and Culture: A Reference Guide*. Westport, CT: Greenwood Press, 2001.

Berkson, Terry. *Corvette Odyssey: The True Story of One Man's Path to Roadster Redemption.* Guilford, CT: Lyons Press, 2004.

Blais, Ellen A. "Gender Issues in Bobbie Ann Mason's *In Country.*" *South Atlantic Review.* 56, no. 2 (1985): 107–118.

Bolge, George S. "The Painting/Sculpture Connection." *Woman's Art Journal.* Web. 3, 2. 1983. 54-56. <http://www.links.jstor.org/sici?sici=02707993>.

Bordo, Susan. *Unbearable Weight: Feminism, Western Culture, and the Body.* Berkeley: University of California Press, 1993.

Bourdieu, Pierre. *Distinction: A Social Critique of the Judgment of Taste.* Translated by Richard Nice. Cambridge: Harvard University Press, 1984.

Bray, Abigail, and Claire Colebrook. "The Haunted Flesh: Corporeal Feminism and the Politics of (Dis)Embodiment." *Signs: Journal of Women in Culture and Society.* 24, no. 1 (1998): 35–67.

Brodie, Kay. "*Geronimo's Bones.*" *Library Journal.* 129, no. 3 (2004): 134–135.

Brooks, James L., director. *Terms of Endearment.* Perf. Shirley MacLaine, Jack Nicholson. Paramount. 1983. Paramount Studios. 2009. DVD.

Brown, Bill. *A Sense of Things: The Object Matter of American Literature.* Chicago: University of Chicago Press, 2003.

Bunge, Nancy. "People Are Equal: An Interview with William Stafford." *Kansas Quarterly.* 24/25, 4/1 (1992/1993): 10–20.

Burston, Paul, and Colin Richardson, eds. Introduction. In *Queer Romance: Lesbians, Gay Men and Popular Culture.* New York: Routledge, 1995. 1–9.

Burton, Jerry. *Corvette: America's Sports Car — Yesterday, Today, Tomorrow.* New York: Hugh Lauter Levin, 2006.

_____. *Zora Arkus-Duntov: The Legend Behind Corvette.* Cambridge, MA: Bentley, 2002.

Butler, Judith. *Bodies That Matter: On the Discursive Limits of "Sex."* New York: Routledge, 1993.

"Cadillac: A History of Innovations Since 1902." *GM Media Online.* Web. 28 April 2009.

Casey, Roger N. *Textual Vehicles: The Automobile in American Literature.* New York: Garland Publishing, 1997.

Chabot, C. Barry. "Joan Didion's *Play It As It Lays* and the Vacuity of the 'Here and Now.'" *Critique.* 21, no. 3 (1979): 53–60.

Chaikivsky, Andrew. "Nasdijj: Seven Years Ago, He Was Born in This Magazine. The Story of a Fraud." *Esquire.* 30 April 2006. Web. 15 June 2009.

Charters, Ann. Introduction. In *On the Road* by Jack Kerouac. New York: Penguin, 2003.

Clarke, Deborah. *Driving Women: Fiction and Automobile Culture in Twentieth Century America.* Baltimore: Johns Hopkins University Press, 2007.

Coale, Samuel. "Didion's Disorder: An American Romancer's Art." *Critique.* 25, no. 3 (1984): 160–170.

Compton, Desiree, and Markie L. C. Blumer. "Seven Pounds." *Journal of Feminist Family Therapy.* 21, no. 2 (2009): 143–146. Web. 15 July 2009.

Cook, Bernie, ed. *Thelma & Louise Live!: The Cultural Afterlife of an American Film.* Austin: University of Texas Press, 2007.

"Coquette." *Oxford English Dictionary Online.* Web. 4 November 2009.

"Corvette." *Oxford English Dictionary Online.* Web. 4 November 2009.

"Corvette Concept Cars." *We Love Corvettes.* Web. 29 January 2010.

"Corvette 2005: A Boy's Dream." Advertisement. *The Corvette Anthology 2007.* Hardyston, NJ: HI-Tech Software. 2006. CD.

Courbet, Gustave. *L'Origine du Monde.* 1866. Painting.

"Dana Forrester." *Pacific Car Art.* Web. 4 February 2010.

Davenport, Steve. "Three Propositions about *On the Road.*" *American Book Review.* 29, no. 1 (2007): 5–6.

Davis, Robert Murray. "The World of John Steinbeck's Joads." *World Literature Today.* 64, no. 3 (1990): 401–404.

Dean, Josh. "'It's Peter Max's Car, Man!': How One Artist's Big PR Dream Left 36 Corvettes in the Dust in a Brooklyn Basement." *New York Magazine.* 9 May 2005. Web. 26 September 2005.

Delgado, Richard, and Jean Stefancic. *Critical Race Theory: an Introduction.* New York: New York University Press, 2001.

Dettelbach, Cynthia Golomb. *In the Driver's Seat: the Automobile in American Literature and Popular Culture.* Westport, CT: Greenwood Press, 1976.

Dey, Tom, director. *Showtime.* Perf. Eddie Murphy, Robert DeNiro. Material Productions. 2002. DVD.

Didion, Joan. "Bureaucrats." *We Tell Ourselves Stories In Order To Live: Collected Nonfiction.* New York: Everyman's Library, 2006. 236–240.

_____. *Play It As It Lays.* New York: Farrar, 1970.

_____. "The Women's Movement." *We Tell Ourselves Stories In Order To Live: Collected Nonfiction.* New York: Everyman's Library, 2006. 257–264.

Dilworth, John. "A Double Content Theory of Artistic Representation." *The Journal of Aesthetics and Art Criticism.* 63, no. 3 (2005): 249–260.

Dobinson, Cheryl, and Kevin Young. "Popular Cinema and Lesbian Interpretative Strategies." *Journal of Homosexuality.* 40, no. 2 (2000): 97–121.

doCarmo, Stephen N. "Bombs From Coke Cans: Appropriating Mass Culture in Bobbie Ann Mason's *In Country.*" *Journal of Popular Culture.* 36, no. 3 (2003): 589–599.

Earl, Harley. "I Dream Automobiles." *Saturday Evening Post.* 227, no. 6 (1954): 17–19.

Endicott, R. Craig. "Top 200 Brands." *Advertising Age.* 68, no. 44 (1997): 44–48.

Fantina, Richard. *Ernest Hemingway: Machismo and Masochism.* New York: Palgrave Macmillan, 2005.

_____. "Hemingway's Masochism, Sodomy, and the Dominant Woman." *Hemingway Review.* 23, no. 1 (2003): 84–105.

Farr, Marie T. "Freedom and Control: Automobiles in American Women's Fiction of the 70s and 80s." *Journal of Popular Culture.* 29, no. 2 (1995): 157–169.

Faulkner, Wendy. "The Technology Question in Feminism: A View from Feminist Technology Studies." *Women's Studies International Forum.* 24, no. 1 (2001): 79–95. Web. 2 January 2010.

"First Drive: Chevrolet Corvette Moray Concept: America's Sports-car Icon Meets Flash Gordon, Italian Style." *Motor Trend.* November 2003. Web. 29 January 2010. <http://www.motortrend.com/>Roadtests/coupes/112_0311_chevrolet_corvette_moray_ concept/html>.

"First Look: '09 ZR1 The Most Potent Corvette Ever!" Cover story. *Autoweek.* 24 December 2007.

Fitzgerald, Craig. "Dagmar Bumpers." *Hemmings Motor News.* Web. 1 October 2006. <http://www.Hemmings.com/hmn/stories/2006/10/01hmn_feature21.html>.

Fitzgerald, F. Scott. *The Great Gatsby.* New York: Scribner. 1925.

Fleming, Robert E. Introduction. In *Free Air* by Sinclair Lewis. Lincoln, NE: University Nebraska Press. 1993.

Fleischer, Matthew. "Navahoax: Did a struggling white writer of gay erotica become one of multicultural literature's most celebrated memoirists — by passing himself off as a Native American?" *LA Weekly.* 26 January 2006. Web. 15 June 2009.

Ford, John, director. *The Grapes of Wrath.* Perf. Henry Fonda, Jane Darwell. Twentieth Century–Fox. 1940. DVD. Twentieth Century–Fox Home Entertainment. 2007.

Fore, Dana. "Life Unworthy of Life?: Masculinity, Disability, and Guilt in *The Sun Also Rises.*" *Hemingway Review.* 26, no. 2 (2007): 74–88.

Forrester, Dana. *Concrete Heaven.* Web. 15 June 2009. <http://www.danaforrester.com> Lithograph.

_____. "Dana Forrester Watercolors-Automotive Art." Web. <http://www.danaforrester.com>.

_____. Telephone interview. 10 January 2010.

_____. "The World of Dana Forrester." Catalog. 2005.

Fowler, Bridget. "Reading Pierre Bourdieu's *Masculine Domination*: Notes Toward an Intersectional Analysis of Gender, Culture and Class." *Cultural Studies.* 17, no. 3/4 (2003): 468–494.

Foxe, Gladys. "'And Nobody Knows What's Going to Happen to Anybody': Fear and Futility in Jack Kerouac's *On the Road* and Why It Is Important." *Psychoanalytic Review.* 95, no. 1 (2008): 45–60.

Frank, T. C., director. *Billy Jack.* Perf. Tom Laughlin, Delores Taylor. National Student Film Corporation. 1971. Warner Home Video. 1999. DVD.

French, Marilyn. *Beyond Power: On Women, Men, and Morals.* New York: Summit, 1985.

From the Earth to the Moon. Cable miniseries; twelve episodes. Home Box Office, Inc. 2005. DVD.

Frumkes, Lewis Burke. "A Conversation with ... Joan Didion." *Writer.* 112, no. 3 (1999): 14–15.

Frye, Marilyn. "Lesbian Feminism and the Gay Rights Movement: Another View of Male Supremacy, Another Separatism." *The Politics of Reality: Essays in Feminist Theory.* Trumansburg, NY: The Crossing Press, 1983. 128–151.

_____. "The Necessity of Differences: Constructing a Positive Category of Women." *Signs: Journal of Women in Culture and Society.* 21, no. 4 (1996): 991–1010.

Gardiner, Judith Kegan, ed. Introduction. *Masculinity Studies and Feminist Theory: New Directions.* New York: Columbia University Press, 2002. 1–29.

Geherin, David J. "Nothingness and Beyond: Joan Didion's *Play It As It Lays.*" *Critique.* 16, no. 1 (1974): 64–78.

Gehman, Richard B. Introduction. In *The Day of the Locust* by Nathanael West. New York: Vail-Ballou Press, 1939.

Geronimo's Bones. Review. *Kirkus Reviews.* 72, no. 2 (2004): 73.

Geronimo's Bones. Review. *Publisher's Weekly.* 251, no. 5 (2004): 66–68.

Gillespie, Joanne S. "Getting Inside S. E. Hinton's *The Outsiders.*" *English Journal.* 95, no. 3 (2006): 44–48.

Gilroy, Paul. "Driving While Black." *Car Cultures.* New York: Berg, 2001. 81–104. Materializing Culture Series.

_____. Interview. "Cosmopolitanism, Blackness, and Utopia: a Conversation with Paul Gilroy." *Transition: an International Review.* 98 (2006). 29 June 2009. <http://www. transition magazine.com/ articles/shelby.htm>.

_____. Interview. "Paul Gilroy, in Conversation." *Darkmatter Journal.* May 2007. Web. 29 June 2009. <http://www.darkmatter101.org/site/2007/05/07/paul-gilroy-in-con versation>.

Goddard, Kevin. "'Looks Maketh the Man': The Female Gaze and the Construction of Masculinity." *The Journal of Men's Studies.* 9, no. 1 (2000): 23–29. 15 August 2009. <http://www.questia.com>.

Groth, Miles. "Laing's Presence." *Janus Head: Journal of Interdisciplinary Studies in Literature, Continental Philosophy, Phenomenological Psychology, and the Arts.* 4, no. 1 (2001). Web. 1 October 2009. <http://www.janushead.org/jinfo.cfm>.

Gutmann, Matthew C. "Trafficking in Men: The Anthropology of Masculinity." *Annual Review of Anthropology.* 26 (1997): 385–409.

Halberstam, Judith. "The Good, the Bad, and the Ugly: Men, Women, and Masculinity." *Masculinity Studies and Feminist Theory: New Directions*. New York: Columbia University Press, 2002. 344–367.

_____. *Female Masculinity*. Durham, NC: Duke University Press, 1998.

Halliday, Jean. "New Corvette Gets Net Intro, TV Push." *Advertising Age*. 68, no. 1 (1997): 3–35.

Hand, Elizabeth. "*Parasites Like Us, You're an Animal, Viskovitz, The Two Sams: Ghost Stories*." *Fantasy and Science Fiction*. 106, no. 3 (2004): 34–40.

Haraway, Donna. "A Cyborg Manifesto: Science, Technology, and Socialist-Feminism in the Late Twentieth Century." In *Simians, Cyborgs and Women: The Reinvention of Nature*. New York: Routledge, 1991. 149–181.

Hazleton, Lesley. *Driving to Detroit: An Automotive Odyssey*. New York: The Free Press, 1998.

Healey, James R. "Zoom, Zoom, Zoom." *USA Today: Money*. 24 February 2004. 1b.

Heasley, Jerry. *Corvette Field Guide: 1953–Present*. Iola, WI: KP Books, 2005.

Heldrich, Philip. "William Stafford's Mythopoetic Kansas." *Midwest Quarterly*. 43, no. 2 (2002): 143–156.

Hemingway, Ernest. *The Sun Also Rises*. New York: Bantam, 1949.

Hildebrandt, Greg. *Yellow Rose of Texas*. Web. <http://www.brothershildebrandt.com>. 15 October 2007. Lithograph.

Hinton, S. E. *The Outsiders*. New York: Speak (Penguin), 1967.

Holmes, Nigel, and Lorraine Moffa. "America in Motion." *American History*. 43, no. 6 (2009): 42–43.

Hooks, Kevin, director. *Passenger 57*. Perf. Wesley Snipes. Warner Brothers. 1992. Film.

Howard, Ron, director. *Apollo 13*. Perf. Tom Hanks, Kevin Bacon, et al. Universal. 1995. Audio commentary. Universal Home Video. 1998. DVD.

Huntley, Kristine. *Geronimo's Bones*. Review. *Booklist*. 100, no. 14 (2004): 1259.

Ingenbleek, Jean-Francois, and Jean Lemaire. "What Is a Sports Car?" *ASTIN Bulletin*. 18, no. 2 (1988): 175–187.

Itten, Theodor. "The Paths of Soul Making: Notes on a Peculiar Psycho-analytic Tradition." *Colloquia — Psychotherapy*. Web. 1 October 2009. <http://www.laingsociety.org/colloquia/psychotherapy/ ittensoulmaking.htm>.

Jamison, DeReef F. "The Relationship between African Self-Consciousness, Cultural Misorientation, Hypermasculinity, and Rap Music Preference." *Journal of African-American Studies*. 9, no. 4 (2006): 45–60.

Jeansonne, Glen. "The Automobile and American Morality." *The Journal of Popular Culture*. 8, no. 1 (1974): 125–131.

Johnson, Adam. *Parasites Like Us*. New York: Penguin, 2003.

Johnson, Joyce. "Remembering Jack Kerouac." *Smithsonian*. 38, no. 6. (2007): 115–121.

Kelm, Rebecca. "*Alison's Automotive Repair Manual*." *Library Journal*. 127, no. 30 (2002): 174.

Kelso, Sylvia. "Take Me for a Ride in Your Man-Eater: Gynophobia in Stephen King's *Christine*." *Para-doxa: Studies in World Literary Genres*. 2, no. 2 (1996): 263–275.

Kerouac, Jack. *On the Road*. New York: Penguin, 1957.

_____. Preface. *Big Sur*. New York: Penguin, 1992.

Khouri, Callie, screenwriter; perf. Susan Sarandon, Geena Davis. *Thelma & Louise*. MGM. 1991. Audio commentary. MGM Home Video. 2001. DVD.

Kimes, Beverly Rae. *Corvette: A Piece of the Action: Impressions of the Marque and the Mystique 1953–1978*. Princeton, NJ: Princeton Publishing, 1977.

_____. *Pioneers, Engineers, and Scoundrels: The Dawn of the Automobile in America*. Warrendale, PA: SAE International, 2005.

Kimmel, Michael S. *Manhood in America: A Cultural History*. New York: Oxford University Press, 2006.

Krist, Gary. "If It's Not One Thing, It's Another." Review. *The New York Times Book Review*. 24 August 2003. 7.

Lackey, Kris. *RoadFrames: The American Highway Narrative*. Lincoln: University of Nebraska Press, 1997.

LaEnvi, Michael, Sr. "The Art of Idar Oils." *Vette Vues Magazine*. July 1999. 33–38. Web. 2 September 2005. <http://www.enriva,com/The_Art_of_Oil/Art/art.html>.

Leber, Michele. *Booklist*. 99, no. 22 (2003): 1953–1954.

Leffingwell, Randy. *Corvette: Fifty Years*. St. Paul, MN: MBI Publishing, 2002.

Leland, John. *Why Kerouac Matters: The Lessons of On the Road (They're Not What You Think)*. New York: Penguin, 2007.

Lewis, Joseph H., director. *Gun Crazy*. Perf. John Dall, Peggy Cummins. Warner Bros. 1949. Warner Bros. Entertainment Inc. 2004. DVD.

Lewis, Sinclair. *Free Air*. Lincoln, NE: University Nebraska Press, 1919.

Lewitt, Sol. "Paragraphs on Conceptual Art [1967]." In *Conceptual Art*, edited by Peter Osborne, London: Phaidon Press, 2002.

Liu, Dennis. "Supercars Across America: 4643 miles, 8 Days, 4 Supercars — McLaren F1* Bertone Mantide* Ferrari Scuderia Spider 16M* Ferrari 612 Scagietti* and Zero Tickets." *Automobile Magazine*. 24, no. 8 (2009): 62–69.

Livingstone, Marc. "Andy Warhol." *Museum of Modern Art*. Web. 5 February 2010.

Loewy, Raymond. *Never Leave Well Enough Alone*. New York: Simon and Schuster, 1951.

Lords, Traci Elizabeth. *Traci Lords: Underneath It All*. New York: Harper, 2003.

Markus, Fred. "The Devil's Own." *Automobile Magazine*. February 2008. 28–33.

"Marshall McLuhan: Key Concepts." *Old Messengers, New Media: The Legacy of Innis and McLuhan*. Library and Archives Canada. Web. 5 May 2009. <http://www.collections canada.gc.ca/innis-mcluhan/002033-2000-e.html>.

Martin, Douglas. "Dagmar, 79, Foxy Blonde, With First-Name Status in 50's." *The New York Times*. Web. 11 October 2001.

Martin, F. David. "Sculpture, Painting, and Damage. The Journal of Aesthetics and Art Criticism. 37, no. 1. 1978: 47-52.

Martin, Man. *Days of the Endless Corvette*. New York: Carroll & Graff, 2007.

———. Telephone interview. 30 November 2009.

Maslin, Janet. "Review/Film: A Cheyenne Mystic Who Transmutes Bitterness." *The New York Times*. 14 March 1989. Web. 31 May 2009. <http://www.nytimes.com/1989/03/24/ movies/review-film-a-cheyenne-mystic-who-transmutes-bitterness.htm>.

Mason, Bobbie Ann. *In Country*. New York: Harper, 1985.

McBride, Joseph, and Susan Shillinglaw. *The Grapes of Wrath*. John Ford, director. Twentieth Century–Fox. 1940. Audio commentary. Fox Home Video. 2002. DVD.

McHugh, Kathleen. "Women in Traffic: L.A. Autobiography." *South Atlantic Quarterly*. 97, no. 2 (1998): 391–412.

McLuhan, Marshall. "*Playboy* Interview: 'Marshall McLuhan — A Candid Conversation with the High Priest of Popcult and Metaphysician of Media.'" *Essential McLuhan*. New York: BasicBooks, 1995. 237–269.

———. *Understanding Media: the Extensions of Man*. Critical Edition. Corte Madera, CA: Gingko Press, 1994.

Mellencamp, Patricia. *A Fine Romance: Five Ages of Film Feminism*. Philadelphia: Temple University Press, 1996.

Mellstrom, Ulf. "Patriarchal Machines and Masculine Embodiment." *Science, Technology, &Human Values.* 27, no. 4, (2002): 460–478.

"Milestone Display with 1.5 millionth Corvette Coming Soon!" National Corvette Museum e-News. Web. 25 September 2009. <http://www.corvettemuseum.org>.

Miller, Daniel. "Driven Societies." *Car Cultures.* New York: Berg, 2001. 1–33. Materializing Culture series.

_____. *Material Cultures: Why Some Things Matter.* Chicago: University of Chicago Press, 1998.

Mills, Katie. *The Road Story and the Rebel: Moving Through Film, Fiction, and Television.* Carbondale, IL: Southern Illinois University Press, 2006.

"Moray: The American Dream Dreamed by Italian Dreamers — Italdesign-Giugario Pays Homage to the Corvette Fifty-Year Era." *Ital Design.* Web. 2 September 2008. <http://www.italdesign.it>.

Motichka, Michele. "Brand Loyalty in the Automotive Community: A Case Study on the Chevrolet Corvette." University of South Florida. School of Mass Communications. 2003. MA thesis.

Muccino, Gabriele, director. *Seven Pounds.* Perf. Will Smith, Rosario Dawson. Columbia. 2008. DVD.

Mulvey, Laura. "Visual Pleasure and Narrative Cinema." *Screen.* 16, no. 3 (1975). Web. 30 July 2009. <http://ww.wiki.brown.edu/confluence/display/MarkTribe/Visual+Pleasure+and+Narrative+Cinema>.

Naremore, James. *More Than Night: Film Noir in Its Contexts.* Berkley: University of California Press, 2008.

Nasdijj. *Geronimo's Bones: A Memoir of My Brother and Me.* New York: Ballantine, 2004.

Nataf, Z. Isiling. "Black Lesbian Spectatorship and Pleasure in Popular Cinema." In *Queer Romance: Lesbians, Gay Men and Popular Culture,* edited by Paul Burston and Colin Richardson. New York: Routledge, 1995. 57–80.

Nava, Mica. *Changing Cultures: Feminism, Youth and Consumerism.* New York: SAGE Publications, 1992.

Neff, Natalie. Editorial. *Autoweek* (online update, by e-mail). 29 April 2009. <http://www.autoweek.com /apps/pbcs.dll/article?AID=/200904291045/FREE/ 904299987>.

"1964 Chevrolet Corvette Sting Ray Coupe." Items 53219166 and 53219167. *GM Photo Store.* Web. 15 Oct. 2005.

"North American International Auto Show 2004." *Car Styling.* 159. 2004. 8–34.

"100 Coolest Cars." *Automobile Magazine.* October 2004. Web. 21 May 2009.

O'Neill, Edward R. "The M-m-mama of Us All: Divas and the Cultural Logic of Late Ca(m)pitalism." *Camera Obscura.* 22 (2007): 10–27.

"Ontological security." *StateMaster Encyclopedia.* Web. 1 October 2009. <http://www.statemaster.com/encyclopedia>.

Orr, Floyd M. *Plastic Ozone Daydream: The Corvette Chronicles.* San Jose, CA: Writers Club Press, 2000.

Osborne, Peter, ed. *Conceptual Art.* London: Phaidon Press, 2002.

Osteen, Mark. "Noir's Cars: Automobility and Amoral Space in American Film Noir." *Journal of Popular Film and Television.* 35, no. 4 (2008): 183–192.

"*Parasites Like Us.*" *Kirkus Reviews.* 71, no. 12 (2003): 826.

Parker, T. Jefferson. *L.A. Outlaws.* New York: Dutton, 2008.

Paul, Bill. *Future Energy: How the New Oil Industry Will Change People, Politics, and Portfolios.* Hoboken, NJ: John Wiley & Sons, 2007.

Peel, Mark, Barbara Caine, and Christina Twomey. "Masculinity, Emotion and Subjectivity: Introduction." *The Journal of Men's Studies.* 15, no. 3 (2007): 247–250.

Perry, Frank, director. *Play It As It Lays.* Perf. Tuesday Weld, Anthony Perkins, et al. Universal. 1972. Film.

Phillips, John. "Misty Eyed in Kentucky." Editorial. *Car and Driver.* January 2008. 26.

Play It As It Lays. Sundance Channel broadcast. 2005. Shocking Videos. DVD. <http://www.revengeismydestiny.com>.

Pulos, Arthur J. *The American Design Adventure 1940–1975.* Cambridge, Massachusetts: M.I.T. Press, 1988.

Queer As Folk. 2000–2005. Showtime Networks, Inc. (cable television) 2006. DVD.

Ratner, Brett, director. *Rush Hour.* Perf. Chris Tucker, Jackie Chan. New Line Cinema. 1998. DVD.

Rhodes, Chip. "The Hollywood Novel: Gender and Lacanian Tragedy in Joan Didion's *Play It As It Lays.*" *Style.* 34, no. 1 (2000): 132–143.

Rising, Margot. *The Purple Corvette.* New York: iUniverse, 2007.

Robbins, Matthew, director. *Corvette Summer.* MGM. 1978. Warner Home Video. 2005. DVD.

Rodriguez, Brenda. "*Seven Pounds.*" *People.* 70, no. 21 (2008): 102.

Rosin, James. "*Route 66*" *The Television Series 1960–1964.* Philadelphia: Autumn Road, 2007.

Rousseau, G. S. "Foucault and the Fortunes of Queer Theory." *The European Legacy.* 5, no. 3 (2000): 401–413.

Route 66. 1960–1964. Roxbury Entertainment. 2005. DVD.

Rudman, Mark. "The Way It Is: New & Selected Poems of William Stafford." *Great River Review.* 47 (2007): 109–111. 15 June 2009.

Saint Martin, Marina. "Art Was His Life and His Life Was Art." *The Gold Coast Bulletin.* 10 November 2007. Web. 5 February 2010.

Samuels, Allsion. "The Gospel of Will Smith." *Newsweek.* 152, no. 23 (2008): 66–67.

Schefter, James. *All Corvettes Are Red: Inside the Rebirth of an American Legend.* New York: Pocket Books, 1996.

Scott, Phillip J. "The Ford Mustang and the Chevrolet Corvette: Icons in American Culture." [MA thesis] 2004. Publication No. AAT 1424366. <http://www.proquest.umi.com/ dissertations/ preview_all1424366>.

Scott, Ridley, director and producer. *Thelma & Louise.* MGM. 1991. Audio commentary. MGM Home Video. 2002. DVD.

Seals, David. "Another Sioux Uprising in the Black Hills." *Grassroots Oyate.* January 16, 2000. Web. June 15, 2009. <http://www.grassrootsoyate.tripod.com/David.htm>.

_____. *The Powwow Highway.* New York: Plume, 1990.

Sedgwick, Eve Kosofsky. *Between Men: English Literature and Homosocial Desire.* New York: Columbia University Press, 1985.

Sherman, Don. "The Mother of All Vettes." *Automobile Magazine.* February 2008. 40–44.

Silk, Gerald. "The Automobile in Art." *Automobile and Culture.* New York: Abrams, 1984.

Sontag, Susan. "Art and Consciousness." Interview (reprint of February 1977). Edited by Bonnie Marranca and Gautam Dasgupta. *Performing Arts Journal: A Journal of Performance and Art.* 27, no. 80 (2005): 1–9.

Spangler, Jason. "We're on a Road to Nowhere: Steinbeck, Kerouac, and the Legacy of the Great Depression." *Studies in the Novel.* 40, no. 3 (2008): 308–327.

Spector-Mersel, Gabriela. "Never-aging Stories: Western Hegemonic Masculinity Scripts." *Journal of Gender Studies.* 15, no. 1 (2006): 67–82.

Spraggins, Johnnie David, Jr. "African-American Masculinity: Power and Expression." *Journal of African-American Men.* 4, no. 3 (1999): 45–72.

Stafford, William. "Old Blue." *The Way It Is: New & Selected Poems*. St. Paul, MN: Graywolf, 1998. 236.

Stein, Jonathan A. *The Performing Art of the American Automobile: The Hendricks Collection on Exhibit at the Gateway Colorado Auto Museum*. Philadelphia: Coachbuilt Press, 2006.

Steinbeck, John. *The Grapes of Wrath*. New York: Penguin, 1939.

_____. "The Grapes of Wrath." (essay reprint) *Literary Cavalcade*. 53, no. 7 (2001): 8–10.

Stern, Jane and Michael. *Auto Ads*. New York: Random House, 1978.

Stewart, Brian. *Red Corvette*. Mesa, AZ: Reignbow Media, 2007.

Sullivan, Nikki. *A Critical Introduction to Queer Theory*. New York: New York University Press, 2003.

Swan, Tony. "Blown Away." *Car and Driver*. February 2008. 32–36.

Telotte, J. P. *Voices in the Dark: The Narrative Patterns of Film Noir*. Urbana: University of Illinois Press, 1989.

Thompson, Steve. "The Big Red Stick." *Autoweek*. Web. 9 March 2009. <www.autoweek.com/apps/ pbcs.dll/article?AID=20090309/C>

Thomson, David. "Frank Perry." *The New Biographical Dictionary of Film*. New York: Knopf, 2002. 676.

Troesser, John. "The Art of Dana Forrester." *Texas Escapes.com*. Web. 4 February 2010.

"2003 Italdesign Corvette Moray Concept Car." *We Love Corvettes*. Web. 29 January 2010. <http://www.welove corvettes.com/concept_cars/2003_moray.html>.

Veblen, Thorstein. *The Theory of the Leisure Class*. New York: Dodo Press, 2005.

Vette, Vicky. "My Biography" and "Tour." *Vicky at Home*. Web. 30 Nov. 2007. <http://www.vickyathome.com>.

"Viagra videos." Web. *Viagra Online*. 29 Nov. 2007. <http://www.viagra.com>.

"Vicky Vette: The MILF Queen Drives Circles Around Starlets Half Her Age." Interview. *Adult Video News*. Web. 20 Nov. 2007. <http://www.avn.com>

Volti, Rudi. *Cars and Culture: The Life Story of a Technology*. Baltimore: Johns Hopkins University Press. 2004.

Walker, John, Ed. *"Play It As It Lays." Halliwell's Film Guide*. 8th ed. New York: Harper Perennial, 1992.

Webster, Larry. "Chevrolet Corvette Z51: In A World of Disappointment, Nothin' but Grins." *Car and Driver*. 50, no. 3 (2004): 44–50.

West, Cornel. *Race Matters*. New York: Vintage, 1993.

White, Kevin. *The First Sexual Revolution: The Emergence of Male Heterosexuality in Modern America*. New York: New York University Press. 1993,

Wiegman, Robyn. "Unmaking: Men and Masculinity in Feminist Theory." In *Masculinity Studies and Feminist Theory: New Directions*, edited by Judith Kegan Gardiner. New York: Columbia University Press, 2002. 31–59.

Wilson, Kevin. "Membership Has Its Privileges." *Autoweek*. 56, no. 36 (2006): 8.

Windschuttle, Keith. "Steinbeck's Myth of the Okies." *The New Criterion*. 20, no. 10 (2002): 24–32.

Wise, Sheila J. "Redefining Black Masculinity and Manhood: Successful Black Gay Men Speak Out." *Journal of African-American Men*. 5, no. 4 (2001): 3–22.

Wolfe, Tom. *The Kandy-Kolored, Tangerine-Flake Streamline Baby*. New York: Picador, 1964.

_____. *The Right Stuff*. New York: Picador, 1979.

Wollheim, Richard. *Art and Its Objects: With Six Supplementary Essays*. 2nd edition. Cambridge: Cambridge University Press, 1980.

Wood, Paul. *Conceptual Art*. New York: Delano Greenidge, 2002.

Woodward, Ian. *Understanding Material Culture*. Los Angeles: Sage, 2007.

Zaleski, Jeff. *"Alison's Automotive Repair Manual."* *Publisher's Weekly.* 249, no. 45 (2002): 39.

Zepke, Stephen. "The Concept of Art When Art Is Not a Concept." *Angelaki: Journal of the Theoretical Humanities.* 2, no. 1 (2006): 157–167.

Zumbrunn, Michael, and Robert Cumberford. *Auto Legends: Classics of Style and Design.* London: Merrell, 2004.

Index

Numbers in **_bold italics_** indicate pages with illustrations.

235